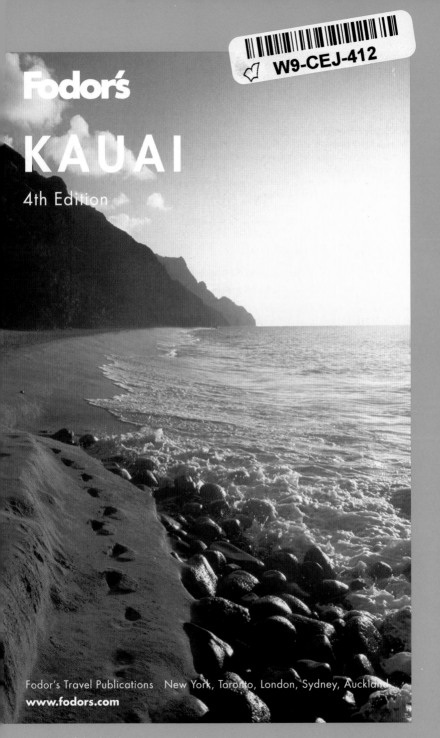

Fodor's

KAUAI

4th Edition

Fodor's Travel Publications   New York, Toronto, London, Sydney, Auckland
www.fodors.com

Portions of this book appear in *Fodor's Hawaii.*

FODOR'S KAUAI

Writers: Lois Ann Ell, Charles E. Roessler, David Simon

Editors: Rachel Klein, Jess Moss, Mark Sullivan

Production Editor: Carrie Parker
Maps & Illustrations: Henry Colomb and Mark Stroud, Moon Street Cartography; David Lindroth, Inc., *cartographers;* Rebecca Baer, *map editor;* William Wu, *information graphics*
Design: Fabrizio La Rocca, *creative director;* Tina Malaney, Chie Ushio, Jessica Walsh, *designers;* Melanie Marin, *associate director of photography;* Jennifer Romains, *photo research*
Cover Photo: (Napali Coast): Quincy Dein/Perspectives/Getty Images
Production Manager: Angela L. McLean

4th Edition

ISBN 978-0-307-92919-8

ISSN 1934-550X

SPECIAL SALES

This book is available at special discounts for bulk purchases for sales promotions or premiums. Special editions, including personalized covers, excerpts of existing books, and corporate imprints, can be created in large quantities for special needs. For more information, write to Special Markets/Premium Sales, 1745 Broadway, MD 3-1, New York, NY 10019, or e-mail specialmarkets@randomhouse.com.

AN IMPORTANT TIP & AN INVITATION

Although all prices, opening times, and other details in this book are based on information supplied to us at press time, changes occur all the time in the travel world, and Fodor's cannot accept responsibility for facts that become outdated or for inadvertent errors or omissions. So **always confirm information when it matters,** especially if you're making a detour to visit a specific place. Your experiences—positive and negative— matter to us. If we have missed or misstated something, **please write to us.** Share your opinion instantly through our online feedback center at fodors.com/contact-us.

PRINTED IN COLOMBIA

10 9 8 7 6 5 4 3 2 1

CONTENTS

1 EXPERIENCE KAUAI 7

What's Where 8
Kauai and Hawaii Today 10
Kauai Planner 12
Kauai Top Attractions. 14
Great Itineraries. 16
When to Go 18
Hawaiian History 19
Hawaiian People and Their
Culture. 20
Kids and Families 22
Top 10 Hawaiian Foods to Try 24
Only in Hawaii. 26
Top 5 Kauai Outdoor Adventures . .28
Top 5 Kauai Beaches. 29
Hawaii and the Environment 30
Top 5 Kauai Scenic Spots 31
Weddings and Honeymoons 32
Cruising the Hawaiian Islands 34

2 EXPLORING KAUAI 35

The North Shore. 40
The East Side. 56
The South Shore. 63
The West Side 67

3 BEACHES 75

The North Shore. 77
The East Side. 87
The South Shore. 93
The West Side 97

4 WATER SPORTS AND TOURS 101

Boat Tours 102
Body Boarding and Bodysurfing . .109
Deep-Sea Fishing 109
Kayaking 112
Kiteboarding 116

Napali Coast: Emerald Queen of Kauai. . 46
Snorkeling in Hawaii 121
Hawaii's Plants 101 139
Birth of the Islands 147
All About Lei. 167
Hula: More Than a Folk Dance. 180
Luau: A Taste of Hawaii 205

Scuba Diving. 116
Snorkeling 119
Stand-Up Paddling 127
Surfing. 128
Whale Watching. 131

**5 GOLF, HIKING, AND OUTDOOR
ACTIVITIES** 133

Aerial Tours. 135
ATV Tours 136
Biking 137
Golf 143
Hiking 146
Horseback Riding 153
Mountain Tubing. 154
Skydiving 155
Tennis 155
Zipline Tours 155

6 SHOPS AND SPAS 159
   Shops 161
   Spas 170
7 ENTERTAINMENT AND
   NIGHTLIFE 175
   Entertainment 176
   Nightlife 179
8 WHERE TO EAT 187
   Kauai Dining Planner 188
   The North Shore 189
   Best Bets for Kauai Dining 190
   The East Side 195
   The South Shore 203
   The West Side 213
9 WHERE TO STAY 215
   Kauai Lodging Planner 216
   The North Shore 217
   Best Bets for Kauai Lodging . . . 218
   The East Side 221
   The South Shore 226
   The West Side 232
   HAWAIIAN VOCABULARY . . . 234
   TRAVEL SMART KAUAI 237
   INDEX 249
   ABOUT OUR WRITERS 256

MAPS

Kauai 38–39
North Shore 42
East Side 57
South Shore 65
West Side 68
Kauai Beaches 78
North Shore Kauai 79
East Side Kauai 87
South Shore Kauai 93
Where to Eat on the
North Shore 193
Where to Eat on the East Side . . . 199
Where to Eat on the South Shore
and West Side 210
Where to Stay on the
North Shore 220
Where to Stay on the East Side . . 225
Where to Stay on the
South Shore and West Side 229

ABOUT THIS BOOK

Our Ratings

At Fodor's, we spend considerable time choosing the best places in a destination so you don't have to. By default, anything we recommend in this book is worth visiting. But some sights, properties, and experiences are so great that we've recognized them with additional accolades. Orange **Fodor's Choice** stars indicate our top recommendations; black stars highlight places we deem **Highly Recommended**; and **Best Bets** call attention to top properties in various categories. Disagree with any of our choices? Care to nominate a new place? Visit our feedback center at www.fodors.com/feedback.

Hotels

Hotels have private bath, phone, TV, and air-conditioning, and do not offer meals unless we specify that in the review. We always list facilities but not whether you'll be charged an extra fee to use them.

Restaurants

Unless we state otherwise, restaurants are open for lunch and dinner daily. We mention dress only when there's a specific requirement and reservations only when they're essential or not accepted—it's always best to book ahead.

Credit Cards

We assume that restaurants and hotels accept credit cards. If not, we'll note it in the review.

Budget Well

Hotel and restaurant price categories from $ to $$$$ are defined in the opening pages of the respective chapters. For attractions, we always give standard adult admission fees; reductions are usually available for children, students, and senior citizens.

Listings
★ Fodor's Choice
★ Highly recommended
⊠ Physical address
✛ Directions or Map coordinates
⌂ Mailing address
☎ Telephone
🖷 Fax
⊕ On the Web
✉ E-mail
🎫 Admission fee
🕐 Open/closed times
Ⓜ Metro stations
⊟ No credit cards

Hotels & Restaurants
🏨 Hotel
🛏 Number of rooms
🛁 Facilities
🍽 Meal plans
✗ Restaurant
🍴 Reservations
👔 Dress code
🚬 Smoking

Outdoors
⛳ Golf
⛺ Camping

Other
☕ Family-friendly
⇨ See also
⊠ Branch address
☞ Take note

Experience
Kauai

1

WHAT'S WHERE

1 North Shore. Dreamy beaches, green mountains, breathtaking scenery, and abundant rain, waterfalls, and rainbows characterize the North Shore, which includes the communities of Kilauea, Princeville, and Hanalei.

2 East Side. This is Kauai's commercial and residential hub, dominated by the island's largest town, Kapaa. The airport, harbor, and government offices are found in the county seat of Lihue.

3 South Shore. Peaceful landscapes, sunny weather, and beaches that rank among the best in the world make the South Shore the resort capital of Kauai. The Poipu resort area is here, along with the main towns of Koloa, Lawai, and Kalaheo.

4 West Side. Dry, sunny, and sleepy, the West Side includes the historic towns of Hanapepe, Waimea, and Kekaha. This area is ideal for outdoor adventurers because it's the entryway to the Waimea Canyon and Kokee State Park, and the departure point for most Napali Coast boat trips.

■ TIP→ On Kauai, the directions "mauka" (toward the mountains) and "makai" (toward the ocean) are often used. Locals tend to refer to highways by name rather than by number.

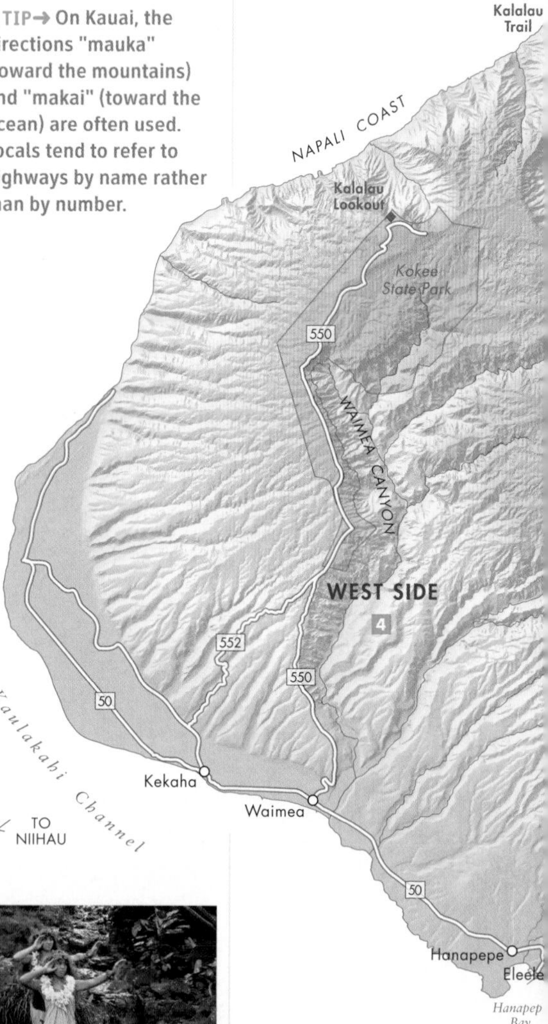

Kalalau Trail

NAPALI COAST

Kalalau Lookout

Kokee State Park

550

WAIMEA CANYON

WEST SIDE
4

552

550

50

Kaulakahi Channel

50

Kekaha

Waimea

↙ TO NIIHAU

50

Hanapepe

Eleele

Hanapepe Bay

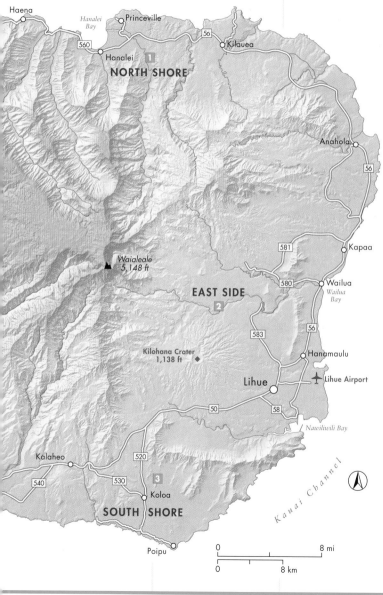

Haena

Hanalei Bay

Princeville

56

Kīlauea

560

Hanalei **1**

NORTH SHORE

Anahola

56

581

Kapaa

Waialeale
5,148 ft

580

Wailua

Wailua Bay

EAST SIDE

2

583

56

Kilohana Crater
1,138 ft

Hanamaulu

Lihue

Lihue Airport

50

58

Nawiliwili Bay

Kalaheo

520

Kauai Channel

540

530

3

Koloa

SOUTH SHORE

Poipu

0   8 mi

0   8 km

KAUAI AND HAWAII TODAY

Despite its small size—about 550 square miles—Kauai has four distinct regions, each with its own unique characteristics. The windward coast, which catches the prevailing trade winds, consists of the North Shore and East Side, while the drier, leeward coast encompasses the South Shore and West Side. One main road nearly encircles the island, except for a 15-mile stretch of sheer cliffs called the Napali Coast.

The center of the island—Mt. Waialeale, completely inaccessible by car and rarely viewable except from above due to nearly year-round cloud cover—is the wettest spot on earth, getting about 450 inches of rain per year.

Hawaiian culture and tradition here have experienced a renaissance over the last few decades. There's a real effort to revive traditions and to respect history as the Islands go through major changes. New developments often have a Hawaiian cultural expert on staff to ensure cultural sensitivity and to educate newcomers.

Nonetheless, development remains a huge issue for all Islanders—land prices are skyrocketing, putting many areas out of reach for the native population. Traffic is becoming a problem on roads that were not designed to accommodate all the new drivers, and the Islands' limited natural resources are being seriously tapped. The government, though sluggish to respond at first, is trying to make development in Hawaii as sustainable as possible.

Sustainability

Although sustainability is an effective buzzword and authentic direction for the Islands' dining establishments, 90% of Hawaii's food and energy is imported.

Most of the land was used for mono-cropping of pineapple or sugarcane, both of which have all but vanished. Sugarcane is now produced in only two plants on Kauai and Maui, while pineapple production has dropped precipitously. Dole, once the largest pineapple company in Hawaii, closed its plants in 1991, and after 90 years, Del Monte stopped pineapple production in 2008. The next year, Maui Land and Pineapple Company also ceased its Maui Gold pineapple operation, although in early 2010 a group of executives took over one third of the land and created a new company. Low cost of labor and transportation from Latin American and Southeast Asian pineapple producers are factors contributing to the industry's demise in Hawaii. Although this proves daunting, it also sets the stage for great agricultural change to be explored.

Back-to-Basics Agriculture

Emulating how the Hawaiian ancestors lived and returning to their simple ways of growing and sharing a variety of foods has become a statewide initiative. Hawaii has the natural conditions and talent to produce far more diversity in agriculture than it currently does.

The seed of this movement thrives through various farmers' markets and partnerships between restaurants and local farmers. Localized efforts such as the Hawaii Farm Bureau Federation are collectively leading the organic and sustainable agricultural renaissance. From home-cooked meals to casual plate lunches to fine-dining cuisine, these sustainable trailblazers enrich the culinary tapestry of Hawaii and uplift the Islands' overall quality of life.

Tourism and the Economy

The over-$10 billion tourism industry represents a third of Hawaii's state income. Naturally, this dependency causes economic hardship as the financial meltdown of recent years affects tourists' ability to visit and spend.

One way the industry has changed has been to adopt more eco-conscious practices, as many Hawaiians feel that development shouldn't happen without regard for impact to local communities and their natural environment.

Belief that an industry based on the Hawaiians' *aloha* should protect, promote, and empower local culture and provide more entrepreneurial opportunities for local people has become more important to tourism businesses. More companies are incorporating authentic Hawaiiana in their programs and aim not only to provide a commercially viable tour but also to ensure that the visitor leaves feeling connected to his or her host.

The concept of *kuleana*, a word for both privilege and responsibility, is upheld. Having the privilege to live in such a sublime place comes with the responsibility to protect it.

Sovereignty

Political issues of sovereignty continue to divide Native Hawaiians, who have formed myriad organizations, each operating with a separate agenda and lacking one collectively defined goal. Ranging from achieving complete independence to solidifying a nation within a nation, existing sovereignty models remain fractured and their future unresolved.

The introduction of the Native Hawaiian Government Reorganization Act of 2009 attempts to set up a legal framework in which Native Hawaiians can attain federal recognition and coexist as a self-governed entity. Also known as the Akaka Bill after Senator Daniel Akaka of Hawaii, this pending bill has been presented before Congress and is still awaiting a vote at the time of this writing.

Rise of Hawaiian Pride

After Hawaii became a state in 1959, a process of Americanization began. Traditions were duly silenced in the name of citizenship. Teaching Hawaiian language was banned from schools and children were distanced from their local customs.

But Hawaiians are resilient people, and with the rise of the civil rights movement they began to reflect on their own national identity, bringing an astonishing renaissance of the Hawaiian culture to fruition.

The people rediscovered language, hula, chanting, and even the traditional Polynesian arts of canoe building and wayfinding (navigation by the stars without use of instruments). This cultural resurrection is now firmly established in today's Hawaiian culture, with a palpable pride that exudes from Hawaiians young and old.

The election of President Barack Obama definitely increased Hawaiian pride and inspired a ubiquitous hope for a better future. The president's strong connection and commitment to Hawaiian values of diversity, spirituality, family, and conservation have restored confidence that Hawaii can inspire a more peaceful, tolerant, and environmentally conscious world.

KAUAI PLANNER

When You Arrive

All commercial and cargo flights use the Lihue Airport, 2 miles east of the town of Lihue. It has just two baggage-claim areas, each with a visitor information center.

A rental car is the best way to get to your hotel, though taxis and some hotel shuttles are available. From the airport it will take you about 15 to 25 minutes to drive to Wailua or Kapaa, 30 to 40 minutes to reach Poipu, and 45 minutes to an hour to get to Princeville or Hanalei.

Visitor Information

Information Hawaii Beach Safety ⊕ www.hawaiibeachsafety.org.

Hawaii Department of Land and Natural Resources ⊕ www.state.hi.us/dlnr.

Kauai Vacation Explorer ⊕ www.kauaiexplorer.com.

Kauai Visitors Bureau ⊠ 4334 Rice St., Suite 101, Lihue ☎ 808/245–3971, 800/262–1400 ⊕ www.kauaidiscovery.com.

Poipu Beach Resort Association ☐ Box 730, Koloa 96756 ☎ 808/742–7444, 888/744–0888 ⊕ www.poipu-beach.org.

Getting Here and Around

Unless you plan to stay strictly at a resort or do all of your sightseeing as part of guided tours, you'll need a rental car. There is bus service on the island, but the buses tend to be slow and run limited hours.

You most likely won't need a four-wheel-drive vehicle anywhere on the island, so save yourself the money. And although convertibles look like fun, the frequent, intermittent rain showers and intense tropical sun make hardtops a better (and cheaper) choice.

If possible, avoid the "rush" hours when the local workers go to and from their jobs. Kauai has some of the highest gas prices in the Islands. *See "Travel Smart Kauai" for more information on renting a car and driving.*

Island Driving Times

It might not seem as if driving from the North Shore to the West Side, say, would take much time, as Kauai is smaller than Oahu, Maui, and certainly the Big Island. But it will take longer than you'd expect, and Kauai roads are subject to some heavy traffic, especially going through Kapaa and Lihue. Here are average driving times that will help you plan your excursions accordingly.

Haena to Hanalei	5 mi/15 min
Hanalei to Princeville	4 mi/10 min
Princeville to Kilauea	5 mi/10 min
Kilauea to Anahola	8 mi/12 min
Anahola to Kapaa	5 mi/10 min
Kapaa to Lihue	10 mi/20 min
Lihue to Poipu	13 mi/25 min
Poipu to Kalaheo	8 mi/15 min
Kalaheo to Hanapepe	4 mi/8 min
Hanapepe to Waimea	7 mi/10 min

Money-Saving Tips

There are ways to travel to paradise even on a budget. Pick up free publications at the airport and at racks all over the island; many of them are filled with money-saving coupons. Access to beaches and most hiking trails on the island is free to the public. Grocery stores and Walmart generally stock postcards and souvenirs; they can be less expensive here than at hotel gift shops. For inexpensive fresh fruit and produce, check out farmers' markets and farm stands along the road—they'll often let you try before you buy.

Dining and Lodging on Kauai

Hawaii is a melting pot of cultures, and nowhere is this more apparent than in its cuisine. From luau and "plate lunch" to sushi and steak, there's no shortage of interesting flavors and presentations.

Whether you're looking for a quick snack or a multicourse meal, we'll help you find the best eating experiences the island has to offer.

There are several top-notch resorts on Kauai, as well as a wide variety of condos, vacation rentals, and bed-and-breakfasts to choose from. Selecting vacation lodging is a tough decision, but fret not—our expert writers and editors have done most of the legwork.

Looking for a tropical forest retreat, a big resort, or a private vacation rental? We'll give you all the details you need to book a place that suits your style. Quick tips: Reserve your room far in advance. Be sure to ask about discounts and special packages (hotel websites often have Internet-only deals).

WHAT IT COSTS

	$	$$	$$$	$$$$
Restaurants	under $17	$17–$26	$27–$35	over $35
Hotels	under $180	$180–$260	$261–$340	over $340

Seeing Napali

Let's put this in perspective: Even if you had only one day on Kauai, we'd still recommend heading to the Napali Coast on Kauai's northwest side. Once you're there, you'll soon realize why no road traverses this series of folding-fan cliffs. That leaves three ways to experience the coastline—by air, by water, or on foot. We recommend all three, in this order: air, water, foot. Each one gets progressively more sensory.

Napali Coast runs 15 miles from Kee Beach, one of Kauai's more popular snorkeling spots, on the island's North Shore to Polihale State Park, the longest stretch of beach in the state, on the West Side of the island.

If you can't squeeze in all three methods—air, water, and foot—or you can't afford all three, we recommend the helicopter tour for those strapped for time and the hiking for those with a low budget. The boat tours are great for family fun.

Whatever way you choose to visit Napali, you might want to keep this awe-inspiring fact in mind: At one time, thousands of Hawaiians lived self-sufficiently in these valleys.

KAUAI
TOP ATTRACTIONS

Napali

(A) Some things defy words, and the Napali Coast is one of them. Besides, *beautiful, verdant, spectacular,* and *amazing* lose their meaning after repeated usage, so forget trying to think of words to describe it, but don't forget to experience Kauai's remote, northwest coastline any which way—by air, water, or trail, preferably all three.

Waimea Canyon Drive

(B) From its start in the west Kauai town of Waimea to the road's end some 20 miles uphill later, at Puu O Kila Lookout, you'll pass through several microclimates—from hot, desertlike conditions at sea level to the cool, deciduous forest of Kokee—and navigate through the traditional Hawaiian system of land division called *ahupuaa.*

Hanalei Bay

(C) Families. Honeymooners. Retirees. Surfers. Sunbathers. Hanalei Bay attracts all kinds, for good reason—placid water in summer; epic surf in winter; the wide, 2-mile-long crescent-shape beach year-round; and the green mountain backdrop striated with waterfalls—also year-round but definitely in full force in winter. And did we mention the atmosphere? Decidedly laid-back.

Spas, Spas, Spas

(D) Kauai is characterized by its rural nature (read: quiet and peaceful), which lends itself nicely to the spa scene on the island. The vast majority of spas could be called rural, too, as they invite the outside in—or would that be the inside out? For a resort spa, ANARA Spa is not only decadent but set in a garden. A Hideaway Spa sits in a grove of old-style plantation homes, and Angeline's traditional Hawaiian spa, Muolaulani, is in her home. The

Halelea Spa at the St. Regis boasts 12 treatment rooms with a variety of massage offerings, including fruit and flower treatments.

Highway 560
(E) This 10-mile stretch of road starting at the Hanalei Scenic Overlook in Princeville rivals all in Hawaii and in 2003 was listed on the National Register of Historic Places, one of only about 100 roads nationwide to meet the criteria. Indeed, the road itself is said to follow an ancient Hawaiian walking trail that skirts the ocean. Today, Route 560 includes 13 historic bridges and culverts, most of which are one-lane wide. Be patient.

River Kayaking
(F) The best part about kayaking Kauai's rivers is that you don't have to be experienced. There are no rapids to run, no waterfalls to jump and, therefore, no excuses for not enjoying the scenic sights from the water. On the East Side, try the Wailua River; if you're on the North Shore, don't miss the Hanalei River. But if you have some experience and are in reasonably good shape, you may choose to create a few lifetime memories and kayak the Napali Coast.

Sunshine Markets
(G) Bananas. Mangos. Papayas. Lemons. Limes. Lychees. The best and freshest fruits, vegetables, flowers—and goat cheese—are found at various farmers' markets around the island. Just don't get there too late in the day—much of the best stuff goes early.

GREAT ITINERARIES

As small as Kauai may be, you still can't do it all in one day: hiking Kalalau Trail, kayaking Wailua River, showering in a waterfall, watching whales at Kilauea Lighthouse, waking to the sunrise above Kealia, touring underwater lava tubes at Tunnels, and shopping for gifts at Koloa Town shops. Rather than trying to check everything off your list in one fell swoop, we recommend choosing your absolute favorite and devoting a full day to the experience.

A Bit of History

Because Hawaiian beliefs are traditionally rooted in nature, much of what you see in Kauai today is built on sacred ground. If you're interested in archaeological remains where sacred ceremonies were held, focus on the Wailua River area. Your best bet is to take a riverboat tour—it's full of kitsch, but you'll definitely walk away with a deeper understanding of ancient Hawaii. Then, head to Lihue's Kauai Museum, where you can pick up a memento of authentic Hawaiian artistry at the gift shop. End your day at Gaylord's restaurant and meander through the historic Kilohana Plantation sugar estate.

Adventure Galore

For big-time adventure, kayak Napali Coast or spend a day learning to fly a microlight. For those whose idea of adventure is a good walk, take the flat, coastal trail along the East Side—you can pick it up just about anywhere starting at the southern end of Lydgate Park, heading north. It'll take you all the way to Anahola, if you desire. After it's all over, recuperate with a massage by the ocean—or in the comfort of your own room, so you can crash immediately afterward.

A Day on the Water

Start your day before sunrise and head west to Port Allen Marina. Check in with one of the tour-boat operators—who will provide you with plenty of coffee to jumpstart your day—and cruise Napali Coast before heading across the Kaulakahi Channel to snorkel the fish-rich waters of Niihau. Slather up with sunscreen and be prepared for a long—and sometimes big—day on the water; you can enjoy a couple of mai tais on the return trip. Something about the sun and the salt air conspires to induce a powerful sense of fatigue—so don't plan anything in the evening. The trip also helps build a huge appetite, so stop at Grinds in Eleele on the way home.

Coastal Drives

If you're staying on the East Side or North Shore, the best drive for ocean vistas is, hands down, Highway 560, which begins at Princeville on the main highway where Highway 56 ends. Stop at the first lookout overseeing Hanalei River valley for a few snapshots; then head down the hill, across the one-lane bridge—taking in the taro fields—and through the town of Hanalei and on to the end of the road at Kee Beach. If you're up for it, enjoy a bit of unparalleled hiking on the Kalalau Trail, go snorkeling at Kee, or simply soak up the sun on the beach, if it's not too crowded. If you're staying on the South Shore or West Side, follow Highway 50 west. You'll start to catch distant ocean vistas from the highway as you head out of the town of Kalaheo and from the coffee fields of Kauai Coffee. Stop here for a sample. You'll come closer to the ocean—and practically reach out and touch it—after you pass through Waimea en route to Kekaha. Although this isn't great swimming water—it's unprotected,

with no reef—there is a long stretch of beach here perfect for walking, running, or simply meandering. Once the paved road ends—if you're brave and your car-rental agreement allows—keep going and you'll eventually come to Polihale, a huge, deserted beach. It'll feel like the end of the world here, so it's a great place to spend a quiet afternoon and witness a spectacular sunset. Just be sure to pack plenty of food, water, and sunscreen before you depart Kekaha—and gas up the car.

Shop Till You Drop

You could actually see a good many of the island's sights by browsing in our favorite island shops. Of course, you can't see the entire island, but this itinerary will take you through Kapaa and north to Hanalei. Don't miss Marta's Boat—high-end clothing for mom and child—across from Foodland in Waipouli. A mile north, Kela's Glass has great art pieces. From there, a leisurely drive north will reveal the rural side of Kauai. If you enjoy tea, sake, or sushi, stop at Kilauea's Kong Lung, where you can stock up on complete place settings for each. Then, head down the road to Hanalei. If you're inspired by surf, stop in Hanalei Surf Company. Our favorite for one-of-a-kind keepsakes—actually antiques and authentic memorabilia—is Yellow Fish Trading Company, and we never head into Hanalei without stopping at On the Road to Hanalei.

Relax Kauai-Style

If you're headed to Kauai for some peace and quiet, you'll want to start your day with yoga at Yoga Hanalei (⊕ *www.yogahanalei.com*) or Kapaa's Bikram Yoga Kauai (⊕ *www.birkamyogakapaa.com*). If you're staying on the South Shore, try yoga on the beach (actually a grassy spot just off the beach) with longtime yoga instructor Joy Zepeda (⊕ *www.aloha-yoga.com*). If it happens to be the second or last Sunday of the month, you might then head to the Lawai International Center (⊕ *www.lawaicenter.org*) for an afternoon stroll among 88 Buddhist shrines. On the North Shore, Limahuli Gardens is the perfect place to wander among native plants. Then watch the sun slip into the sea on any west-facing beach and call it a day with a glass of wine.

Have a Little Romance

We can't think of a better way to ensure a romantic vacation for two than to pop a bottle of champagne and walk the Mahaulepu shoreline at sunrise, hand in hand with a loved one. Make this a Sunday and follow your walk with brunch at the Grand Hyatt. Then spend the afternoon luxuriating with facials, body scrubs, and massage in the Hyatt ANARA Spa's Garden Treatment Village, in a private, thatched hut just for couples. That'll put you in the mood for a wedding ceremony or renewal of vows on the beach followed by a sunset dinner overlooking the ocean at the Beach House restaurant. Can it get any more romantic than this?

WHEN TO GO

Long days of sunshine and fairly mild year-round temperatures make Hawaii an all-season destination. Most resort areas are at sea level, with average afternoon temperatures of 75°F–80°F during the coldest months of December and January; during the hottest months of August and September the temperature often reaches 90°F. Only at high elevations does the temperature drop into the colder realms, and only at mountain summits does it reach freezing.

Kauai is beautiful in every season, but if you must have good beach weather, you should plan to visit between June and October. The rainy season runs from November through February, with the windward or east and north areas of the island receiving most of the rainfall. Nights can be chilly from November through March. Rain is possible throughout the year, of course, but it rarely rains everywhere on the island at once. If it's raining where you are, the best thing to do is head to another side of the island, usually south or west.

If you're a beach lover, keep in mind that big surf can make many North Shore beaches unswimmable during winter months, while the South Shore gets its large swells in summer. If you want to see the humpback whales, February is the best month, though they arrive as early as October and a few may still be around in early April. In winter, Napali Coast boat tours can be rerouted due to high seas, the Kalalau Trail can become very wet and muddy or, at times, impassable, and sea kayaking is not an option. If you have your heart set on visiting Kauai's famed coast you may want to visit in the drier, warmer months (May–September).

Hawaiian Holidays

If you happen to be in the Islands on March 26 or June 11, you'll notice light traffic and busy beaches—these are state holidays not celebrated anywhere else. March 26 recognizes the birthday of Prince Jonah Kuhio Kalanianaole, a member of the royal line who served as a delegate to Congress and spearheaded the effort to set aside homelands for Hawaiian people. June 11 honors the first island-wide monarch, Kamehameha I; locals drape his statues with lei and stage elaborate parades. May 1 isn't an official holiday, but it's the day when schools and civic groups celebrate the quintessential Island gift, the flower lei. Statehood Day is celebrated on the third Friday in August (admission to the Union was August 21, 1959). Check the daily *Garden Island* paper for other events.

Climate

Moist trade winds drop their precipitation on the North Shore and East Side of the island, creating tropical climates, while the South Shore and West Side mainly remain hot and dry.

Average maximum and minimum temperatures for Kauai are listed *below*; the temperatures throughout the Hawaiian Islands are similar.

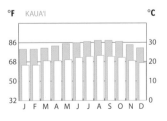

HAWAIIAN HISTORY

Hawaiian history is long and complex; a brief survey can put into context the ongoing renaissance of native arts and culture.

The Polynesians

Long before both Christopher Columbus and the Vikings, Polynesian seafarers set out to explore the vast stretches of the open ocean in double-hulled canoes. From western Polynesia, they traveled back and forth between Samoa, Fiji, Tahiti, the Marquesas, and the Society Isles, settling on the outer reaches of the Pacific, Hawaii, and Easter Island, as early as AD 300. The golden era of Polynesian voyaging peaked around AD 1200, after which the distant Hawaiian Islands were left to develop their own unique cultural practices and subsistence in relative isolation.

The Islands' symbiotic society was deeply intertwined with religion, mythology, science, and artistry. Ruled by an *alii,* or chief, each settlement was nestled in an *ahupuaa*, a pie-shaped land division from the uplands where the alii lived, through the valleys and down to the shores where the commoners resided. Everyone contributed, whether it was by building canoes, catching fish, making tools, or farming land.

A United Kingdom

When the British explorer Captain James Cook arrived in 1778, he was revered as a god upon his arrival and later killed over a stolen boat. With guns and ammunition purchased from Cook, the Big Island chief, Kamehameha the Great, gained a significant advantage over the other alii. He united Hawaii into one kingdom in 1810, bringing an end to the frequent interisland battles that dominated Hawaiian life.

Tragically, the new kingdom was beset with troubles. Native religion was abandoned, and *kapu* (laws and regulations) were eventually abolished. The European explorers brought foreign diseases with them, and within a few short decades the Native Hawaiian population was decimated.

New laws regarding land ownership and religious practices eroded the underpinnings of pre-contact Hawaii. Each successor to the Hawaiian throne sacrificed more control over the Island kingdom. As Westerners permeated Hawaiian culture, Hawaii became more riddled with layers of racial issues, injustice, and social unrest.

Modern Hawaii

Finally in 1893, the last Hawaiian monarch, Queen Liliuokalani, was overthrown by a group of Americans and European businessmen and government officials, aided by an armed militia. This led to the creation of the Republic of Hawaii, and it became a U.S. territory for the next 60 years. The loss of Hawaiian sovereignty and the conditions of annexation have haunted the Hawaiian people since the monarchy was deposed.

Pearl Harbor was attacked in 1941, which engaged the United States immediately into World War II. Tourism, from its beginnings in the early 1900s, flourished after the war and naturally inspired rapid real estate development in Waikiki. In 1959, Hawaii officially became the 50th state. Statehood paved the way for Hawaiians to participate in the American democratic process, which was not universally embraced by all Hawaiians. With the rise of the civil rights movement in the 1960s, Hawaiians began to reclaim their own identity, from language to hula.

HAWAIIAN PEOPLE AND THEIR CULTURE

By October 2010, Hawaii's population was more than 1.3 million with the majority of residents living on Oahu. Nine percent are Hawaiian or other Pacific Islander, almost 40% are Asian American, 9% are Latino, and about 25% Caucasian. Nearly a fifth of the population list two or more races, making Hawaii the most diverse state in the United States.

Among individuals 18 and older, about 84% finished high school, half attained some college, and 26% completed a bachelor's degree or higher.

The Role of Tradition

The kingdom of Hawaii was ruled by a spiritual class system. Although the *alii*, or chief, was believed to be the direct descendent of a deity or god, high priests, known as *kahuna*, presided over every imaginable aspect of life and *kapu* (taboos) that strictly governed the commoners.

Each part of nature and ritual was connected to a deity—Kane was the highest of all deities, symbolizing sunlight and creation; Ku was the god of war; Lono represented fertility, rainfall, music, and peace; Kanaloa was the god of the underworld or darker spirits. Probably the most well known by outsiders is Pele, the goddess of fire.

The kapu not only provided social order, they also swayed the people to act with reverence for the environment. Any abuse was met with extreme punishment, often death, as it put the land and people's *mana*, or spiritual power, in peril.

Ancient deities play a huge role in Hawaiian life today—not just in daily rituals, but in the Hawaiians' reverence for their land. Gods and goddesses tend to be associated with particular parts of the land, and most of them are connected with

many places, thanks to the body of stories built up around each.

One of the most important ways the ancient Hawaiians showed respect for their gods and goddesses was through the hula. Various forms of the hula were performed as prayers to the gods and as praise to the chiefs. Performances were taken very seriously, as a mistake was thought to invalidate the prayer, or even to offend the god or chief in question. Hula is still performed both as entertainment and as prayer; it is not uncommon for a hula performance to be included in an official government ceremony.

Who Are the Hawaiians Today?

To define the Hawaiians in a page, let alone a paragraph, is nearly impossible. Those considered to be indigenous Hawaiians are descendants of the ancient Polynesians who crossed the vast ocean and settled Hawaii. According to the government, there are Native Hawaiians or native Hawaiians (note the change in capitalization), depending on a person's background.

Federal and state agencies apply different methods to determine Hawaiian lineage, from measuring blood percentage to mapping genealogy. This has caused turmoil within the community because it excludes many who claim Hawaiian heritage. It almost guarantees that, as races intermingle, even those considered Native Hawaiian now will eventually disappear on paper, displacing generations to come.

Modern Hawaiian Culture

Perfect weather aside, Hawaii might be the warmest place anyone can visit. The Hawaii experience begins and ends with *aloha,* a word that envelops love, affection, and mercy, and has become a salutation for hello and good-bye. Broken

down, *alo* means "presence" and *ha* means "breath"—the presence of breath. It's to live with love and respect for self and others with every breath. Past the manicured resorts and tour buses, aloha is a moral compass that binds all of Hawaii's people.

Hawaii is blessed with some of the most unspoiled natural wonders, and aloha extends to the land, or *aina*. Hawaiians are raised outdoors and have strong ties to nature. They realize as children that the ocean and land are the delicate source of all life. Even ancient gods were embodied by nature, and this reverence has been passed down to present generations who believe in *kuleana,* their privilege and responsibility.

Hawaii's diverse cultures unfold in a beautiful montage of customs and arts—from music, to dance, to food. Musical genres range from slack key to *Jawaiian* (Hawaiian reggae) to *hapa-haole* (Hawaiian music with English words). From George Kahumoku's Grammy-worthy laid-back strumming, to the late Iz Kamakawiwoole's "Somewhere over the Rainbow," to Jack Johnson's more mainstream tunes, contemporary Hawaiian music has definitely carved its ever-evolving niche.

The Merrie Monarch Festival is celebrating almost 50 years of worldwide hula competition and education. The fine-dining culinary scene, especially in Honolulu, has a rich tapestry of ethnic influences and talent. But the real gems are the humble hole-in-the-wall eateries that serve authentic cuisines of many ethnic origins in one plate, a deliciously mixed plate indeed.

And perhaps, the most striking quality in today's Hawaiian culture is the sense of family, or *ohana*. Sooner or later, almost everyone you meet becomes an uncle or auntie, and it is not uncommon for near strangers to be welcomed into a home as a member of the family.

Until the last century, the practice of *hanai,* in which a family essentially adopts a child, usually a grandchild, without formalities, was still prevalent. While still practiced to a somewhat lesser degree, the *hanai,* which means to feed or nourish, still resonates within most families and communities.

How to Act Like a Local

Adopting local customs is a firsthand introduction to the Islands' unique culture. So live in T-shirts and shorts. Wear cheap rubber flip-flops, but call them slippers. Wave people into your lane on the highway, and, when someone lets you in, give them a wave of thanks in return. Never, ever blow your horn, even when the pickup truck in front of you is stopped for a long session of "talk story" right in the middle of the road.

Holoholo means to go out for the fun of it—an aimless stroll, ride, or drive. "Wheah you goin', braddah?" "Oh, holoholo." It's local speak for Sunday drive, no plan, it's not the destination but the journey. Try setting out without an itinerary. Learn to *shaka*: pinky and thumb extended, middle fingers curled in, waggle sideways. Eat white rice with everything. When someone says, "Aloha!" answer, "Aloha no!" ("And a real big aloha back to you"). And, as the locals say, "No make big body" ("Try not to act like you own the place").

KIDS AND FAMILIES

With dozens of adventures, discoveries, and fun-filled beach days, Hawaii is a blast with kids. Even better, the things to do here do not appeal only to small fry. The entire family, parents included, will enjoy surfing, discovering a waterfall in the rain forest, and snorkeling with sea turtles. And there are plenty of organized activities for kids that will free parents' time for a few romantic beach strolls.

Choosing a Place to Stay

Resorts: All the big resorts make kids' programs a priority, and it shows. When you are booking your room, ask about "kids eat free" deals and the number of kids' pools at the resort. Also check out the size of the groups in the children's programs, and find out whether the cost of the programs includes lunch, equipment, and activities.

On the North Shore the best bet is the St. Regis Princeville Resort, where kids can spend the day (without their parents) exploring local sea life with a marine biologist. The Kauai Marriott Resort is a good choice on the East Side, and on the South Shore both the Grand Hyatt Kauai and Sheraton Kauai Resort have kids' programs.

Condos: Condo and vacation rentals are a fantastic value for families vacationing in Hawaii. You can cook your own food, which is cheaper than eating out and sometimes easier (especially if you have a finicky eater in your group), and you'll get twice the space of a hotel room for about a quarter of the price. If you decide to go the condo route, be sure to ask about the size of the complex's pool (some try to pawn a tiny soaking tub off as a pool) and whether barbecues are available. One of the best parts of staying in your own place is having a sunset family barbecue by the pool or overlooking the ocean.

On the North Shore, there are numerous condo resort choices in Princeville, including Hanalei Bay Resort with eight tennis courts and two pools. On the South Shore, Outrigger Kiahuna Plantation is a family favorite, with an excellent location that includes a swimmable beach adjacent to a grassy field great for picnics.

Ocean Activities

Hawaii is all about getting your kids outside—away from TV and video games. And who could resist the turquoise water, the promise of spotting dolphins or whales, and the fun of body boarding or surfing?

On the Beach: Most people like being in the water, but toddlers and school-age kids tend to be especially enamored of it. The swimming pool at your condo or hotel is always an option, but don't be afraid to hit the beach with a little one in tow. There are several beaches in Hawaii that are nearly as safe as a pool—completely protected bays with pleasant white-sand beaches. As always, use your judgment, and heed all posted signs and lifeguard warnings.

Generally calm beaches to try include Anini Beach and Hanalei Bay Beach Park on the North Shore, Lydgate State Park and Kalapaki Beach on the East Side, Poipu Beach Park on the South Shore, and Salt Pond Beach Park on the West Side.

On the Waves: Surf lessons are a great idea for older kids, especially if Mom and Dad want a little quiet time. Beginner lessons are always on safe and easy waves and last anywhere from two to four hours.

The Blue Seas Surf School is best for beginners, and you can book your kids a 1½-hour lesson for $75.

The Underwater World: If your kids are ready to try snorkeling, Hawaii is a great place to introduce them to the underwater world. Even without the mask and snorkel, they'll be able to see colorful fish darting this way and that, and they may also spot turtles and dolphins at many of the island beaches.

Get your kids used to the basics at Lydgate State Park on the island's East Side, where there's no threat of a current. On its guided snorkel tours, SeaFun Kauai will show kids of all ages how to identify marine life and gives great beginner instruction.

Land Activities

In addition to beach experiences, Hawaii has rain forests, botanical gardens, numerous aquariums (Oahu and Maui take the cake), and even petting zoos and hands-on children's museums that will keep your kids entertained and out of the sun for a day.

On the North Shore, kids will love Na Aina Kai, a garden with a 16-foot-tall Jack and the Beanstalk bronze sculpture, gecko maze, tree house, kid-size train, and tropical jungle, and on the East Side is Smith's Tropical Paradise, a 30-acre botanical garden.

Horseback riding is a popular family activity, and most of the tours on Kauai move slowly, so no riding experience is required. Kids as young as two can ride at Esprit de Corps.

When it rains on Kauai, kids don't have to stay indoors. ATV tours are the activity of choice. Try Kauai ATV Tours, which has two-passenger "Mud Bugs" to accommodate families with kids ages five and older.

After Dark

At night, younger kids get a kick out of luaus, and many of the shows incorporate young audience members, adding to the fun. The older kids might find it all a bit lame, but there are a handful of new shows in the Islands that are more modern, incorporating acrobatics, lively music, and fire dancers. If you're planning on hitting a luau with a teen in tow, we highly recommend going the modern route—try Luau Kalamaku in Lihue. The best luau for young kids on Kauai is Smith's Tropical Paradise, in Wailua. A tram tour takes families through the botanical garden before dinner, and the show starts with some high-tech pyrotechnics. Also, guests actually leave their dinner tables to walk to the amphitheater, which means young ones don't have to sit still the entire evening.

TOP 10 HAWAIIAN FOODS TO TRY

Food in Hawaii is a reflection of the state's diverse cultural makeup and tropical location. Fresh seafood, organic fruits and vegetables, free-range beef, and locally grown products are the hallmarks of Hawaii regional cuisine. Its preparations are drawn from across the Pacific Rim, including Japan, the Philippines, Korea, and Thailand—and "local food" is a cuisine in its own right. Don't miss Hawaiian-grown coffee, either, whether it's smooth Kona from the Big Island or coffee grown on other islands.

Saimin

The ultimate hangover cure and the perfect comfort food during Hawaii's mild winters, *saimin* ranks at the top of the list of local favorites. In fact, it's one of the few dishes deemed truly local, having been highlighted in cookbooks since the 1930s. Saimin is an Asian-style noodle soup so ubiquitous, it's even on McDonald's menus statewide. In mom-and-pop shops, a large melamine bowl is filled with homemade *dashi*, or chicken broth, and wheat-flour noodles and then topped off with strips of omelet, green onions, bright pink fish cake and *char siu* (Chinese roast pork) or canned luncheon meat, such as SPAM. Add shoyu and chili pepper water, lift your chopsticks and slurp away.

SPAM

Speaking of SPAM, Hawaii's most prevalent grab-and-go snack is SPAM *musubi*. Often displayed next to cash registers at groceries and convenience stores, the glorified rice ball is rectangular, topped with a slice of fried SPAM and wrapped in *nori* (seaweed). Musubi is a bite-sized meal in itself. But just like sushi, the rice part hardens when refrigerated. So it's best to gobble it up, right after purchase.

Hormel Company's SPAM actually deserves its own recognition—way beyond as a mere musubi topping. About 5 million cans are sold per year in Hawaii and the Aloha State even hosts a festival in its honor. It's inexpensive protein and goes a long way when mixed with rice, scrambled eggs, noodles or, well, anything. The spiced luncheon meat gained popularity in World War II days, when fish was rationed. Gourmets and those with aversions to salt, high cholesterol, or high blood pressure may cringe at the thought of eating it, but SPAM in Hawaii is here to stay.

Manapua

Another savory snack is *manapua*, fist-sized dough balls fashioned after Chinese *bao* (a traditional Chinese bun) and stuffed with fillings such as *char siu* (Chinese barbeque) pork and then steamed. Many mom-and-pop stores sell them in commercial steamer display cases along with pork hash and other dim sum. Modern-day fillings include curry chicken.

Fresh Ahi or Tako Poke

There's nothing like fresh ahi or *tako* (octopus) *poke* to break the ice at a backyard party, except, of course, the cold beer handed to you from the cooler. The perfect pupu, poke (pronounced poh-kay) is basically raw seafood cut into bite-sized chunks and mixed with everything from green onions to roasted and ground kukui nuts. Other variations include mixing the fish with chopped round onion, sesame oil, seaweed, and chili pepper water. Shoyu is the constant. These days, grocery stores sell a rainbow of varieties such as kimchi crab and anything goes, from adding mayonnaise to tobiko caviar. Fish lovers who want to take it to the next level order sashimi, the best cuts of ahi sliced and dipped in a mixture of shoyu and wasabi.

Tropical Fruits

Tropical fruits such as apple banana and strawberry papaya are plucked from trees in Island neighborhoods and eaten for breakfast—plain or with a squeeze of fresh lime. Give them a try; the banana tastes like an apple and the papaya's rosy flesh explains its name. Locals also love to add their own creative touches to exotic fruits. Green mangoes are pickled with Chinese five spice, and Maui Gold pineapples are topped with li hing mui powder (heck, even margarita glasses are rimmed with it). Green papaya is tossed in a Vietnamese salad with fish paste and fresh prawns.

Plate Lunch

It would be remiss not to mention the plate lunch as one of the most beloved dishes in Hawaii. It generally includes two scoops of sticky white rice, a scoop of macaroni or macaroni-potato salad, heavy on the mayo, and perhaps kimchi or *koko* (salted cabbage). There are countless choices of main protein such as chicken *katsu* (fried cutlet), fried mahimahi and beef tomato. The king of all plate lunches is the Hawaiian plate. The main item is laulau or kalua pig and cabbage along with poi, *lomilomi* salmon, chicken long rice, and sticky white rice.

Bento Box

The bento box gained popularity back in the plantation days, when workers toiled in the sugarcane fields. No one brought sandwiches to work then. Instead it was a lunch box with the ever-present steamed white rice, pickled *ume* (plum) to preserve the rice, and main meats such as fried chicken or fish. Today, many stores sell prepackaged bentos or you may go to an *okazuya* (Japanese deli) with a hot buffet counter and create your own.

Malasadas

The Portuguese have contributed much to Hawaii cuisine in the form of sausage, soup, and sweetbread. But their most revered food is *malasadas*, hot, deep-fried doughnuts rolled in sugar. Malasadas are crowd-pleasers. Buy them by the dozen, hot from the fryer, placed in brown paper bags to absorb the grease. Or bite into gourmet malasadas at restaurants, filled with vanilla or chocolate cream.

Shave Ice

Much more than just a snow cone, shave ice is what locals crave after a blazing day at the beach or a hot-as-Hades game of soccer. If you're lucky, you'll find a neighborhood store that hand-shaves the ice, but it's rare. Either way, the counter person will ask you first if you'd like ice cream and/or adzuki beans scooped into the bottom of the cone or cup. Then they shape the ice to a giant mound and add colorful fruit syrups. First-timers should order the Rainbow, of course.

Crack Seed

There are dozens of varieties of crack seed in dwindling specialty shops and at the drug stores. Chinese call the preserved fruits and nuts *see mui* but somehow the Pidgin English version is what Hawaiians prefer. Those who like hard candy and salty foods will love li hing mangoes and rock salt plums, and those with an itchy throat will feel relief from the lemon strips. Peruse large glass jars of crack seed sold in bulk or smaller hanging bags—the latter make good gifts to give to friends back home.

ONLY IN HAWAII

Traveling to Hawaii is as close as an American can get to visiting another country while staying within the United States. There's much to learn and understand about the state's indigenous culture, the hundred years of immigration that resulted in today's blended society, and the tradition of aloha that has welcomed millions of visitors over the years.

Aloha Shirt

To go to Hawaii without taking an aloha shirt home is almost sacrilege. The first aloha shirts from the 1920s and 1930s—called "silkies"—were classic canvases of art and tailored for the tourists. Popular culture caught on in the 1950s, and they became a fashion craze. With the 1960s' more subdued designs, Aloha Friday was born, and the shirt became appropriate clothing for work, play, and formal occasions. Because of its soaring popularity, cheaper and mass-produced versions became available.

Hawaiian Quilt

Although ancient Hawaiians were already known to produce fine *kapa* (bark) cloth, the actual art of quilting originated from the missionaries. Hawaiians have created designs to reflect their own aesthetic, and bold patterns evolved over time. They can be pricey because the quilts are intricately made by hand and can take years to finish. These masterpieces are considered precious heirlooms that reflect the history and beauty of Hawaii.

Popular Souvenirs

Souvenir shopping can be intimidating. There's a sea of Island-inspired and often kitschy merchandise, so we'd like to give you a breakdown of popular and fun gifts that you might encounter and consider bringing home. If authenticity is important to you, be sure to check labels and ask shopkeepers. Museum shops are good places for authentic, Hawaiian-made souvenirs.

Fabrics. Purchased by the yard or already made into everything from napkins to bedspreads, modern Hawaiian fabrics make wonderful keepsakes.

Home accessories. Deck out your kitchen or dining room in festive luau style with bottle openers, pineapple mugs, tiki glasses, shot glasses, slipper and surfboard magnets, and salt-and-pepper shakers.

Lei and shell necklaces. From silk or polyester flower lei to kukui or puka shell necklaces, lei have been traditionally used as a welcome offering to guests (although the artificial ones are more for fun, as real flowers are always preferable).

Lauhala products. *Lauhala* weaving is a traditional Hawaiian art. The leaves come from the hala, or pandanus, tree and are hand-woven to create lovely gift boxes, baskets, bags, and picture frames.

Spa products. Relive your spa treatment at home with Hawaiian bath and body products, many of them manufactured with ingredients found only on the Islands.

Vintage Hawaii. You can find vintage photos, reproductions of vintage postcards or paintings, heirloom jewelry, and vintage aloha wear in many specialty stores.

Luau

The luau's origin, which was a celebratory feast, can be traced back to the earliest Hawaiian civilizations. In the traditional luau, the taboo or *kapu* laws were very strict, requiring men and women to eat separately. However, in 1819 King Kamehameha II broke the great taboo and shared a feast with women and commoners ushering in the modern-era luau. Today, traditional luau usually commemorate a

child's first birthday, graduation, wedding, or other family occasion. They also are a Hawaiian experience that most visitors enjoy, and resorts and other companies have incorporated the fire-knife dance and other Polynesian dances into their elaborate presentations.

Nose flutes

The nose flute is an instrument used in ancient times to serenade a lover. For the Hawaiians, the nose is romantic, sacred, and pure. The Hawaiian word for kiss is *honi*. Similar to an Eskimo's kiss, the noses touch on each side sharing one's spiritual energy or breath. The Hawaiian term, *ohe hano ihu*, simply translated to "bamboo," with which the instrument is made; "breathe," because one has to gently breathe through it to make soothing music; and "nose," as it is made for the nose and not the mouth.

Slack-Key Guitar and the Paniolo

Kihoalu, or slack-key music, evolved in the early 1800s when King Kamehameha III brought in Mexican and Spanish vaqueros to manage the overpopulated cattle that had run wild on the Islands. The vaqueros brought their guitars and would play music around the campfire after work. When they left, supposedly leaving their guitars to their new friends, the Hawaiian *paniolo*, or cowboys, began to infuse what they learned from the vaqueros with their native music and chants, and so the art of slack-key music was born.

Today, the paniolo culture thrives where ranchers have settled.

Ukulele

The word *ukulele* literally translates to the "the jumping flea" and came to Hawaii in the 1880s by way of the Portuguese and Spanish. Once a fading art form, today it brings international kudos as a solo instrument, thanks to tireless musicians and teachers who have worked hard to keep it by our fingertips.

One such teacher is Roy Sakuma. Founder of four ukulele schools and a legend in his own right, Sakuma and his wife Kathy produced Oahu's first Ukulele Festival in 1971. Since then, they've brought the tradition to the Big Island, Kauai, and Maui. The free event annually draws thousands of artists and fans from all over the globe.

Hula

"Hula is the language of the heart, therefore the heartbeat of the Hawaiian people." —Kalakaua, the Merrie Monarch. Thousands—from tots to seniors—devote hours each week to hula classes. All these dancers need some place to show off their stuff. The result is a network of hula competitions (generally free or very inexpensive) and free performances in malls and other public spaces. Many resorts offer hula instruction.

TOP 5 KAUAI OUTDOOR ADVENTURES

Kauai's spectacular scenery makes getting outdoors a must-do activity for most people.

There are endless options here for spending time outside enjoying waterfalls, rivers, coastlines, and canyons, but here are a few of our favorites.

Tour Napali Coast by Boat

Every one of the Hawaiian Islands possesses something spectacularly unique to it and this stretch of folding cliffs is it for Kauai. To see it, though, you'll want to hop aboard a boat. You may opt for a leisurely ride aboard a catamaran or a more adventurous inflatable raft. Some tours offer the opportunity to stop for snorkeling or a walk through an ancient fishing village.

Kayak the Wailua River

The largest river in all Hawaii, the Wailua River's source is the center of the island—a place known as Mt. Waialeale—the wettest spot on earth. And yet it's no Mighty Mississippi. There are no rapids to run. And that makes it a great waterway on which to learn to kayak. Guided tours will take you to a remote waterfall. Bring the whole family on this one.

Hike the Kalalau Trail

The Sierra Club allegedly rates this famous, cliffside trail a difficulty level of 9 out of 10. But don't let that stop you. You don't have to hike the entire 11 miles. A mile hike will reward you with scenic ocean views—in winter, you might see breaching whales—and sights of soaring seabirds and tropical plant life dotting the trail sides. Wear sturdy shoes, pack your camera, and be prepared to ooh and aah.

Enjoy a Helicopter Ride

If you drive from Kee Beach to Polihale, you may think you've seen all of Kauai, but we're here to tell you there's more scenic beauty awaiting you. Lots more. Save up for this one. It's not cheap, but a helicopter ride over the Garden Island will make you think you're watching a movie with 3D glasses. For breathtaking photos with no glass reflection, or if you just want a thrill, consider a doorless helicopter tour.

Zipline over the Trees

It may not feel natural to take a running leap over the ledge of a valley, but it sure is fun. Guides clip your harness to wires and slow you down for landings, leaving you free to enjoy ocean and mountain views as you "fly" over treetops and across valleys. Most outfitters offer a shorter "express" version of their signature tours, though we recommend the full tour so you have time to catch your breath—you're sure to lose it screaming.

TOP 5 KAUAI BEACHES

With more than 50 miles of sandy shores—more than any other Hawaiian island—Kauai is a beach bum's dream. It's easy to give in to "Hawaii time" and spend your trip relaxing on the sand. Here are some of our top places to park your beach towel.

Haena Beach Park (Tunnels Beach)

Even if all you do is sit on the beach, you'll leave here happy. The scenic beauty is unsurpassed, with verdant mountains serving as a backdrop to the turquoise ocean. Snorkeling here is the best on the island during the calm, summer months. When the winter's waves arrive, surfers line up on the outside break.

Hanalei Bay Beach Park

When you dream of Hawaii, this is what comes to mind: A vast bay rimmed by a wide beach and waterfalls draping distant mountains. Everyone finds something to do here—surf, kayak, swim, sail, sunbathe, walk, and celebrity-watch. Like most North Shore beaches in Hawaii, Hanalei switches from calm waters in summer to big waves in winter.

Mahaulepu Beach

You'll have to drive through private property to reach this gem, though the beach—like all in Hawaii—is public. The 2-mile stretch is unlike anything else you'll find on Kauai. The land is rugged, with limestone cliffs, caves, and sand dunes. Although swimming here isn't always recommended, it's a great spot to wander around or take a hike along the Mahaulepu Heritage Trail, a beautiful coastal path.

Poipu Beach Park

The *keiki* (children's) swimming hole makes Poipu a great family beach, but it's also popular with snorkelers and moderate to experienced surfers. And although Poipu is considered a tourist destination, Kauai residents come out on the weekends, adding a local flavor. Watch for the endangered Hawaiian monk seals; they like it here, too.

Polihale State Park

If you're looking for remote, if you're looking for guaranteed sun, if you're thinking of camping on the beach, drive down the bumpy 5-mile-long road to the westernmost point of Kauai. Be sure to stay for the sunset. Unless you're an experienced water person, we advise staying out of the water due to a steep, onshore break. You can walk for miles along this beach, the longest in Hawaii.

HAWAII AND THE ENVIRONMENT

Sustainability. It's a word rolling off everyone's tongues these days. In a place known as the most remote island chain in the world (check your globe), Hawaii relies heavily on the outside world for food and material goods—estimates put the percentage of food arriving on container ships as high as 90. Like many places, though, efforts are afoot to change that. And you can help.

Shop Local Farms and Markets

From Kauai to the Big Island, farmers' markets are cropping up, providing a place for growers to sell fresh fruits and vegetables. There is no reason to buy imported mangoes, papayas, avocadoes, and bananas at grocery stores, when the ones you'll find at farmers' markets are not only fresher and bigger but tastier, too. Some markets allow the sale of fresh-packaged foods—salsa, say, or smoothies—and the on-site preparation of food—like pork *laulau* (pork, beef and fish or chicken with taro, or luau, leaves wrapped and steamed in *ti* leaves) or roasted corn on the cob—so you can make your run to the market a dining experience.

Not only is the locavore movement vibrantly alive at farmers' markets, but Hawaii's top chefs are sourcing more of their produce—and fish, beef, chicken, and cheese—from local providers as well. You'll notice this movement on restaurant menus, featuring Kilauea greens or Hamakua tomatoes or locally caught mahimahi.

And while most people are familiar with Kona coffee farm tours on Big Island, if you're interested in the growing slow-food movement in Hawaii, you'll be heartened to know many farmers are opening up their operations for tours—as well as sumptuous meals.

Support Hawaii's Merchants

Food isn't the only sustainable effort in Hawaii. Buying local goods like art and jewelry, Hawaiian heritage products, crafts, music, and apparel is another way to "green up" the local economy. The County of Kauai helps make it easy with a program called **Kauai Made** (⊕ *www. kauaimade.net*), which showcases products made on Kauai, by Kauai people, using Kauai materials. The Maui Chamber of Commerce does something similar with **Made in Maui** (⊕ *www.madeinmaui. com*). Think of both as the Good Housekeeping Seal of Approval for locally made goods.

Then there are the crafty entrepreneurs who are diverting items from the trash heap by repurposing garbage. Take Oahu's **Muumuu Heaven** (⊕ *www.muumuuheaven. com*). They got their start by reincarnating vintage aloha apparel into hip new fashions. **Kini Beach** (⊕ *www.kinibeach. com*) collects discarded grass mats and plastic inflatables from Waikiki hotels and uses them to make pricey bags and totes.

Choose Green Tour Operators

Conscious decisions when it comes to Island activities go a long way to protecting Hawaii's natural world. The **Hawaii Ecotourism Association** (⊕ *www.hawaiiecotourism. org*) recognizes tour operators for, among other things, their environmental stewardship. The **Hawaii Tourism Authority** (⊕ *www. hawaiitourismauthority.org*) recognizes outfitters for their cultural sensitivity. Winners of these awards are good choices when it comes to guided tours and activities.

TOP 5 KAUAI SCENIC SPOTS

Verdant valleys, epic cliffs, plunging waterfalls, and majestic canyons are just a few of the features that you'll find on Kauai. You might almost get used to the stunning green mountains that jut out of the land as you drive from place to place—almost. There are countless places to stop and take in the view; here are some of our favorites. Just don't forget a camera.

Hanalei Valley Overlook

On the way to Hanalei (about 1,000 yards west of the Princeville Shopping Center), this pull-off provides views of Hanalei River winding its way through wet *loi* (taro patches) framed by jagged green mountains. If you're staying on the North Shore, don't just stop here once. The colors will change over the course of a day, or with the weather.

Kee Beach

At the end of the road on the North Shore, Kee Beach is as close as you can get to the fabled cliffs of Bali Hai. Surrounded by palm and almond trees, this stretch of white-sand beach is a great spot for viewing sunsets. The Kalalau Trail begins here; if you're up for an uphill hike, the first quarter-mile or so of the trail takes you to a perch with views of both Kee and the misty cliffs of Napali.

Kilauea Lighthouse

Albatrosses, great frigate birds, and nene are just a few species among the thousands of seabirds that nest along the cliffs surrounding the Kilauea Lighthouse. This is the northernmost point on Kauai—in fact, it's the northernmost point in the main Hawaiian Islands. You'll get sweeping views of the North Shore here. If you hang around for a little while in winter, you're almost sure to see a whale pass by.

Opaekaa Falls

It would be tough to visit Kauai without seeing a waterfall; after rain it seems like every mountain is laced with white streaks of water. Opaekaa is one of our favorites because it's always running, rain or shine. Water from the mighty Wailua River falls more than 100 feet in a lush green setting. The lookout to the left before you reach the parking lot for the waterfall overlook takes in the scenic Wailua River Valley.

Waimea Canyon

The oft-used term "breathtaking" does not do justice to your first glimpse of Waimea Canyon (sometimes called the Grand Canyon of the Pacific). Narrow waterfalls tumble thousands of feet to streams that cut through the rust-color volcanic soil. There are plenty of spots along Route 550 to stop and stare at the canyon's awesome beauty—we recommend using the designated lookouts; they have parking and restrooms. Impressive vistas don't stop at the rim of the canyon. Continue on to the end of the road to Kalalau Lookout for a view through the clouds of otherworldly Kalalau Valley.

WEDDINGS AND HONEYMOONS

There's no question that Hawaii is one of the country's foremost honeymoon destinations. Romance is in the air here, and the white, sandy beaches, turquoise water, swaying palm trees, balmy tropical breezes, and perpetual sunshine put people in the mood for love. It's easy to understand why Hawaii is fast becoming a popular wedding destination as well, especially as the cost of airfare is often discounted, new resorts and hotels entice visitors, and as of January 2012 the state now recognizes and grants civil unions. A destination wedding is no longer exclusive to celebrities and the superrich. You can plan a traditional ceremony in a place of worship followed by a reception at an elegant resort, or you can go barefoot on the beach and celebrate at a luau. There are almost as many wedding planners in the Islands as real estate agents, which makes it oh-so-easy to wed in paradise, and then, once the knot is tied, stay and honeymoon as well.

The Big Day

Choosing the Perfect Place. When choosing a location, remember that you really have two choices to make: the ceremony location and where to have the reception, if you're having one. For the former, there are beaches, bluffs overlooking beaches, gardens, private residences, resort lawns, and, of course, places of worship. As for the reception, there are these same choices, as well as restaurants and even luau. If you decide to go outdoors, remember the seasons—yes, Hawaii has seasons. If you're planning a winter wedding outdoors, be sure you have a backup plan (such as a tent), in case it rains. Also, if you're planning an outdoor wedding at sunset—which is very popular—be sure you match the time of your ceremony to the time the sun sets at that time of year. If

you choose an indoor spot, be sure to ask for pictures of the location when you're planning. You don't want to plan a pink wedding, say, and wind up in a room that's predominantly red. Or maybe you do. The point is, it should be your choice.

Finding a Wedding Planner. If you're planning to invite more than a minister and your loved one to your wedding ceremony, seriously consider an on-island wedding planner who can help select a location, help design the floral scheme and recommend a florist as well as a photographer, help plan the menu and choose a restaurant, caterer, or resort, and suggest any Hawaiian traditions to incorporate into your ceremony. And more: Will you need tents, a cake, music? Maybe transportation and lodging? Many planners have relationships with vendors, providing packages—which mean savings.

If you're planning a resort wedding, most have on-site wedding coordinators; however, there are many independents around the Islands and even those who specialize in certain types of ceremonies—by locale, size, religious affiliation, and so on. A simple "Hawaii weddings" Google search will reveal dozens. What's important is that you feel comfortable with your coordinator. Ask for references—and call them. Share your budget. Get a proposal—in writing. Ask how long they've been in business, how much they charge, how often you'll meet with them, and how they select vendors. Request a detailed list of the exact services they'll provide. If your idea of your wedding doesn't match their services, try someone else. If you can afford it, you might want to meet the planner in person.

Getting Your License. The good news about marrying in Hawaii is that no

waiting period, no residency or citizenship requirements, and no blood tests or shots are required. However, both the bride and groom must appear together in person before a marriage-license agent to apply for a marriage license. You'll need proof of age—the legal age to marry is 18. (If you're 19 or older, a valid driver's license will suffice; if you're 18, a certified birth certificate is required.) Upon approval, a marriage license is immediately issued and costs $60, cash only. After the ceremony, your officiant will mail the marriage license to the state. Approximately four months later, you will receive a copy in the mail. (For $10 extra, you can expedite this process. Ask your marriage-license agent when you apply.) For more detailed information, visit ⊕ *www.ehawaii.gov.*

Also—this is important—the person performing your wedding must be licensed by the Hawaii Department of Health, even if he or she is a licensed minister. Be sure to ask.

Wedding Attire. In Hawaii, basically anything goes, from long, formal dresses with trains to white bikinis. Floral sundresses are fine, too. For the men, tuxedos are not the norm; a pair of solid-colored slacks with a nice aloha shirt is. In fact, tradition in Hawaii for the groom is a plain white aloha shirt (they do exist) with slacks or long shorts and a colored sash around the waist. If you're planning a wedding on the beach, barefoot is the way to go.

If you decide to marry in a formal dress and tuxedo, you're better off making your selections on the mainland and hand-carrying them aboard the plane. Yes, it can be a pain, but ask your wedding-gown retailer to provide a special carrying bag. After all, you don't want to chance losing your wedding dress in a wayward piece of luggage. And when it comes to fittings, again, that's something to take care of before you arrive in Hawaii.

Local customs. The most obvious traditional Hawaiian wedding custom is the lei exchange in which the bride and groom take turns placing a lei around the neck of the other—with a kiss. Bridal lei are usually floral, whereas the groom's is typically made of *maile*, a green leafy garland that drapes around the neck and is open at the ends. Brides often also wear a *lei poo*—a circular floral headpiece. Other Hawaiian customs include the blowing of the conch shell, hula, chanting, and Hawaiian music.

The Honeymoon

Do you want champagne and strawberries delivered to your room each morning? A breathtaking swimming pool in which to float? A five-star restaurant in which to dine? Then a resort is the way to go. If, however, you prefer the comforts of a home, try a bed-and-breakfast. A small inn is also good if you're on a tight budget or don't plan to spend much time in your room. On the other hand, maybe you want your own private home in which to romp naked—or just laze around recovering from the wedding planning. Maybe you want your own kitchen so you can whip up a gourmet meal for your loved one. In that case, a private vacation-rental home is the answer. Or maybe a condominium resort. That's another beautiful thing about Hawaii: the lodging accommodations are almost as plentiful as the beaches, and there's one that will perfectly match your tastes and your budget.

CRUISING THE HAWAIIAN ISLANDS

Cruising has become extremely popular in Hawaii. For first-time visitors, it's an excellent way to get a taste of all the Islands; and if you fall in love with one or even two Islands, you know how to plan your next trip.

Cruising to Hawaii

Carnival Cruises. They call them "fun ships" for a reason—Carnival is all about keeping you busy and showing you a good time, both on board and on shore. Great for families, Carnival always plans plenty of kid-friendly activities, and their children's program rates high with the little critics. Carnival offers itineraries starting in Los Angeles, Ensenada, Vancouver, and Honolulu. Their ships stop on Maui (Kahului), the Big Island (Kailua-Kona and Hilo), Oahu, and Kauai. ☎ 888/227–6482 ⊕ www.carnival.com.

Holland America. The grande dame of cruise lines, Holland America has a reputation for service and elegance. Holland America's Hawaii cruises leave from and return to San Diego, California, with a brief stop at Ensenada. In Hawaii, the ship ties up at port in Maui (Lahaina), the Big Island (Hilo), Oahu, and Kauai (Nawiliwili). Holland America also offers longer itineraries (30-plus days) that include Hawaii, Tahiti, and the Marquesas and depart from or return to San Diego, Seattle, or Vancouver. ☎ 877/932–4259 ⊕ www.hollandamerica.com.

Princess Cruises. Princess strives to offer affordable luxury. Their prices start out a little higher, but you get more bells and whistles (affordable balcony rooms, nicer decor, more restaurants to choose from, personalized service). They're not fantastic for kids, but they do a great job of keeping teenagers occupied. *Golden Princess, Sapphire Princess,* and *Star Princess*

sail from Los Angeles on a 14-day round-trip voyage with calls at Hilo on the Big Island, Honolulu, Kauai, and Lahaina on Maui, plus Ensenada, Mexico. There are also 15-day cruises out of San Francisco. In addition, the line offers longer cruises—up to 29 day—that include stops in Hawaii and the South Pacific. ☎ 800/774–6237 ⊕ www.princess.com.

Cruising within Hawaii

American Safari Cruises. Except for the summer months when its yachts cruise Alaska, American Safari Cruises offers round-trip, eight-day, seven-night interisland cruises departing from Lahaina, Maui. The *Safari Explorer* accommodates only 36 passengers; its smaller size allows it to dock at Moloka'i and Lana'i in addition to a stop on the island of Hawaii. The cruise is all-inclusive, with even shore excursions, water activities, and a massage included as part of the deal. ☎ 888/862–8881 ⊕ www.americansafaricruises.com.

Hawaii Nautical. Offering a completely different sort of experience, Hawaii Nautical provides private multiple-day interisland cruises on their catamarans, yachts, and sailboats. Prices are higher, but service is completely personal, right down to the itinerary. ☎ 808/234–7245 ⊕ www.hawaiinautical.com.

Norwegian Cruise Lines. Norwegian is the only major operator to offer interisland cruises in Hawaii. *Pride of America* sails year-round and offers seven day itineraries within the Islands stopping on Maui, Oahu, the Big Island (Hilo), and overnighting on Kauai. The ship has a vintage Americana theme and a big family focus with lots of connecting staterooms and suites. ☎ 800/327–7030 ⊕ www.ncl.com.

Exploring Kauai

WORD OF MOUTH

"Napali, Napali, and Napali—by air, by boat, and by hikes. All are worth it. Also remember Kokee is actually more of seeing Napali. Waimea is okay but Kokee is exceptional."

—lifeisbeautiful

Updated by
Charles E.
Roessler

Even a nickname like "The Garden Island" fails to do justice to Kauai's beauty. Verdant trees grow canopies over the few roads, and brooding mountains are framed by long, sandy beaches, coral reefs, and sheer sea cliffs. Pristine trade winds moderate warm daily temperatures while offering comfort for deep, refreshing sleep through gentle nights.

The main road tracing Kauai's perimeter takes you past much more scenery than would seem possible on one small island. Chiseled mountains, thundering waterfalls, misty hillsides, dreamy beaches, lush vegetation, and small towns make up the physical landscape. Perhaps the most stunning piece of scenery is a place no road will take you—the breathtakingly beautiful Napali Coast, which runs along the northwest side of the island.

For adventure seekers, Kauai offers everything from difficult hikes to helicopter tours. The island has top-notch spas and golf courses, and its beaches are known to be some of the most beautiful in the world. Even after you've spent days lazing around drinking mai tais or kayaking your way down a river, there's still plenty to do, as well as see: Plantation villages, a historic lighthouse, wildlife refuges, a fern grotto, a colorful canyon, and deep rivers are all easily explored.

■TIP→ While exploring the island, try to take advantage of the many roadside scenic overlooks and pull over to take in the constantly changing view. Don't try to pack too much into one day. Kauai is small, but travel is slow. The island's sights are divided into four geographic areas, in clockwise order: the North Shore, the East Side, the South Shore, and the West Side.

GEOLOGY

Kauai is the oldest and northernmost of the main Hawaiian Islands. Five million years of wind and rain have worked their magic, sculpting fluted sea cliffs and whittling away at the cinder cones and caldera that prove its volcanic origin. Foremost among these is Waialeale, one of the wettest spots on Earth. Its approximate 450-inch annual rainfall feeds the mighty Wailua River, the only navigable waterway in Hawaii. The

DID YOU KNOW?

You'll find a welcome respite at gorgeous and secluded Kalalau Beach when you reach the end of the arduous 11-mile Kalalau Trail.

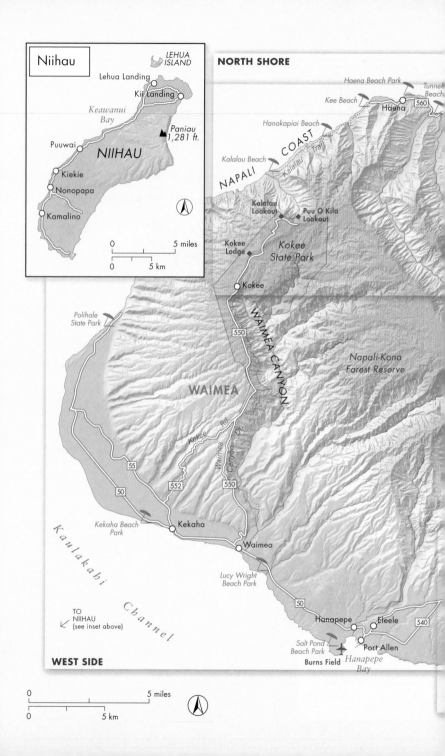

Niihau

LEHUA
ISLAND

Lehua Landing

Kii Landing

Keawanui Bay

Puuwai

NIIHAU

▲ Paniau
1,281 ft.

Kiekie

Nonopapa

Kamalino

0   5 miles

0   5 km

Haena Beach Park

Kee Beach   Tunnel
Beach
Haena   560

Hanakapiai Beach

NAPALI COAST

Kalalau Beach   *Kalalau Trail*

Kalalau
Lookout   Puu O Kila
Lookout

Kokee
Lodge   *Kokee State Park*

Kokee

Polihale
State Park

WAIMEA CANYON

550

Napali-Kona Forest Reserve

WAIMEA

Kokee Rd.

Waimea Canyon Dr.

55

50   552   550

Kekaha Beach
Park

Kekaha

Waimea

Lucy Wright
Beach Park

50

Kaulakahi Channel

TO
NIIHAU
(see inset above)

Hanapepe   Eleele   540

Salt Pond
Beach Park   Port Allen

Burns Field   *Hanapepe Bay*

0   5 miles

0   5 km

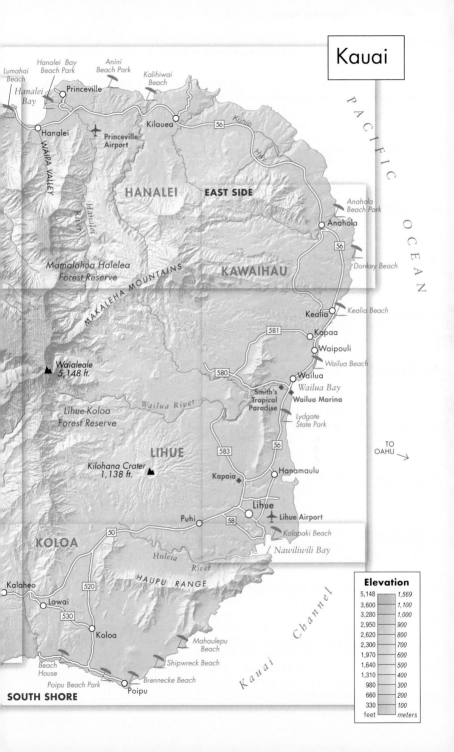

Kauai

PACIFIC OCEAN

Lumahai Beach
Hanalei Bay Beach Park
Anini Beach Park
Kalihiwai Beach
Hanalei Bay
Princeville
Hanalei
Kilauea
56
Kohio Hwy
Princeville Airport
WAIPA VALLEY
HANALEI
EAST SIDE
Anahola Beach Park
Anahola
56
Hanalei River
Mamalahoa Halelea Forest Reserve
KAWAIHAU
Donkey Beach
MAKALEHA MOUNTAINS
Kealia
Kealia Beach
581
Kapaa
Waipouli
Wailua Beach
Waialeale 5,148 ft.
580
Wailua
Lihue-Koloa Forest Reserve
Wailua River
Smith's Tropical Paradise
Wailua Bay
Wailua Marina
Lydgate State Park
LIHUE
Kilohana Crater 1,138 ft.
583
Kapaia
56
Hanamaulu
TO OAHU →
Lihue
Lihue Airport
Puhi
58
Kalapaki Beach
KOLOA
50
Huleia River
Nawiliwili Bay
HAUPU RANGE
Kalaheo
Lawai
520
530
Koloa
Mahaulepu Beach
Shipwreck Beach
Kauai Channel
Beach House
Poipu Beach Park
Brennecke Beach
Poipu
SOUTH SHORE

Elevation	
5,148	1,569
3,600	1,100
3,280	1,000
2,950	900
2,620	800
2,300	700
1,970	600
1,640	500
1,310	400
980	300
660	200
330	100
feet	meters

vast Alakai Swamp soaks up rain like a sponge, releasing it slowly into the watershed that gives Kauai its emerald sheen.

FLORA AND FAUNA

Kauai offers some of the best birding in the state, due in part to the absence of the mongoose. Many nene (the endangered Hawaiian state bird) reared in captivity have been successfully released here, along with an endangered forest bird called the puaiohi. The island is also home to a large colony of migratory nesting seabirds and has two refuges protecting endangered Hawaiian waterbirds. Kauai's most noticeable fowl, however, is the wild chicken. A cross between jungle fowl (*moa*) brought by the Polynesians and domestic chickens and fighting cocks that escaped during the last two hurricanes, they are everywhere, and the roosters crow when they feel like it, not just at dawn. Consider yourself warned.

HISTORY

Kauai's residents have had a reputation for independence since ancient times. Called "the separate kingdom," Kauai alone resisted King Kamehameha's charge to unite the Hawaiian Islands. In fact, it was only by kidnapping Kauai's king, Kaumualii, and forcing him to marry Kamehameha's widow that the Garden Isle was joined to the rest of Hawaii. That spirit lives on today as Kauai residents try to resist the lure of tourism dollars captivating the rest of the Islands. Local building rules maintain that no structure may be taller than a coconut tree, and Kauai's capital city, Lihue, is still more small town than city.

THE NORTH SHORE

The North Shore of Kauai includes the environs of Kilauea, Princeville, Hanalei, and Haena. Traveling north on Route 56 from the airport, the coastal highway crosses the Wailua River and the busy towns of Wailua and Kapaa before emerging into a decidedly rural and scenic landscape, with expansive views of the island's rugged interior mountains. As the two-lane highway turns west and narrows, it winds through spectacular scenery and passes the posh resort community of Princeville before dropping down into Hanalei Valley. Here it narrows further and becomes a federally recognized scenic roadway, replete with one-lane bridges (the local etiquette is for six or seven cars to cross at a time, before yielding to those on the other side), hairpin turns, and heart-stopping coastal vistas. The road ends at Kee, where the ethereal rain forests and fluted sea cliffs of Napali Coast Wilderness State Park begin.

Napali Coast is considered the jewel of Kauai, and for all its greenery, it would surely be an emerald. After seeing the coast, many are at a loss for words, because its beauty is so overwhelming. Others resort to poetry. Pulitzer Prize–winning poet W.S. Merwin wrote a book-length poem, "The Folding Cliffs," based on a true story set in Napali. *Napali* means "the cliffs," and while it sounds like a simple name, it's quite an apt description. The coastline is cut by a series of impossibly small valleys, like fault lines, running to the interior, with the resulting cliffs seeming to fold back on themselves like an accordion-folded fan made of green velvet.

In winter Kauai's North Shore receives more rainfall than other areas of the island. Don't let this deter you from visiting. The clouds drift over the mountains of Namolokama creating a mysterious mood and then, in a blink, disappear, rewarding you with mountains laced with a dozen waterfalls or more. The views of the mountain—as well as the sunsets over the ocean—from the St. Regis Bar, adjacent to the lobby of the St. Regis Princeville Resort, are fantastic.

The North Shore attracts all kinds—from celebrities to surfers. In fact, the late Andy Irons, three-time world surfing champion, along with his brother Bruce and legend Laird Hamilton grew up riding waves along the North Shore.

HANALEI, HAENA, AND WEST

Haena is 40 miles northwest of Lihue; Hanalei is 5 miles southeast of Haena.

Crossing the historic one-lane bridge into Hanalei reveals old-world Hawaii, including working taro farms, poi making, and evenings of throwing horseshoes at Black Pot Beach Park—found unmarked (as many places are on Kauai) at the east end of Hanalei Bay Beach Park. Although the current real-estate boom on Kauai has attracted mainland millionaires to build estate homes on the few remaining parcels of land in Hanalei, there's still plenty to see and do. It's *the* gathering place on the North Shore. Restaurants, shops, and people-watching here are among the best on the island, and you won't find a single brand name, chain, or big-box store around—unless you count surf brands like Quiksilver and Billabong.

The beach and river at Hanalei offer swimming, snorkeling, body boarding, surfing, and kayaking. Those hanging around at sunset often congregate at the Hanalei Pavilion, where a husband-and-wife-slack-key-guitar-playing combo makes impromptu appearances. There's an old rumor, since quashed by the local newspaper, the *Garden Island*, that says Hanalei was the inspiration for the song "Puff the Magic Dragon," performed by the 1960s singing sensation Peter, Paul & Mary. Even with the newspaper's clarification, some tours still point out the shape of the dragon carved into the mountains encircling the town.

Once you pass through Hanalei town, the road shrinks even more as you skirt the coast and pass through Haena. Blind corners, quick turns, and one-lane bridges force slow driving along this scenic stretch across the Lumahai and Wainiha valleys.

GETTING HERE AND AROUND

There is only one road leading beyond Princeville to Kee Beach at the western end of the North Shore: Route 560. Hanalei's commercial stretch fronts this route, and you'll find parking at the shopping compounds on each side of the road. After Hanalei, parking is restricted to two main areas, Haena Beach Park and a new lot at Haena State Park, and there are few pullover areas along Route 560. Traffic is usually light, though the route can become congested right after sunset.

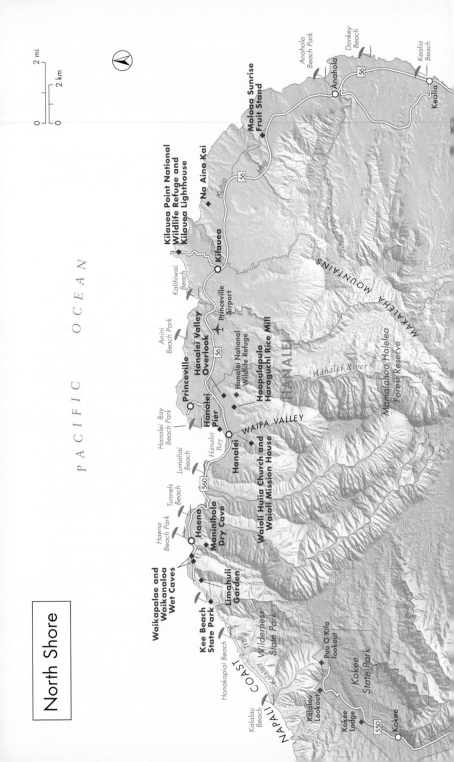

North Shore

PACIFIC OCEAN

2 mi
2 km

Anahola Beach Park
Donkey Beach
Kealia Beach

Anahola
56
Kealia

Moloaa Sunrise Fruit Stand

Kilauea Point National Wildlife Refuge and Kilauea Lighthouse

Na Aina Kai

Kuhio

56

Kilauea

Kalihiwai Beach

Princeville Airport

Anini Beach Park

Hanalei Valley Overlook

MAKALEHA MOUNTAINS

Princeville

56

Hanalei National Wildlife Refuge

Hoopulapula Haraguchi Rice Mill

HANALEI

Hanalei River

Hanalei Bay Beach Park

Hanalei Pier

WAIPA VALLEY

Mamalahoa Halelea Forest Reserve

Hanalei Bay

Hanalei

Lumahai Beach

560

Tunnels Beach

Haena Beach Park

Maniniholo Dry Cave

Waioli Huiia Church and Waioli Mission House

Haena

Waikapalae and Waikanaloa Wet Caves

Kee Beach State Park

Limahuli Garden

Hanakapiai Beach

Kalalau Trail

Napali Coast Wilderness State Park

Puu O Kila lookout

Kalalau Beach

NAPALI COAST

Kalalau Lookout

Kokee State Park

Kokee Lodge

550

Kokee

EXPLORING
TOP ATTRACTIONS

Hanalei Valley Overlook. Dramatic mountains and a patchwork of neat taro farms bisected by the wide Hanalei River make this one of Hawaii's loveliest sights. The fertile Hanalei Valley has been planted in taro since perhaps AD 700, save for a century-long foray into rice that ended in 1960. (The historic Haraguchi Rice Mill is all that remains of the era.) Many taro farmers lease land within the 900-acre Hanalei National Wildlife Refuge, helping to provide wetland habitat for four species of endangered Hawaiian water birds. ⊠ *Rte. 56, across from Foodland, Princeville.*

★ **Kee Beach State Park.** This stunning, and often overcrowded, beach marks the start of majestic Napali Coast. The 11-mile **Kalalau Trail** begins near the parking lot, drawing day hikers and backpackers. Another path leads from the sand to a stone hula platform dedicated to **Laka,** the goddess of hula, which has been in use since ancient times. This is a sacred site that should be approached with respect; it's inappropriate for visitors to leave offerings at the altar, which is tended by students in a local hula *halau* (school). Local etiquette suggests observing from a distance. Most folks head straight for the sandy beach and its dreamy lagoon, which is great for snorkeling when the sea is calm. ⊠ *Drive to western end of Rte. 560.*

WORTH NOTING

Hanalei Pier. Built in 1892, the historic Hanalei Pier is a landmark seen from miles across the bay. It came to fame when it was featured in the award-winning 1957 movie *South Pacific.* Kids use it as a diving board, fishermen fish, picnickers picnic. It's a great spot for a leisurely stroll. ⊠ *In Hanalei, turn makai at Aku Rd. and drive 1 block to Weli Weli Rd. Turn right. Drive to end of road, park, and walk left to beach.*

Hoopulapula Haraguchi Rice Mill. Rice grew in the taro fields of Hanalei valley for almost 80 years—beginning in the 1880s and ending in the early 1960s. Today, this history is embodied in the Haraguchi family, whose ancestors threshed, hulled, polished, separated, graded, and bagged rice in their 3,500-square-foot rice mill, which was demolished once by fire and twice by hurricanes. Rebuilt to the exacting standards of the National Register of Historic Places, the mill—and neighboring taro fields—is now open for tours on a very limited schedule. The family still farms taro on the onetime rice paddies and also operates the Hanalei Taro & Juice kiosk in Hanalei town. Reservations are required for the tour. ⊠ *Located next to Kayak Kauai right as you enter Hanalei town 5-5070 Kuhio Hwy.* ☎ *808/651–3399* ⊕ *www.haraguchiricemill. org* 🖾 *$87* ☾ *Wed. for tours only; kiosk Mon.–Sat. 11–3.*

DID YOU KNOW?

In summer, Hanalei Bay is calm enough for the *keiki* (children), but in winter it's top surfers only, as this beach has one of the biggest onshore surf breaks in the state.

Limahuli Garden. Narrow Limahuli Valley, with its fluted mountain peaks and ancient stone taro terraces, creates an unparalleled setting for this botanical garden and nature preserve. Dedicated to protecting native plants and unusual varieties of taro, it represents the principles of conservation and stewardship held by its founder, Charles "Chipper" Wichman. Limahuli's primordial beauty and strong *mana* (spiritual power) eclipse the extensive botanical collection. It's one of the most gorgeous spots on Kauai and the crown jewel of the National Tropical Botanical Garden, which Wichman now heads. Call ahead to reserve a guided tour, or tour on your own. Be sure to check out the quality gift shop and revolutionary compost toilet, and be prepared to walk a somewhat steep hillside. ⊠ *Rte. 560, Haena* ☎ *808/826–1053* ⊕ *www.ntbg. org* ✍ *Self-guided tour $15, guided tour $30 (reservations required)* ⏲ *Tues.–Sat. 9:30–4.*

Maniniholo Dry Cave. Kauai's north shore caves echo an enchanting, almost haunting, alternative to sunny skies and deep blue seas. Steeped in legend, Maniniholo Dry Cave darkens and becomes more claustrophobic as you glide across its sandy floor, hearing the drips down the walls and wondering at its past. Legend has it that Maniniholo was the head fisherman of the Menehune—Kauai's quasi-mythical first inhabitants. After gathering too much food to carry, his men stored the excess in the dry cave overnight. When he returned in the morning, the food had vanished and he blamed the imps living in the cracks of the cave. He and his men dug into the cliff to find and destroy the imps, leaving behind the cave. Across the highway from Maniniholo Dry Cave is Haena State Park. ⊠ *Rte. 560, Haena.*

Waikapalae and Waikanaloa Wet Caves. These wet caves are smaller (and wetter) than Maniniholo but are still visually worth a short jaunt. Said to have been dug by Pele, goddess of fire, these watering holes used to be clear, clean, and great for swimming. Now stagnant, they're nevertheless a photogenic example of the many haunting natural landmarks of Kauai's North Shore. Waikanaloa is visible right beside the highway, near the end of the road. Waikapalae is back a few hundred yards and is accessed by a five-minute uphill walk. ⊠ *Western end of Rte. 560.*

Waioli Huiia Church. Designated a National Historic Landmark, this little church—affiliated with the United Church of Christ—doesn't go unnoticed right alongside Route 560 in downtown Hanalei, and its doors are often wide open (from 9 to 5, give or take) inviting inquisitive visitors in for a look around. Like the Waioli Mission House next door, it's an exquisite representation of New England architecture crossed with Hawaiian thatched buildings. During Hurricane Iniki's visit in 1992, which brought sustained winds of 160 mph and wind gusts up to 220 mph, this little church was lifted off its foundation but, thankfully, lovingly restored. Services are held at 10 am on Sunday with many hymns sung in Hawaiian. ⊠ *5-5393A Kuhio Hwy., located at mile marker 3 on Rte. 560, Hanalei* ☎ *808/826–6253.*

Waioli Mission House. This 1837 home was built by missionaries William and Mary Alexander. Its tidy New England architecture and formal koa-wood furnishings epitomize the prim and proper missionary

Continued on page 54

NAPALI COAST: EMERALD QUEEN OF KAUAI

If you're coming to Kauai, Napali ("cliffs" in Hawaiian) is a major must-see. More than 5 million years old, these sea cliffs rise thousands of feet above the Pacific, and every shade of green is represented in the vegetation that blankets their lush peaks and folds. At their base, there are caves, secluded beaches, and waterfalls to explore.

The big question is how to explore this gorgeous stretch of coastline. You can't drive to it, through it, or around it. You can't see Napali from a scenic lookout. You can't even take a mule ride to it. The only way to experience its magic is from the sky, the ocean, or the trail.

FROM THE SKY

If you've booked a helicopter tour of Napali, you might start wondering what you've gotten yourself into on the way to the airport. Will it feel like being on a small airplane? Will there be turbulence? Will it be worth all the money you just plunked down?

Your concerns will be assuaged on the helipad, once you see the faces of those who have just returned from their journey: Everyone looks totally blissed out. And now it's your turn.

Climb on board, strap on your headphones, and the next thing you know the helicopter gently lifts up, hovers for a moment, and floats away like a spider on the wind—no roaring engines, no rumbling down a runway. If you've chosen a flight with music, you'll feel as if you're inside your very own IMAX movie.

Pinch yourself if you must, because this is the real thing. Your pilot shares history, legend, and lore. If you miss something, speak up: pilots love to show off their island knowledge. You may snap a few pictures (not too many or you'll miss the eyes-on experience!), nudge a friend or spouse, and point at a whale breeching in the ocean, but mostly you stare, mouth agape. There is simply no other way to take in the immensity and greatness of Napali but from the air.

Helicopter flight over Napali Coast

GOOD TO KNOW

Helicopter companies depart from the north, east, and west side of the island. Most are based in Lihue, near the airport.

If you want more adventure—and air—choose one of the helicopter companies that flies with the doors off.

Some companies offer flights without music. Know the experience you want ahead of time. Some even sell a DVD of your flight, so you don't have to worry about taking pictures.

Wintertime rain grounds some flights; plan your trip early in your stay in case the flight gets rescheduled.

IS THIS FOR ME?

Taking a helicopter trip is the most expensive way to see Napali—as much as $280 for an hour-long tour.

Claustrophobic? Choose a boat tour or hike. It's a tight squeeze in the helicopter, especially in one of the middle seats.

Short on time? Taking a helicopter tour is a great way to see the island.

WHAT YOU MIGHT SEE

■ Nualolo Kai (an ancient Hawaiian fishing village) with its fringed reef

■ The 300-foot Hanakapiai Falls

■ A massive sea arch formed in the rock by erosion

■ The 11-mile Kalalau Trail threading its way along the coast

■ The amazing striations of aa and pahoehoe lava flows that helped push Kauai above the sea

FROM THE OCEAN

Napali from the ocean is two treats in one: spend a good part of the day on (or in) the water, and gaze up at majestic green sea cliffs rising thousands of feet above your head.

There are three ways to see it: a mellow pleasure-cruise catamaran allows you to kick back and sip a mai tai; an adventurous raft (Zodiac) tour will take you inside sea caves under waterfalls, and give you the option of snorkeling; and a daylong outing in a kayak is a real workout, but then you can say you paddled 16 miles of coastline.

Any way you travel, you'll breathe ocean air, feel spray on your face, and see pods of spinner dolphins, green sea turtles, flying fish, and, if you're lucky, a rare Hawaiian monk seal.

Napali stretches from Kee Beach in the north to Polihale beach on the West Side. If your departure point is Kee, you are already headed toward the lush Hanakapiai Valley. Within a few minutes, you'll see caves and waterfalls galore. About halfway down the coast just after the Kalalau Trail ends, you'll come to an immense arch—formed where the sea eroded the less dense basaltic rock—and a thundering 50-foot waterfall. And as the island curves near Nualolo State Park, you'll begin to notice less vegetation and more rocky outcroppings.

(left and top right) Kayaking on Napali Coast
(bottom right) Dolphin on Napali Coast

GOOD TO KNOW

If you want to snorkel, choose a morning rather than an afternoon tour—preferably during a summer visit—when seas are calmer.

If you're on a budget, choose a non-snorkeling tour.

If you want to see whales, take any tour, but be sure to plan your vacation for December through March.

If you're staying on the North Shore or East Side, embark from the North Shore. If you're staying on the South Shore, it might not be worth your time to drive to the north, so head to the West Side.

IS THIS FOR ME?

Boat tours are several hours long, so if you have only a short time on Kauai, a helicopter tour is a better alternative.

Even on a small boat, you won't get the individual attention and exclusivity of a helicopter tour.

Prone to seasickness? A large boat can be surprisingly rocky, so be prepared.

WHAT YOU MIGHT SEE

■ Hawaii's state fish—the humuhumunukunukuapuaa— otherwise known as the reef triggerfish

■ Waiahuakua Sea Cave, with a waterfall coming through its roof

■ Tons of marine life, including dolphins, green sea turtles, flying fish, and humpback whales, especially in February and March

■ Waterfalls—especially if your trip is after a heavy rain

FROM THE TRAIL

If you want to be one with Napali—feeling the soft red earth beneath your feet, picnicking on the beaches, and touching the lush vegetation—hiking the Kalalau Trail is the way to do it.

Most people hike only the first 2 miles of the 11-mile trail and turn around at Hanakapiai. This 4-mile round-trip hike takes three to four hours. It starts at sea level and doesn't waste any time gaining elevation. (Take heart—the uphill lasts only a mile and tops out at 400 feet; then it's downhill all the way.) At the half-mile point, the trail curves west and the folds of Napali Coast unfurl.

Along the way you might share the trail with feral goats and wild pigs. Some of the vegetation is native; much is introduced.

After the 1-mile mark the trail begins its drop into Hanakapiai. You'll pass a couple of streams of water trickling across the trail, and maybe some banana, ginger, the native uluhe fern, and the Hawaiian ti plant. Finally the trail swings around the eastern ridge of Hanakapiai for your first glimpse of the valley and then switchbacks down the mountain. You'll have to boulder-hop across the stream to reach the beach. If you like, you can take a 4-mile, round-trip fairly strenuous side trip from this point to the gorgeous Hanakapiai Falls.

(left) Awaawapuhi mountain biker on razor-edge ridge
(top right) Feral goats in Kalalau Valley
(bottom right) Napali Coast

GOOD TO KNOW

Wear comfortable, amphibious shoes. Unless your feet require extra support, wear a self-bailing sort of shoe (for stream crossings) that doesn't mind mud. Don't wear heavy, waterproof hiking boots.

During winter the trail is often muddy, so be extra careful; sometimes it's completely inaccessible.

Don't hike after heavy rain—flash floods are common.

If you plan to hike the entire 11-mile trail (most people do the shorter hike described at left) you'll need a permit to go past Hanakapiai.

IS THIS FOR ME?

Of all the ways to see Napali (with the exception of kayaking the coast), this is the most active. You need to be in decent shape to hit the trail.

If you're vacationing in winter, this hike might not be an option due to flooding—whereas you can take a helicopter or boat trip year-round.

WHAT YOU MIGHT SEE

■ Big dramatic surf right below your feet

■ Amazing vistas of the cool blue Pacific

■ The spectacular Hanakapiai Falls; if you have a permit don't miss Hanakoa Falls, less than 1/2 mile off the trail

■ Wildlife, including goats and pigs

■ Zany-looking ohia trees, with aerial roots and long, skinny serrated leaves known as hala. Early Hawaiians used them to make mats, baskets, and canoe sails.

influence, while the informative guided tours offer a fascinating peek into the private lives of Kauai's early white residents. Half-hour guided tours are available for $10 on Tuesday, Thursday, and Saturday from 9 to 3. ■TIP➔ If no one is there when you arrive, don't despair; just ring the bell by the chimney. ✉ *Kuhio Hwy., Hanalei* ☎ 808/245–3202 ≡ *$10* ☉ *Tues., Thurs., and Sat. 9–3.*

PRINCEVILLE, KILAUEA, AND AROUND

Princeville is 4 miles northeast of Hanalei; Kilauea is 5 miles east of Princeville.

Built on a bluff offering gorgeous sea and mountain vistas, including Hanalei Bay, Princeville is the creation of a 1970s resort development. The area is anchored by a few large hotels, world-class golf courses, and lots of condos and time-shares.

Five miles down Route 56, a former plantation town, Kilauea, maintains its rural flavor in the midst of unrelenting gentrification encroaching all around it. Especially noteworthy are its historic lava-rock buildings, including **Christ Memorial Episcopal Church** on Kolo Road and, on Keneke and Kilauea Road (commonly known as Lighthouse Road), the Kong Lung Company, which is now an expensive shop.

GETTING HERE AND AROUND

There is only one main road through the Princeville resort area, so maneuvering a car here can be a nightmare. If you're trying to find a smaller lodging unit, be sure to get specific driving directions. Ample parking is available at the Princeville Shopping Center at the entrance to the resort. Kilauea is about 5 miles east on Route 56. There's a public parking lot in the town center as well as parking at the end of Kilauea Road for access to the lighthouse.

EXPLORING

Fodor'sChoice
★

Kilauea Point National Wildlife Refuge and Kilauea Lighthouse. A beacon for sea traffic since it was built in 1913, this National Historic Landmark has the largest clamshell lens of any lighthouse in the world. It's within a national wildlife refuge, where thousands of seabirds soar on the trade winds and nest on the steep ocean cliffs. Seeing endangered nene geese, white- and red-tailed tropic birds, and more (all identifiable by educational signboards) as well as native plants, dolphins, humpback whales, huge winter surf, and gorgeous views of the North Shore are well worth the modest entry fee. The gift shop has a great selection of books about the island's natural history and an array of unique merchandise, with all proceeds benefiting education and preservation efforts. ✉ *Kilauea Lighthouse Rd., Kilauea* ☎ 808/828–0168 ⊕ *www.fws.gov/kilaueapoint* ≡ *$5* ☉ *Daily 10–4.*

> **WORD OF MOUTH**
>
> "The lighthouse, however, was inexpensive and unbelievably beautiful. Tons of frigate birds, tropical birds, even shearwater babies in nests along the pathway. And the views…Ahhh, the views. If you go to the building near the lighthouse, you can borrow binoculars, definitely a must. We were able to watch a turtle rolling around in the surf." —HawaiiVirgin

Be sure to set aside time to catch a sunset over Napali Coast from Kee Beach on Kauai's North Shore.

Moloaa Sunrise Fruit Stand. Don't let the name fool you; they don't open at sunrise (more like 7:30 am, so come here after you watch the sun appear elsewhere). And it's not just a fruit stand. Breakfast is light and includes bagels, granola, smoothies, coffee, espresso, cappuccino, latte, and, of course, tropical-style fresh juices (pineapple, carrot, watermelon, guava, even sugarcane, in season). This is also a great spot to get out and stretch, take in the mountain view, and pick up sandwiches to go. Select local produce is available, although the variety is not as good as at the island's farmers' markets. What makes this fruit stand different is the fresh, natural ingredients like multigrain breads and *nori* (seaweed) wraps. ⊠ *Just past mile marker 16 makai on Rte. 56* ☎ *808/822–1441* ⊙ *Mon.–Sat. 7:30–5, Sun. 10–5.*

☾ ★ **Na Aina Kai.** One small sign along the highway is all that promotes this once-private garden gone big time. Joyce Doty's love for plants and art now spans 240 acres and includes 13 different gardens, a hardwood plantation, a canyon, lagoons, a Japanese teahouse, a Poinciana maze, a waterfall, and a sandy beach. Throughout are more than 100 bronze sculptures, reputedly one of the nation's largest collections. One popular project is a children's garden with a 16-foot-tall Jack and the Beanstalk bronze sculpture, gecko maze, tree house, kid-size train and, of course, a tropical jungle. Located in a residential neighborhood and hoping to maintain good neighborly relations, the garden, which is now a non-profit organization, limits tours (guided only). Tour lengths vary widely, from 1½ to 5 hours. Reservations are strongly recommended. ⊠ *Rte. 56, north of mile marker 21, turn makai onto Wailapa Rd. and follow* *signs, Kilauea ☎ 808/828–0525 ⊕ www.naainakai.org ✉ $35 for 1½-hr guided stroll to $85 for 5-hr hiking tour ☉ Tues.–Fri., call ahead for hrs.*

THE EAST SIDE

The East Side encompasses Lihue, Wailua, and Kapaa. It's also known as the Coconut Coast, as there was once a coconut plantation where today's aptly named Coconut Marketplace is located. A small grove still exists on both sides of the highway. *Mauka*, a fenced herd of goats keeps the grass tended; on the *makai* side, you can walk through the grove, although it's best not to walk directly under the trees—falling coconuts can be dangerous. Lihue is the county seat, and the whole East Side is the island's center of commerce, so early-morning

and late-afternoon drive times (or rush hour) can get congested. (Because there's only one main road, if there's a serious traffic accident the entire roadway may be closed, with no way around. Not to worry; it's a rarity.)

KAPAA AND WAILUA

Kapaa is 16 miles southeast of Kilauea; Wailua is 3 miles southwest of Kapaa.

Old Town Kapaa was once a plantation town, which is no surprise—most of the larger towns on Kauai once were. Old Town Kapaa is made up of a collection of wooden-front shops, some built by plantation workers and still run by their progeny today. Kapaa houses the two biggest grocery stores on the island, side by side: Foodland and Safeway. It also offers plenty of dining options for breakfast, lunch, and dinner, and gift shopping. To the south, Wailua comprises a few restaurants and shops, a few midrange resorts along the coastline, and a housing community *mauka*.

GETTING HERE AND AROUND
Turn to the right out of the airport at Lihue for the road to Wailua. A bridge—under which the very culturally significant Wailua River gently flows—marks the beginning of town. It quickly blends into Kapaa; there's no real demarcation. Careful, though—the zone between Lihue and Wailua has been the site of many car accidents. Pay attention and drive carefully, always knowing where you are going and when to turn off.

EXPLORING
TOP ATTRACTIONS
★ **Opaekaa Falls.** The mighty Wailua River produces many dramatic waterfalls, and Opaekaa (pronounced oh-pie-kah-ah) is one of the best. It plunges hundreds of feet to the pool below and can be easily viewed

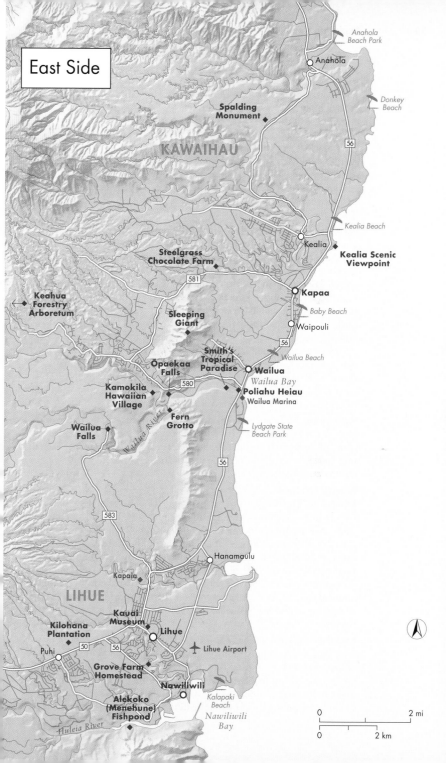

East Side

Anahola
Beach Park

Anahola

Donkey
Beach

56

KAWAIHAU

Spalding
Monument

Kealia Beach

Kealia

Kealia Scenic
Viewpoint

Steelgrass
Chocolate Farm

581

Kapaa

Baby Beach

Keahua
Forestry
Arboretum

Sleeping
Giant

Waipouli

56

Wailua Beach

Smith's
Tropical
Paradise

Opaekaa
Falls

580

Wailua

Wailua Bay

Poliahu Heiau

Kamokila
Hawaiian
Village

Wailua Marina

Wailua River

Fern
Grotto

Lydgate State
Beach Park

Wailua
Falls

56

583

Hanamaulu

Kapaia

LIHUE

Kauai
Museum

Lihue

Kilohana
Plantation

50

Lihue Airport

Puhi

56

Grove Farm
Homestead

Nawiliwili

Kalapaki
Beach

Alekoko
(Menehune)
Fishpond

Nawiliwili
Bay

Huleia River

0   2 mi

0   2 km

from a scenic overlook with ample parking. *Opaekaa* means "rolling shrimp," which refers to tasty native crustaceans that were once so abundant they could be seen tumbling in the falls. ■TIP→ Just before reaching the parking area for the waterfalls, turn left into a scenic pullout for great views of the Wailua River valley and its march to the sea. ✉ *Kuamoo Rd., from Rte. 56, turn mauka onto Kuamoo Rd. and drive 1½ miles Wailua.*

Poliahu Heiau. Storyboards near this ancient *heiau* (sacred site) recount the significance of the many sacred structures found along the Wailua River. It's unknown exactly how the ancient Hawaiians used Poliahu Heiau—one of the largest pre-Christian temples on the island—but legend says it was built by the Menehune because of the unusual stonework found in its walled enclosures. From this site, drive downhill toward the ocean to *pohaku hanau*, a two-piece birthing stone said to confer special blessings on all children born there, and *pohaku piko*, whose crevices were a repository for umbilical cords left by parents seeking a clue to their child's destiny, which reportedly was foretold by how the cord fared in the rock. Some Hawaiians feel these sacred stones shouldn't be viewed as tourist attractions, so always treat them with respect. Never stand or sit on the rocks or leave any offerings. ✉ *Rte. 580, Kuamoo Rd., Wailua.*

Wailua Falls. You may recognize this impressive cascade from the opening sequences of the *Fantasy Island* television series. Kauai has plenty of noteworthy waterfalls, but this one is especially gorgeous, easy to find, and easy to photograph. ✉ *End of Rte. 583, Maalo Rd. In Kapaia 4 miles from Rte. 56.*

WORTH NOTING

Fern Grotto. The Fern Grotto has a long history on Kauai. For some reason, visitors seem to like it. It's really nothing more than a yawning lava tube swathed in lush fishtail ferns 3 miles up the Wailua River. Though it was significantly damaged after Hurricane Iniki and again after heavy rains in 2006, the greenery has completely recovered. Smith's Motor Boat Services is the only way to legally see the grotto. You can access the entrance with a kayak, but if boats are there, you may not be allowed to land. ✉ *Kapaa, depart from Wailua Marina on mauka side of Rte. 56, just south of Wailua River* ☎ 808/821–6893 🎫 $20 ⊙ *Daily departures 9:30–3:30.*

Kamokila Hawaiian Village. The village is dramatically ensconced at the base of a steep, long, winding road right beside the Wailua River. Of course, in the days of King Kaumualii, there wasn't a road, just access by boat, and so it made the perfect hideout for his war canoes tucked away in this crook of the Wailua River. Today, there's a replica Hawaiian village in place of war canoes—numerous thatched-roof structures

Taking a riverboat tour to Fern Grotto to see a fishtail fern-covered lava tube is a popular family activity.

and abundant plant life. Yet, the lack of human activity here makes it seem abandoned, which may be why Hollywood found it an appealing location for the movie *Outbreak*. ✉ *Kapaa, turn mauka on Kuamoo Rd. in Wailua, drive 1½ miles, turn left across from Opaekaa Falls* ☎ *808/823–0559* ✉ *$5* ⊙ *Daily 9–5.*

Keahua Forestry Arboretum. Tree-lined and grassy, this is a perfect spot for a picnic—and there are lots of picnic tables scattered throughout the parklike setting. A shallow, cascading stream makes a fun spot for kids to splash, although the water's a bit chilly. A 1-mile walking trail meanders through mango, monkeypod, and eucalyptus trees. This is an exceptionally peaceful place—good for yoga and meditation—that is, unless the resident roosters decide to crow. ■ TIP➔ If it looks like rain, don't follow the road across the stream; it often floods, and could leave you stranded on one side. ✉ *Wailua, take Kuamoo Rd. mauka 6½ miles* ⊙ *Daily dawn–dusk.*

Kealia Scenic Viewpoint. Between mile markers 9 and 10 on Highway 56 is this ocean overlook, perfect for spotting whales during their winter migration. In fact, on three Saturdays in winter, the Hawaiian Islands Humpback Whale National Marine Sanctuary conducts its annual whale count from this spot, one of several around the island. The lookout was rebuilt and doubled in size a few years ago, and it's now easy to hop on the cement bike and walking path just below for a coastal stroll or ride. Most days you can see clear to Lihue and beyond. If you packed them, bring your binoculars. ✉ *Kapaa.*

Sleeping Giant. Although its true name is Nounou, this landmark mountain ridge is better known as the Sleeping Giant because of its resemblance to a very large man sleeping on his back. Legends differ on whether the giant is Puni, who was accidentally killed by rocks launched at invading canoes by the Menehune, or Nunui, a gentle creature who has not yet awakened from the nap he took centuries ago after building a massive temple and enjoying a big feast. ⊠ *Kapaa* ✛ *Mauka Rte. 56, about 1 mile north of Wailua River, backing Kapaa* .

COASTAL PATH

Ke Ala Hele Makalae, a bike-and-pedestrian path, hugs a good portion of the East Side coastline in the Kapaa area. It's being built in sections, and the completed version is expected to run all the way from Lihue to Anahola. For now, the most accessible portion begins at Lydgate Park and loops south toward the golf course for 2½ miles. The most scenic section currently runs from north Kapaa town past Kealia Beach and north toward Anahola. A walk or ride lets you feel the cool sea air, and it's a great way to meet local folks, who love using the path.

☼ **Smith's Tropical Paradise.** Nestled next to Wailua Marina along the mighty Wailua River, this 30-acre botanical and cultural garden offers a glimpse of exotic foliage, including fruit orchards, a bamboo rain forest, and tropical lagoons. Take the tram and enjoy a narrated tour or stroll along the mile-long pathways. It's a popular spot for wedding receptions and other large events, and its four-times-weekly luau is one of the island's oldest and best. ⊠ *Just south of Wailua River, mauka, on Rte. 56, Kapaa* ☎ 808/821–6895 ⊕ *www.smithskauai.com* ✍ *$6* ☉ *Daily 8:30–4.*

Spalding Monument. The Colonel Zephaniah Spalding monument commemorates the Civil War veteran who purchased this splendid property overlooking an area from Anahola to Kapaa in 1876 and soon established what became the Kealia Sugar Plantation. Turn onto Kealia Road just after mile marker 10 for an off-the-beaten-track 4½-mile scenic detour. Immediately on your right are a small post office and a snack and surf shop and, on your left, rodeo grounds often in use on summer weekends. The road ascends, and 2½ miles later you'll reach a grassy area with the concrete remains of a onetime monument. It's a nice spot to picnic or to simply gaze at the nearby grazing horses. If you're an early riser, this is a great spot to watch the sun rise; if not, check the local newspaper for the next full moon and bring a bottle of wine. Continue on another bumpy 2 miles, and you'll reconnect with Highway 56 near the town of Anahola.

Steelgrass Chocolate Farm. Hawaii is the only state in the country where *theobroma cacao* grows. As every chocolate connoisseur knows, the tree that grows the precious seed that becomes chocolate is the cacao tree. The Lydgates are on a mission to grow cacao on family farms all over the island with the hopes of one day starting a co-op that will produce Kauai Homegrown Chocolate. For now, you can tour this organic farm (in addition to cacao, they grow vanilla, timber, bamboo, and many tropical fruits) and learn how chocolate is made, "from branch to bar," as they put it. The three-hour tour includes, of course, plenty of chocolate tastings. Reservations are required for the morning tour, which begins Monday, Wednesday, and Friday at 9 am. Children 12

One of the best places for a luau is here at Smith's Tropical Paradise.

and under are free. ✉ *Located above the town of Kapaa (directions provided at time of reservation)* ☎ *808/821–1857* ⊕ *www.steelgrass. org* ✉ *$60* ⊘ *Mon., Wed., Fri. for tours only.*

LIHUE

7 miles southwest of Wailua.

The commercial and political center of Kauai County, which includes the islands of Kauai and Niihau, Lihue is home to the island's major airport, harbor, and hospital. This is where you can find the state and county offices that issue camping and hiking permits and the same fast-food eateries and big-box stores that blight the mainland. The county is seeking help in reviving the downtown; for now, once your business is done, there's little reason to linger in lackluster Lihue.

GETTING HERE AND AROUND
Route 56 leads into Lihue from the north and Route 50 comes here from the south and west. The road from the airport (where Kauai's car rental agencies are) leads to the middle of Lihue. Many of the area's stores and restaurants are on and around Rice Street, which also leads to Kalapaki Bay and Nawiliwili Harbor.

EXPLORING
Alekoko (Menehune) Fishpond. No one knows just who built this intricate aquaculture structure in the Huleia River. Legend attributes it to the Menehune, a mythical—or real, depending on whom you ask—ancient race of people known for their small stature, industrious nature, and superb stoneworking skills. Volcanic rock was cut and fit together into

THE BEST SIGHTSEEING TOURS

Aloha Kauai Tours. You get *way off the beaten track* on these four-wheel-drive van excursions. Choose from several options, including the half-day Backroads Tour covering mostly haul-cane roads behind the locked gates of Grove Farm Plantation, and the half-day Rainforest Tour, which follows the Wailua River to its source, Mt. Waialeale. The expert guides are some of the best on the island. Rates are $80. ☒ *Check in at Kilohana Plantation on Rte. 50 in Puhi* ☎ *808/245–6400, 800/452–1113* ⊕ *www.alohakauaitours.com.*

Roberts Hawaii Tours. The Round-the-Island Tour, sometimes called the Wailua River–Waimea Canyon Tour, gives a good overview of half the island, including Fort Elisabeth and Opaekaa Falls. Guests are transported in air-conditioned, 25-passenger minibuses. The $79.50 trip includes a boat ride up the Wailua River to the Fern Grotto and a visit to the lookouts above Waimea Canyon. ☎ *808/245–9101, 800/831–5541* ⊕ *www.robertshawaii.com.*

Waimea Historic Walking Tour. Led by a *kupuna,* a respected Hawaiian elder, this 2½- to 3-hour tour begins promptly at 9:30 am, every Monday at the West Kauai Visitor Center. While sharing her personal remembrances, Aletha Kaohi leads an easy walk that explains Waimea's distinction as a recipient of the 2006 National Trust for Historic Preservation Award. The tour is free, but a reservation is required. ☒ *Waimea* ☎ *808/338–1332.*

massive walls 4 feet thick and 5 feet high, forming an enclosure for raising mullet and other freshwater fish that has endured for centuries. ☒ *Hulemalu Rd., Niumalu.*

Grove Farm Homestead. Guided tours of this carefully restored 80-acre country estate offer a fascinating and authentic look at how upper-class Caucasians experienced plantation life in the mid-19th century. The tour focuses on the original home, built by the Wilcox family in 1860 and filled with a quirky collection of classic Hawaiiana. You can also see the workers' quarters, farm animals, orchards, and gardens that reflect the practical, self-sufficient lifestyle of the island's earliest Western inhabitants. Tours of the homestead are conducted twice a day, three days a week. To protect the historic building and its furnishings, tours may be canceled on very wet days. ■ TIP→ With a six-person limit per tour, reservations are essential. ☒ *Rte. 58, Nawiliwili Rd.* ⌂ *Box 1631 96766* ☎ *808/245–3202* ⊕ *www.grovefarm.net* ☒ *$20* ☉ *Tours Mon., Wed., and Thurs. at 10 and 1.*

Kauai Museum. Maintaining a stately presence on Rice Street, the historic museum building is easy to find. It features a permanent display, "The Story of Kauai," which provides a competent overview of the Garden Island and Niihau, tracing the Islands' geology, mythology, and cultural history. Local artists are represented in changing exhibits in the second-floor Mezzanine Gallery. The recently expanded gift shop alone is worth a visit, with a fine collection of authentic Niihau shell lei, feather hatband lei, hand-turned wooden bowls, reference books,

SUNSHINE MARKETS

If you want to rub elbows with the locals and purchase fresh produce and flowers at very reasonable prices, head for Sunshine Markets, also known as Kauai's farmers' markets. These busy markets are held weekly, usually in the afternoon, at locations all around the island. They're good fun, and they support neighborhood farmers. Arrive a little early, bring dollar bills to speed up transactions and your own shopping bags to carry your produce, and be prepared for some pushy shoppers. Farmers are usually happy to educate visitors about unfamiliar fruits and veggies, especially when the crowd thins. ☎ 808/241–6303 ⊕ www.kauai.gov.

North Shore Sunshine Markets ✉ Waipa, mauka of Rte. 560 north of Hanalei after mile marker 3, Hanalei

☉ Tues. 2 pm ✉ Kilauea Neighborhood Center, on Keneke St., Kilauea ☉ Thurs. 4:30 pm ✉ Hanalei Community Center ☉ Sat. 9:30 am noon.

East Side Sunshine Markets ✉ Vidinha Stadium, Lihue, ½ mile south of airport on Rte. 51 ☉ Fri. 3 pm ✉ Kapaa, turn mauka on Rte. 581/ Olohena Rd. for 1 block ☉ Wed. 3 pm.

South Shore Sunshine Markets ✉ Ballpark, Koloa, north of intersection of Koloa Road and Rte. 520 ☉ Mon. noon.

West Side Sunshine Markets ✉ Kalaheo Community Center, on Papalina Rd. just off Kaumualii Hwy., Kalaheo ☉ Tues. 3 pm ✉ Hanapepe Park, Hanapepe ☉ Thurs. 3 pm ✉ Kekaha Neighborhood Center, Elepaio Rd., Kekaha ☉ Sat. 9 am.

and other quality arts, crafts, and gifts, many of them locally made. ✉ 4428 Rice St. ☎ 808/245–6931 ☒ $10 ☉ Mon.–Sat. 9–5, closed Sun.

🕐 **Kilohana Plantation.** This estate dates back to 1896, when plantation manager Albert Spencer Wilcox first developed it as a working cattle ranch. His nephew, Gaylord Parke Wilcox, took over in 1936, building Kauai's first mansion. Today the 16,000-square-foot, Tudor-style home houses specialty shops, art galleries, and 22 North, a pretty restaurant with courtyard seating. Nearly half the original furnishings remain, and the gardens and orchards were replanted according to the original plans. You can tour the grounds for free; children enjoy visiting the farm animals. A train runs 2½ miles through 104 acres of lands representing the agricultural story of Kauai—then and now. ✉ 3-2087 Kaumualii Hwy. (Rte. 50) ☎ 808/245–5608 ☉ Mon.–Sat. 9:30–9:30, Sun. 9:30–3:30.

THE SOUTH SHORE

As you follow the main road south from Lihue, the landscape becomes lush and densely vegetated before giving way to drier conditions that characterize Poipu, the South Side's major resort area. Poipu owes much of its popularity to a steady supply of sunshine and a string of sandy beaches, although the beaches are smaller and more covelike than those on the West Side. With its extensive selection of accommodations, services, and activities, the South Shore attracts more visitors than any other area of Kauai. It's also attracting developers with big plans for the

Stop by the farmers' market in Kapaa to pick up locally grown mangoes and other fruits.

onetime sugarcane fields that are nestled in this region and enveloped by mountains. There are few roads in and out, and local residents are concerned about increased traffic as well as noise and dust pollution as a result of chronic construction. If you're planning to stay on the South Side, be sure to ask if your hotel, condo, or vacation rental will be impacted by the ongoing development during your visit.

Both Poipu and nearby Koloa (site of Kauai's first sugar mill) can be reached via Route 520 (Maluhia Road) from the Lihue area. Route 520 is known locally as Tree Tunnel Road, due to the stand of eucalyptus trees lining the road that were planted at the turn of the 20th century by Walter Duncan McBryde, a Scotsman who began cattle ranching on Kauai's South Shore. The canopy of trees was ripped to literal shreds twice—in 1982 during Hurricane Iwa and again in 1992 during Hurricane Iniki. And, true to Kauai, both times the trees grew back into an impressive tunnel. It's a distinctive way to announce, "You are now on vacation," for there's a definite feel of leisure in the air here. There's still plenty to do—snorkel, bike, walk, horseback ride, take an ATV tour, surf, scuba dive, shop, and dine—everything you'd want on a tropical vacation. From the west, Route 530 (Koloa Road) slips into downtown Koloa, a string of fun shops and restaurants, at an intersection with the only gas station on the South Shore.

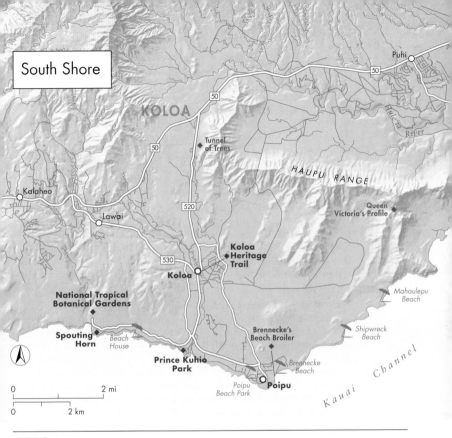

KOLOA

11 miles southwest of Lihue.

Hawaii's lucrative foray into sugar was born in this sleepy town, where the first sugar was milled back in 1830. You can still see the mill's old stone smokestack. Little else remains, save for the charming plantation-style buildings that have kept Koloa from becoming a tacky tourist trap for Poipu-bound visitors. The original small-town character has been preserved by converting historic structures along the main street into boutiques, restaurants, and shops. Placards describe the original tenants and life in the old mill town. Look for Koloa Fish Market, which offers poke and sashimi takeout, and Progressive Expressions, a popular local surf shop.

EXPLORING

Koloa Heritage Trail. Throughout the South Shore, you'll find brass plaques with details of 14 historical stops along the 10-mile route Koloa Heritage Trail—bike it, hike it, or drive it, your choice. You'll learn about Koloa's whaling history, sugar industry, ancient Hawaiian cultural sites, the island's volcanic formation, and more. Pick up a free self-guided trail map at most any shop in Koloa town.

POIPU

2 miles southeast of Koloa.

Thanks to its generally sunny weather and a string of golden-sand beaches dotted with oceanfront lodgings, Poipu is a top choice for many visitors. Beaches are user-friendly, with protected waters for *keiki* (children) and novice snorkelers, lifeguards, clean restrooms, covered pavilions, and a sweet coastal promenade ideal for leisurely strolls. Some experts have even ranked Poipu Beach Park number one in the nation. It depends on your preferences, of course, though it certainly does warrant high accolades.

GETTING HERE AND AROUND

Poipu is the one area on Kauai where you could get by without a car, though that could mean an expensive taxi ride from the airport and limited access to other parts of the island. To reach Poipu by car, follow Poipu Road south from Koloa. After the traffic circle, the road curves to follow the coast, leading to some of the popular South Shore beaches.

EXPLORING

National Tropical Botanical Gardens (*NTBG*). Tucked away in Lawai Valley, these gardens include lands and a cottage once used by Hawaii's Queen Emma for a summer retreat. Visitors can take a self-guided tour of the rambling 252-acre **McBryde Gardens** to see and learn about plants collected throughout the tropics. It is known as a garden of "research and conservation." The 100-acre **Allerton Gardens,** which can be visited only on a guided tour, artfully display statues and water features that were originally developed as part of a private estate. Reservations are required for tours of Allerton Gardens, but not for the self-guided tours of McBryde Gardens. The visitor center has a high-quality gift shop with botany-theme merchandise.

Besides harboring and propagating rare and endangered plants from Hawaii and elsewhere, NTBG functions as a scientific research and education center. The organization also operates gardens in Limahuli, on Kauai's North Shore, and in Hana, on Maui's east shore. ⊠ *Lawai Rd., across from Spouting Horn parking lot* ☎ *808/742–2623* ⊕ *www. ntbg.org* ☞ *McBryde self-guided tour $15, Allerton guided tour $45* ⊙ *McBryde Gardens daily at 12:45 ($25). Allerton Gardens tours (by reservation) daily at 9, 10, 1, and 2. Sunset Tour Tues, Thur., Sat ($70).*

QUICK
BITES

Brennecke's Beach Broiler. Stop in at Brennecke's Beach Broiler, a long-time fixture on the beach in Poipu. After a day of sun, this is a perfect spot to chill out with a mango margarita or mai tai, paired with a yummy pupu platter. ⊠ *2100 Hoone Rd.* ☎ *808/742–7588.*

Prince Kuhio Park. A triangle of grass behind the Prince Kuhio condominiums honors the birthplace of Kauai's beloved Prince Jonah Kuhio Kalanianaole. Known for his kind nature and good deeds, he lost his chance at the throne when Americans staged an illegal overthrow of Queen Liliuokalani in 1893 and toppled Hawaii's constitutional monarchy. This is a great place to view wave riders surfing a popular break known as PKs and to watch the sun sink into the Pacific. ⊠ *Lawai Rd..*

Spouting Horn. If the conditions are right, you can see a natural blowhole in the reef behaving like Old Faithful, shooting saltwater high into the air and making a cool, echoing sound. It's most dramatic during big summer swells, which jam large quantities of water through an ancient lava tube with great force. ■ TIP→ Stay on the paved walkways, as rocks can be slippery and wave action unpredictable. Vendors hawk inexpensive souvenirs and collectibles in the parking lot. You may find good deals on shell jewelry, but ask for a certificate of authenticity to ensure it's a genuine Niihau shell lei before paying the higher price that these intricate creations command. ⊠ *At end of Lawai Rd.*

THE WEST SIDE

Exploring the West Side is akin to visiting an entirely different world. The landscape is dramatic and colorful: a patchwork of green, blue, black, and orange. The weather is hot and dry, the beaches are long, the sand is dark. Niihau, a private island and the last remaining place in Hawaii where Hawaiian is spoken exclusively, can be glimpsed offshore. This is rural Kauai, where sugar is making its last stand and taro is still cultivated in the fertile river valleys. The lifestyle is slow, easy, and traditional, with many folks fishing and hunting to supplement their diets. Here and there modern industry has intruded into this pastoral scene: huge generators turn oil into electricity at Port Allen; scientists cultivate experimental crops of genetically engineered plants in Kekaha; the navy launches rockets at Mana to test the "Star Wars" missile defense system; and NASA mans a tracking station in the wilds of Kokee. It's a region of contrasts that simply shouldn't be missed.

Heading west from Lihue or Poipu, you pass through a string of tiny towns, plantation camps, and historic sites, each with a story to tell of centuries past. There's Hanapepe, whose coastal salt ponds have been harvested since ancient times; Kaumakani, where the sugar industry still clings to life; Fort Elisabeth, from which an enterprising Russian tried to take over the island in the early 1800s; and Waimea, where Captain Cook made his first landing in the Islands, forever changing the face of Hawaii.

From Waimea town you can head up into the mountains, skirting the rim of magnificent Waimea Canyon and climbing higher still until you reach the cool, often-misty forests of Kokee State Park. From the vantage point at the top of this gemlike island, 3,200 to 4,200 feet above sea level, you can gaze into the deep, verdant valleys of the North Shore and Napali Coast. This is where the "real" Kauai can still be found: the native plants, insects, and birds that are found nowhere else on earth.

HANAPEPE

15 miles west of Poipu.

In the 1980s Hanapepe was fast becoming a ghost town, its farm-based economy mirroring the decline of agriculture. Today it's a burgeoning art colony with galleries, crafts studios, and a lively art-theme street fair on Friday nights. The main street has a new vibrancy enhanced by

West Side

PACIFIC OCEAN

NAPALI COAST

Kee Beach State Park

Haena

560

Hanalei Bay

Hanalei

Hanakapiai Beach

Kalalau Trail

Puu O Kila Lookout

Kalalau Lookout

Kokee Lodge

Kokee

Kokee State Park

550

Polihale State Park

Napali-Kona Forest Reserve

WAIMEA CANYON

WAIMEA

Kokee Rd.

55

552

550

Canyon Dr.

Waimea Dr.

Menehune Ditch

KOLOA

Kekaha Beach Park

Kekaha

50

West Kauai Visitor and Technology Center

Waimea

Hanapepe Valley and Canyon Lookout

Kalaheo

Fort Elisabeth

Hanapepe Walking Tour

50

Hanapepe Swinging Bridge

50

530

540

Kukuiolono Park

Kaulakahi Channel

Lapperts Ice Cream

Hanapepe

Eleele

TO NIIHAU

Salt Pond Beach Park

Burn's Field

Port Allen

Hanapepe Bay

Kauai Coffee Visitor Center and Museum

0   5 miles

0   5 km

the restoration of several historic buildings. The emergence of Kauai Coffee as a major West Side crop and expanded activities at Port Allen, now the main departure point for tour boats, also gave the town's economy a boost.

GETTING HERE AND AROUND

Hanapepe, locally known as Kauai's "biggest little town," is just past the Eleele Shopping Center on the main highway (Route 50). A sign leads you to the town center, where street parking is easy and there's an enjoyable walking tour.

EXPLORING

QUICK BITES

Lappert's Ice Cream. It's not ice cream on Kauai if it's not Lappert's Ice Cream. Guava, macadamia nut, pineapple, mango, coconut, banana—Lappert's is the ice-cream capital of Kauai. Warning: Even at the factory store in Hanapepe, the prices are no bargain. But, hey, you gotta try it. ⊠ *On Hwy. 50 mauka, Hanapepe* ☎ *808/335–6121* ⊕ *www.lappertshawaii.com.*

Hanapepe Swinging Bridge. This bridge may not be the biggest adventure on Kauai, but it's enough to make your heart hop. It's considered a historic suspension bridge even though it was rebuilt in 1996 after the original was destroyed—like so much of the island—by Hurricane Iniki. What is interesting about this bridge is that it's not just for show; it actually provides the only access to taro fields across the Waimea River. If you're in the neighborhood, it's worth a stroll. ⊠ *Located mauka in downtown Hanapepe next to Banana Patch Studios' parking lot.*

Hanapepe Valley and Canyon Lookout. This dramatic divide and fertile river valley once housed a thriving Hawaiian community of taro farmers, with some of the ancient fields still in cultivation today. From the lookout, you can take in the farms on the valley floor with the majestic mountains as a backdrop. ⊠ *Rte. 50.*

Hanapepe Walking Tour. This 1½ mile self-guided walking tour takes you to 14 different plaques with historic photos and stories mounted on buildings throughout Hanapepe town. Businesses and shops in town sell a map of the tour for $2; however, you can often pick one up free with a coupon found in many guidebooks on promotional-brochure rack stands. ⊠ *Hanapepe town.*

Kauai Coffee Visitor Center and Museum. Two restored camp houses, dating from the days when sugar was the main agricultural crop on the Islands, have been converted into a museum, visitor center, and gift shop. About 3,400 acres of McBryde sugar land have become Hawaii's largest coffee plantation. You can walk among the trees, view old grinders and roasters, watch a video to learn how coffee is processed, sample various estate roasts, and check out the gift store. The center offers a 15-minute or so self-guided tour with well-marked signs through a small coffee grove. From Eleele, take Highway 50 in the direction of Waimea Canyon and veer right onto Highway 540, west of Kalaheo. It's located 2½ miles from the Highway 50 turnoff. ⊠ *870 Halawili Rd., Kalaheo* ☎ *808/335–0813* ⊕ *www.kauaicoffee.com* 🎫 *Free* ☉ *Daily 9–5.*

DID YOU KNOW?

The Kalalau Lookout is a great place to snap a photo before you start off your hike to Puu O Kila.

Kukuiolono Park. Translated as "Light of the God Lono," Kukuiolono has serene Japanese gardens, a display of significant Hawaiian stones, and spectacular panoramic views. This quiet hilltop park is one of Kauai's most scenic areas and an ideal picnic spot. There's also a small golf course. ✉ *Papalina Rd., Kalaheo* ☎ *808/332–9151* 🎫 *Free* ⊘ *Daily 6:30–6:30.*

WAIMEA, WAIMEA CANYON, AND AROUND

Waimea is 7 miles northwest of Hanapepe; Waimea Canyon is approximately 10 miles northeast of Waimea.

Waimea is a serene, pretty town that has the look of the Old West and the feel of Old Hawaii, with a lifestyle that's decidedly laid-back. It's an ideal place for a refreshment break while sightseeing on the West Side. The town played a major role in Hawaiian history since 1778, when Captain James Cook became the first European to set foot on the Hawaiian Islands. Waimea was also the place where Kauai's King Kaumualii acquiesced to King Kamehameha's unification drive in 1810, averting a bloody war. The town hosted the first Christian missionaries, who hauled in massive timbers and limestone blocks to build the sturdy Waimea Christian Hawaiian and Foreign Church in 1846. It's one of many lovely historic buildings preserved by residents who take great pride in their heritage and history.

North of Waimea town, via Route 550, you'll find the vast and gorgeous Waimea Canyon, also known as the Grand Canyon of the Pacific. The spectacular vistas from the lookouts along the road culminate with an overview of Kalalau Valley. There are various hiking trails leading to the inner heart of Kauai. A camera is a necessity in this region.

GETTING HERE AND AROUND

Route 50 continues northwest to Waimea and Kekaha from Hanapepe. You can reach Waimea Canyon and Kokee State Park from either town—the way is clearly marked. Some pull-off areas on Route 550 are fine for a quick view of the canyon, but the designated lookouts have bathrooms and parking.

EXPLORING

Fort Elisabeth. The ruins of this stone fort, built in 1816 by an agent of the imperial Russian government named Anton Scheffer, are reminders of the days when Scheffer tried to conquer the island for his homeland, or so one story goes. Another claims that Scheffer's allegiance lay with King Kaumualii, who was attempting to regain leadership of his island nation from the grasp of Kamehameha the Great. The crumbling walls of the fort are not particularly interesting, but the sign loaded with historical information is. ✉ *Rte. 50, Waimea.*

★ **Kalalau Lookout.** At the end of the road, high above Waimea Canyon, Kalalau Lookout marks the start of a 1-mile (one-way) hike to **Puu O Kila Lookout.** On a clear day at either spot, you can see a dreamy landscape of gaping valleys, sawtooth ridges, waterfalls, and turquoise seas, where whales can be seen spouting and breaching during the winter months. If clouds block the view, don't despair—they tend to blow through fast, giving you time to snap that photo of a lifetime. You may

DID YOU KNOW?

It's possible to see vast stretches of the Kalalau Valley from Kokee State Park, which is about 4,000 feet above sea level.

spot wild goats clambering on the sheer, rocky cliffs, and white tropic birds. If it's very clear to the northwest, look for the shining sands of Kalalau Beach, gleaming like golden threads against the deep blue of the Pacific. ⊠ *Waimea Canyon Dr., 4 miles north of Kokee State Park.*

★ **Kokee State Park.** This 4,345-acre wilderness park is 4,000 feet above sea level, an elevation that affords you breathtaking views in all directions. You can gain a deeper appreciation of the island's rugged terrain and dramatic beauty from this vantage point. Large tracts of native ohia and koa forest cover much of the land, along with many varieties of exotic plants. Hikers can follow a 45-mile network of trails through diverse landscapes that feel wonderfully remote—until the tour helicopters pass overhead. The state recently introduced a 20-year master plan for the park that included significant development (think a 40- to 60-room lodge in a sacred meadow), but after community input meetings, the plan was scaled back.

Kokee Natural History Museum. When you arrive at the park, Kokee Natural History Museum is a great place to start your visit. The friendly staff is knowledgeable about trail conditions and weather, while informative displays and a good selection of reference books can teach you more about the unique attributes of the native flora and fauna. You may also find that special memento or gift you've been looking for. ⊠ *Rte. 550* ☎ *808/335–9975* 🖅 *Donations accepted* ⊙ *Daily 9–4:30* ⊠ *Kaumakani–Hanapepe, Hanapepe* ⊕ *www.kokee.org.*

QUICK
BITES

Kokee Lodge. There's only one place to buy food and hot drinks in Kokee State Park, and that's the dining room of rustic Kokee Lodge. It's known for its corn bread, of all things. Peruse the gift shop for T-shirts, postcards, or campy Kokee memorabilia. ⊠ *Kokee State Park, 3600 Kokee Rd., mile marker 15, Kokee* ☎ *808/335–6061* ⊙ *No dinner.*

Fodor'sChoice
★

Waimea Canyon. Carved over countless centuries by the Waimea River and the forces of wind and rain, Waimea Canyon is a dramatic gorge nicknamed the "Grand Canyon of the Pacific"—but not by Mark Twain, as many people mistakenly think.

Hiking and hunting trails wind through the canyon, which is 3,600 feet deep, 2 miles wide, and 10 miles long. The cliff sides have been sharply eroded, exposing swatches of colorful soil. The deep red, brown, and green hues are constantly changing in the sun, and frequent rainbows and waterfalls enhance the natural beauty.

This is one of Kauai's prettiest spots, and it's worth stopping at both the **Puu ka Pele** and **Puu hinahina** lookouts. Clean public restrooms and parking are at both lookouts. ⊠ *Waimea.*

West Kauai Visitor and Technology Center. Local photos and informational computers with touch screens bring the island's history and attractions to life at the West Kauai Vistor and Technology Center. Weekly events include lei making, a walking tour, and a crafts fair. Call for a schedule. ⊠ *9565 Kaumualii Hwy. (Rte. 50), Waimea* ☎ *808/338–1332* ⊕ *www.wkbpa.org* 🖅 *Free* ⊙ *Weekdays 9:30–4.*

3

Beaches

WORD OF MOUTH

"An early-morning walk on Kee beach watching the mist rise on the cliffs is one of my best Kauai memories."

—aloha

Updated by
Charles E.
Roessler

With more sandy beaches per mile of coastline than any other Hawaiian Island, Kauai could be nicknamed the Sandy Island just as easily as it's called the Garden Island. Totaling more than 50 miles, Kauai's beaches make up 44% of the island's shoreline—almost twice that of Oahu, second on this list. It is, of course, because of Kauai's age as the eldest sibling of the inhabited Hawaiian Islands, allowing more time for water and wind erosion to break down rock and coral into sand.

But not all Kauai's beaches are the same. Each beach is unique unto itself, for that day, that hour. Conditions, scenery, and intrigue can change throughout the day and certainly throughout the year, transforming, say, a tranquil lakelike ocean setting in summer into monstrous waves drawing internationally ranked surfers from around the world in winter.

There are sandy beaches, rocky beaches, wide beaches, narrow beaches, skinny beaches, and alcoves. Generally speaking, surf kicks up on the North Shore in winter and the South Shore in summer, although summer's southern swells aren't nearly as frequent or big as the northern winter swells that attract those surfers. Kauai's longest and widest beaches are found on the North Shore and West Side and are popular with beachgoers, although during winter's rains, everyone heads to the dryer South and West Sides. The East Side beaches tend to be narrower and have onshore winds less popular with sunbathers, yet fishers abound. Smaller coves are characteristic of the South Shore and attract all kinds of water lovers year-round, including monk seals.

In Hawaii, all beaches are public, but their accessibility varies greatly. Some require an easy ½-mile stroll, some require a four-wheel-drive vehicle, others require boulder hopping, and one takes an entire day of serious hiking. And then there are those "drive-in" beaches onto which you can literally pull up and park your car. Kauai is not Disneyland, so don't expect much signage to help you along the way. One of the

No matter what time of year you visit Kauai, there's a good chance you'll have a beach all to yourself.

top-ranked beaches in the whole world—Hanalei—doesn't have a single sign in town directing you to the beach. Furthermore, the majority of Kauai's beaches on Kauai's vast coastline are remote, offering no facilities. ■TIP→ If you want the convenience of restrooms, picnic tables, and the like, stick to county beach parks.

THE NORTH SHORE

If you've ever dreamed of Hawaii—and who hasn't—you've dreamed of Kauai's North Shore. *Lush, tropical,* and *abundant* are just a few words to describe this rugged and dramatic area. And the views to the sea aren't the only attraction—the inland views of velvety-green valley folds and carved mountain peaks will take your breath away. Rain is the reason for all the greenery on the North Shore, and winter is the rainy season. Not to worry, though; it rarely rains *everywhere* on the island at one time. ■TIP→ The rule of thumb is to head south or west when it rains in the north.

The waves on the North Shore can be big—and we mean huge—in winter, drawing crowds to witness nature's spectacle. By contrast, in summer the waters can be completely serene.

The beaches in this section are listed in order from west to east.

Fodor's Choice
★
Kalalau. This oft-described Garden of Eden awaits the intrepid hiker who traverses 11 arduous miles along sea cliff faces, through muddy coastal valleys, and across sometimes-raging streams—all the while schlepping food provisions and camping gear. The trek requires 6 to 10 hours of hiking, making it an adventure indeed. With serious planning

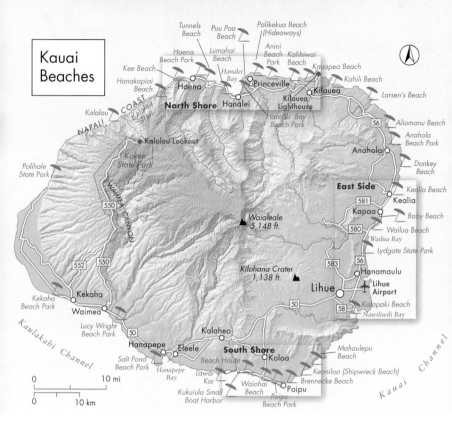

Kauai Beaches

North Shore

Tunnels Beach
Puu Poa Beach
Palikekua Beach (Hideaways)
Anini Beach Park
Kalihiwai Beach
Kee Beach
Haena Beach Park
Lumahai Beach
Hanalei Beach
Hanakapiai Beach
Kauapea Beach
Hanalei Bay
Haena
Hanalei
Kahili Beach
Princeville
Kilauea
Kilauea Lighthouse
NAPALI COAST
Kalalau Trail
Larsen's Beach
Kalalau
Hanalei Bay Beach Park

Kalalau Lookout

Aliomanu Beach

Kokee State Park

Anahola Beach Park

Anahola

Polihale State Park

Donkey Beach

Waialeale 5,148 ft.

East Side

Kealia Beach

WAIMEA CANYON

581

Kealia

Kapaa

Baby Beach

580

Wailua Beach

Wailua Bay

Lydgate State Park

Kilohana Crater 1,138 ft.

583

56

Hanamaulu

552

550

Lihue

Lihue Airport

50

Kekaha Beach Park
Kekaha
Waimea

58

Kalapaki Beach

Nawiliwili Bay

Lucy Wright Beach Park

Kalaheo

50

Hanapepe
Eleele

South Shore

Mahaulepu Beach

Beach House
Koloa

Kaulakahi Channel

Salt Pond Beach Park
Hanapepe Bay
Lawai Kai
Waiohai Beach
Poipu
Poipu Beach Park

Keoniloa (Shipwreck Beach)

Brennecke Beach

Kauai Channel

Kukuiula Small Boat Harbor

| 0 | 10 mi |
| 0 | 10 km |

and preparation, the effort is worth it. Another option is to paddle in to the beach—summer only, though; otherwise the surf is way too big. Located at the end of the trail with the same name, Kalalau is a remote, wilderness beach along the 15 miles of spectacular Napali Coast, itself a 6,500-acre state park. The beach is anchored by a *heiau* (a stone platform used as a place of worship) on one end and a waterfall on the other. The safest hiking to and swimming at the beach takes place during the summer months when the rains abate, so the trail can dry out, and when the North Shore's famous winter surf recedes, revealing an expansive beach cupped by low, vegetated sand dunes and a large walk-in cave on the western edge. Day hikes into the valley offer waterfalls, freshwater swimming pools, and wild, tropical fruits, as well as illegal campers forsaking society. Don't be mistaken: Camping permits are required. **Amenities:** none. **Best For:** solitude; sunset; nudists; walking. ⊠ *Trailhead starts at end of Rte. 560, 7 miles west of Hanalei* ⊕ *www. hawaiistateparks.org.*

Hanakapiai Beach. If you're not up for the 11-mile haul to Kalalau Beach, then hike 2 miles along Napali Coast's Kalalau Trail to Hanakapiai Beach. It'll take about 1½ hours. Just don't get in the water. Ever. The water here is what locals like to call "confused." It has something to do with the radical change in water depth and sheer cliff walls creating

North Shore Kauai

wicked currents, rogue waves, backwash, under-
tow, cross waves, and rip currents. Instead, enjoy
a picnic away from the ocean's edge. In the winter
when the surf eats up the beach, this might mean
perching on the lava-rock boulders backing the
sand. To reach the beach, you'll have to boulder-
hop across a stream. During heavy rains or even
just after, the stream can flood, stranding hikers
on the wrong side. This has resulted in helicopter
rescues, so don't cross unless the boulders are vis-
ibly exposed. **Amenities:** toilets. **Best For:** solitude;
sunset. ⊠ *Trailhead starts at end of Rte. 560, 7 miles west of Hanalei*
⊕ *www.hawaiistateparks.org.*

BEACHES KEY	
🏻	*Restroom*
🚿	*Showers*
🏄	*Surfing*
🤿	*Snorkel/Scuba*
👫	*Good for kids*
P	*Parking*

Kee Beach. Highway 560 on the North Shore literally dead-ends at this
beach, which is also the trailhead for the famous Kalalau Trail and the
site of an ancient *heiau* dedicated to hula. The beach is protected by a
reef—except during high surf—creating a small sandy-bottom lagoon
and making it a popular snorkeling destination. If there's a current, it's
usually found on the western edge of the beach as the incoming tide
ebbs back out to sea. Makana (a prominent peak also known as Bali
Hai after the blockbuster musical *South Pacific*) is so artfully arranged,
you'll definitely want to capture the memory, so don't forget your camera. The popularity of this beach often makes parking quite difficult.
Start extra early or, better yet, arrive at the end of the day, in time
to witness otherworldly sunsets sidelighting Napali Coast. **Amenities:**
lifeguards; parking; showers, toilets. **Best For:** swimming; snorkeling;
sunset; walking. ⊠ *End of Rte. 560, 7 miles west of Hanalei.*

Fodor's Choice
★

Haena Beach Park (*Tunnels Beach*). This is a drive-up beach park popular
with campers year-round. The wide bay here—named Makua and commonly known as Tunnels—is bordered by two large reef systems creating favorable waves for surfing during peak winter conditions. In July
and August, waters at this same beach are as calm as a lake, usually, and
snorkelers enjoy the variety of fish life found in a hook-shape reef made
up of underwater lava tubes, on the east end of the bay. ■**TIP→ During
the summer months only, this is a premier snorkeling site on Kauai.** It's not
unusual to find a food vendor parked here selling sandwiches and drinks
out of a converted bread van. **Amenities:** food and drink; lifeguards;
parking; showers; toilets. **Best For:** walking; snorkeling; surfing. ⊠ *Near
end of Rte. 560, across from lava-tube sea caves, after stream crossing.*

Lumahai Beach. Famous because it's the beach where Nurse Nellie washes that man out of her hair in *South Pacific*, Lumahai Beach's setting is all you've ever dreamed Hawaii to be. That's the drawing card, and if you're adventurous and safety-conscious, a visit here is definitely worth it. The challenges are that it's hard to find, there's little parking, and there's a steep hike in; also, too many people misjudge the waves, even those never intending to set foot in the water. There's a year-round surge of onshore waves, massive sand movements (especially around the river mouth), and a steep foreshore assaulted by strong currents. Like the mythical creature from the deep, rogue waves have actually washed up on lava-rock outcroppings and pulled sightseers out to sea. Our advice: Look from the safety of the scenic overlook or walk on *dry* sand only. Or, take advantage of Lumahai's length and find adequate parking ½ mile Farther, where the river comes in. **Amenities:** none. **Best For:** solitude; walking; sunset. ☒ *On winding section of Rte. 560 west of Hanalei, east of mile marker 5* ✛ *Park on makai side of road and walk down steep path to beach.*

> ### WORD OF MOUTH
>
> "Watch a sunset, walk Hanalei Bay in the morning, become mesmerized by the Kauai blue waters and just enjoy the beauty that surrounds you." —jojuice

☺ Fodor's Choice ★ **Hanalei Bay Beach Park.** This 2-mile, crescent beach surrounds a spacious bay that is quintessential Hawaii. After gazing out to sea and realizing you have truly arrived in paradise, look landward. The site of the mountains, ribboned with waterfalls, will take your breath away. All this beauty accounts for why coastal expert "Dr. Beach" named Hanalei number one in the U.S. in 2009. In winter Hanalei Bay boasts some of the biggest onshore surf breaks in the state, attracting world-class surfers. The beach itself is wide enough to have safe real estate for your beach towel even in winter. In summer the bay is transformed—calm waters lap the beach, sailboats moor in the bay, and outrigger-canoe paddlers ply the sea. Pack the cooler, haul out the beach umbrellas, and don't forget the beach toys, because Hanalei Bay is worth scheduling for an entire day, maybe two. **Amenities:** lifeguards; parking; showers; toilets. **Best For:** surfing; swimming; walking; windsurfing. ☒ *Weli Weli Rd., in Hanalei, turn makai at Aku Rd. and drive 1 block to Weli Weli Rd. Parking areas are on makai side of Weli Weli Rd.*

Puu Poa Beach. The coastline along the community of Princeville is primarily made up of sea cliffs with a couple of pockets of beaches. The sea cliffs end with a long, narrow stretch of beach just east of the Hanalei River and at the foot of the St. Regis Princeville Resort. Public access is via 100-plus steps around the back of the hotel; hotel guests can simply take the elevator down to sea level. The beach itself is subject to the hazards of winter's surf, narrowing and widening with the surf height. On calm days, snorkeling is good thanks to a shallow reef system pocked with sand. Sometimes a shallow sandbar extends across the river to Black Pot Beach Park, part of the Hanalei Beach system, making it easy to cross the river. On high-surf days, the outer edge of the reef near the river draws internationally ranked surfers. The resort's pool is off-limits to nonguests, but the restaurants and bars are not. **Amenities:** food and drink, parking. **Best For:** surfing; snorkeling; sunset. ⊠ *Follow Ka Haku Rd. to end; park in public parking on right just before hotel's entrance; cross street for beach access, Princeville.*

Pali Ke Kua Beach (*Hideaways Beach*). This is actually two very small pocket beaches separated by a narrow rocky point. The beach area itself is narrow and can all but disappear in wintertime. However, in summer, the steep, rocky trail (don't trust the rusty handrails and rotting ropes) that provides access reduces the number of beachgoers, at times creating a deserted beach feel. With patches of reef and a combination sandy/rocky bottom, the swimming and snorkeling can be good, although winter's high surf creates dangerous conditions. ■TIP→ Don't attempt the trail after a heavy rain—it turns into a mudslide. **Amenities:** parking. **Best For:** surfing; snorkeling; sunset. ⊠ *Follow Ka Haku Rd. to end; park in public parking on right just before hotel's entrance; follow dirt trail between parking lot and condominium complex, Princeville.*

Anini Beach Park. A great family park, Anini is unique in that it features one of the longest and widest fringing reefs in all Hawaii, creating a shallow lagoon that is good for snorkeling and following the occasional turtle. It is quite safe in all but the highest of winter surf. The reef follows the shoreline for some 2 miles and extends 1,600 feet offshore at its widest point. During times of low tide—usually occurring around the full moon of the summer months—much of the reef is exposed. Anini is inarguably the windsurfing mecca of Kauai, even for beginners, and it also attracts participants in the growing sport of kiteboarding. **Amenities:** food and drink; parking; showers; toilets. **Best For:** walking; swimming; windsurfing; sunrise. ⊠ *Anini Rd., turn makai off Rte. 56 onto Kalihiwai Rd., on Hanalei side of Kalihiwai Bridge; follow road left at "Y" to reach Anini Rd. and beach.*

Kalihiwai Beach. A winding road leads down a cliff face to this picture-perfect beach. A jewel of the North Shore, Kalihiwai Beach is on par with Hanalei, just without the waterfall-ribbon backdrop. It's another one of those drive-up beaches, so it's very accessible. Most people park on the sand under the grove of ironwood trees. Families set up camp for the day at the west end of the beach, near the stream, where young kids like to splash and older kids like to body board. On the eastern edge of the beach, from which the road descends, there's a locals' favorite surf spot during winter's high surf. The onshore break can be dangerous during this time. During the calmer months of summer, Kalihiwai Beach is a good choice for beginning board riders and swimmers. The

toilets here are the portable kind. No showers. **Amenities:** parking; toilets. **Best For:** surfing; swimming; walking. ⊠ *Kalihiwai Rd., turn makai off Rte. 56 onto Kalihiwai Rd. on Kilauea side of Kalihiwai Bridge.*

Kauapea Beach (*Secret Beach*). This beach went relatively unknown—except by some intrepid fishermen, of course—for a long time, hence the common reference to it as "Secret Beach." You'll understand why once you stand on the shore of Kauapea and see the solid wall of rock 100 feet high, maybe more, that cups the length of the beach, making it fairly inaccessible. For the hardy, there is a steep hike down the western end. From there, if you make the long trek across the

beach—toward Kilauea Point National Wildlife Refuge—and if you arrive just after sunrise, you may witness a school of dolphins just offshore. You may also run across a gathering of another kind on the beach—nudists. Because of its remote location, Kauapea is popular with nude sunbathers, although the county is trying to curtail the shedding of clothes here. A consistent onshore break makes swimming here questionable. **Amenities:** parking. **Best For:** solitude; walking; surfing. ⊠ *Turn makai onto Kalihiwai Rd. just past the turnoff for Kilauea; take second dirt road to its end; park and follow dirt trail.*

★ **Kahili Beach** (*Rock Quarry*). You wouldn't know it today, but this beach on Kilauea Bay was once an interisland steamer landing and a rock quarry. Today, it's a fairly quiet beach, although when the surf closes out many other North Shore surf spots, the break directly offshore from Kilauea Stream near the abandoned quarry is still rideable. For the regular oceangoer, summer's your best bet, although the quickly sloping ocean bottom doesn't make for great swimming or snorkeling. The stream estuary is quite beautiful, and the ironwood trees and false kamani growing in the generous sand dunes at the rear of the beach provide protection from the sun. Kids like to play here, as do soaring great frigate birds overhead. In March 2006, the streambed emptying into the ocean here grew to immense proportions when Ka Loko Dam broke, sending a wall of water—as well as life and property—to the sea. **Amenities:** none. **Best For:** surfing; walking; solitude. ⊠ *Turn makai onto Wailapa Rd.; drive for ½ mile and turn left onto dirt road, following it to its end, Kilauea.*

Larsen's Beach. The long, wide fringing reef here is this beach's trademark. The waters near shore are often too shallow for swimming; if you go in, wear a rash guard to protect against prickly sea urchins and sharp coral on the bottom. High surf during the winter of 2009 blew out a

BEACH SAFETY ON KAUAI

Hawaii's world-renowned, beautiful beaches can be extremely dangerous at times due to large waves and strong currents—so much so that the state rates wave hazards using three signs: a yellow square (caution), a red stop sign (high hazard), and a black diamond (extreme hazard). Signs are posted and updated three times daily or as conditions change.

Visiting beaches with lifeguards is strongly recommended, and you should swim only when there's a normal caution rating. Never swim alone or dive into unknown water or shallow breaking waves. If you're unable to swim out of a rip current, tread water and wave your arms in the air to signal for help.

Even in calm conditions, there are other dangerous things in the water to be aware of, including razor-sharp coral, jellyfish, eels, and sharks, to name a few.

Jellyfish cause the most ocean injuries, and signs are posted along beaches when they're present. Reactions to a sting are usually mild (burning sensation, redness, welts); however, in some cases they can be severe (breathing difficulties). If you're stung, pick off the tentacles, rinse the affected area with water, and apply ice.

The chances of getting bitten by a shark in Hawaiian waters are very low; sharks attack swimmers or surfers three or four times per year. Of the 40 species of sharks found near Hawaii, tiger sharks are considered the most dangerous because of their size and indiscriminate feeding behavior. They're easily recognized by their blunt snouts and vertical bars on their sides.

Here are a few tips to reduce your shark-attack risk:

■ Swim, surf, or dive with others at beaches patrolled by lifeguards.

■ Avoid swimming at dawn, dusk, and night, when some shark species may move inshore to feed.

■ Don't enter the water if you have open wounds or are bleeding.

■ Avoid murky waters, harbor entrances, areas near stream mouths (especially after heavy rains), channels, or steep drop-offs.

■ Don't wear high-contrast swimwear or shiny jewelry.

■ Don't swim near dolphins, which are often prey for large sharks.

■ If you spot a shark, leave the water quickly and calmly; never provoke or harass a shark, no matter how small.

The website ⊕ www.oceansafety. soest.hawaii.edu/index.asp provides statewide beach hazard maps as well as weather and surf advisories.

section of reef, creating some tricky currents for the novice oceangoer. And there have been a number of drownings and near-drownings here. A recent land disagreement cut off the traditional trail down to the beach. Now, like many other North Shore beaches, this one requires a hike along a steep, rocky trail. ⚠ Slippery when wet. **Amenities:** parking. **Best For:** solitude; sunrise; nudists. ⊠ *Turn makai at north intersection of Koolau Rd.; drive 1¼ miles to dirt turnoff on left marked*

by a slender pole and a "beach access" sign in black lettering. Park at end of road, Kilauea.

THE EAST SIDE

The East Side of the island is considered the "windward" side, a term you'll often hear in weather forecasts. It simply means the side of the island receiving onshore winds. The wind helps break down rock into sand, so there are plenty of beaches here. Unfortunately, only a few of those beaches are protected, so many are not ideal for beginning ocean-goers, though they are perfect for long sunrise ambles. On super-windy days, kiteboarders sail along the east shore, sometimes jumping waves and performing acrobatic maneuvers in the air.

The beaches below are listed in order from north to south.

Aliomanu Beach. Because of the time change, most visitors to Hawaii awake before the sun rises. Enjoy those early hours by heading to the easily accessible and lesser-known Aliomanu Beach for a long morning walk and witness that great, orange orb emerging over the ocean's horizon. The waters off Aliomanu Beach are protected by the fringing reef 100 yards or so out to sea, making snorkeling as good as at many more popular areas; however, currents can be tricky, especially near the stream tucked in the beach's elbow toward the northern end, and at the river mouth on the southern end that demarcates Aliomanu Beach from its neighbor, Anahola Beach. A good walk is to start at the river mouth and head north, skirting a seawall midway; aqua shoes are recommended, especially for rounding the rocky point at the northern tip. ■TIP→ With its shallow waters, this is a popular fishing and family beach, so stick to weekdays if you want quiet. **Amenities:** parking. **Best For:** walking; solitude; sunrise. ⊠ *Turn makai just north of mile marker 14 on Aliomanu Rd.; park in dirt parking lot where road bends 90 degrees to the left.*

Anahola Beach Park. Anahola is known as the most Hawaiian of all communities on Kauai, so Anahola Beach Park is definitely a locals' hangout, especially for families with small children. A child's first birthday is considered a big bash (including rented tents, picnic tables, and catered luau food) for family and friends in Hawaii, and this is a popular location for the celebration. The shallow and calm water at the beach road's end is tucked behind a curving finger of land and perfect for young ones. As the beach winds closer to the river mouth, there's less protection

DID YOU KNOW?

Lydgate State Park is one of our favorite beaches on the East Side. Families love the protected saltwater pools, picnic areas, and playgrounds designed by local children.

and a shore break favorable for body boarders if the trades are light or kona (south) winds are present. Children like to frolic in the river, and pole fishermen often set up at the river mouth. On Tuesday around 5 pm, you might catch Puna Dawson's hula *halau* (school) meeting. She welcomes visitors to watch and participate. If you come at sunrise, the view of Kalalea Mountains with the Anahola River trailing in front of it makes for a good photographic opportunity. **Amenities:** lifeguards; parking; showers; toilets; camping. **Best For:** swimming; partiers; snorkeling; surfing. ⊠ *Turn makai just south of mile marker 14 on Anahola Rd. and drive 1 mile.*

Donkey Beach. This beach has one of the most unusual names of all on Kauai and is rarely known by its proper Hawaiian name, Paliku. Lihue Plantation Company once kept a herd of mules and donkeys in the pasture adjacent to the beach, hence the nickname. It's a popular spot for au naturel sunbathers, and if the waves are right, body boarders and surfers might be spotted offshore. However, the waters here are rough and not recommended for swimming and snorkeling. Instead, we suggest a morning walk or mountain-bike trek along the easy trail that overlooks the beach. Start at the northern end of Kealia Beach (or in Kapaa town for a longer walk or bike ride) and head north. The trail splinters just past Donkey Beach and then splinters again; however, it does go all the way to Anahola Beach. **Amenities:** parking; toilets. **Best For:** surfing; solitude; sunrise; nudists. ⊠ *Just north of Kealia Kai subdivision entrance on Rte. 56, turn makai into parking lot. Hike down to beach.*

Kealia Beach. A half-mile long and adjacent to the highway heading north out of Kapaa, Kealia Beach attracts body boarders and surfers year-round (possibly because the local high school is just up the hill). Kealia is not generally a great beach for swimming or snorkeling. The waters are usually rough and the waves crumbly because of an onshore break (no protecting reef) and northeasterly trade winds. A scenic lookout on the southern end, accessed off the highway, is a superb location for saluting the morning sunrise or spotting whales during winter. A level, paved trail follows the coastline north and is one of the most scenic coastal trails on the island for walking, running, and biking. **Amenities:** lifeguards; parking; showers; toilets. **Best For:** surfing; swimming; walking; sunrise. ⊠ *Rte. 56, at mile marker 10, Kapaa.*

☾ **Baby Beach.** There aren't many swimming beaches on Kauai's East Side; however, this one usually ranks highly with mothers of small children because there's a narrow lagoonlike area between the beach and the near-shore reef perfect for small children. Of course, in winter, watch for east and northeast swells that would not make this such a safe option. There are no beach facilities—no lifeguards, so watch your babies. There is an old-time shower spigot available to rinse the saltwater. **Amenities:** parking; showers. **Best For:** swimming; sunrise. ⊠ *In Kapaa, turn mauka at the Chevron gas station onto Keaka Rd., then left on Moamakai Rd. Parking is off-street between Makaha and Panihi Rds.*

Wailua Beach. Some say the first Polynesians to migrate to Hawaii landed at Wailua Beach. At the river's mouth, petroglyphs carved on boulders

BEST BEACHES

He says "to-mah-toe," and she says "to-may-toe." When it comes to beaches on Kauai, the meaning behind that axiom holds true: People are different. What rocks one person's world wreaks havoc for another's. Here are some additional tips on how to choose a beach that's right for you.

BEST FOR FAMILIES

Lydgate State Park, East Side. The kid-designed playground, the protected swimming pools, and Kamalani Bridge guarantee you will not hear these words from your child: "Mom, I'm bored."

Poipu Beach Park, Poipu, South Shore. The *keiki* (children's) pool and lifeguards make this a safe spot for kids. The near-perpetual sun isn't so bad, either.

BEST STAND-UP PADDLING

Anini Beach Park, North Shore. The reef and long stretch of beach give beginners to stand-up paddling a calm place to give this new sport a try. You won't get pummeled by waves here.

Wailua Beach, East Side. On the East Side, the Wailua River bisects the beach and heads inland 2 miles, providing stand-up paddlers with a long and scenic stretch of water before they have to figure out how to turn around.

BEST SURFING

Hanalei Bay Beach Park, North Shore. In winter, Hanalei Bay offers a range of breaks, from beginner to advanced. Hanalei is where surfing legends such as Laird Hamilton and the Irons Brothers—international surf champions—began their shredding careers as they grew up surfing these waters.

Waiohai Beach, South Shore. Surf instructors flock to this spot with their students for its gentle, near-shore break. Then, as students advance, they can paddle out a little farther to an intermediate break—if they dare.

BEST SUNSETS

Kee Beach, North Shore. Even in winter, when the sun sets in the south and out of view, you won't be disappointed here, because the "magic hour," as photographers call the time around sunset, paints Napali Coast with a warm gold light.

Polihale State Park, West Side. This due-west-facing beach may be tricky to get to, but it does offer the most unobstructed sunset views on the island. The fact that it's so remote means you won't have strangers in your photos, but you will want to depart right after sunset or risk getting lost in the dark.

BEST FOR SEEING AND BEING SEEN

Haena Beach Park, North Shore. Behind those gated driveways and heavily foliaged yards that line this beach live—at least, part-time—some of the world's most celebrated music and movie moguls. Need we say more?

Hanalei Bay Beach Park, North Shore. We know we tout this beach often, but it deserves the praise. It's a mecca for everyone—regular joes, surfers, fishers, young, old, locals, visitors, and, especially, the famous. You may also recognize Hanalei Bay from the movie *The Descendants*.

are sometimes visible during low-surf and -tide conditions. Surfers, body boarders, and bodysurfers alike enjoy this beach year-round thanks to its dependable waves (usually on the north end); however, because of Hawaii's northeast trade winds, these waves are not the "cleanest" for surf aficionados. Many families spend the weekend days under the Wailua Bridge at the river mouth, even hauling out their portable grills and tables to go with their beach chairs. The great news about Wailua Beach is that it's almost impossible to miss; however, parking can be a challenge. **Amenities:** parking; showers; toilets. **Best For:** swimming; surfing; walking; windsurfing. ⊠ *The best parking for the north end of the beach is on Papaloa Rd. behind the Shell station. For the southern end of the beach, the best parking is in the Wailua River State Park (where toilets—the portable kind—are also found). To get there, turn mauka on Kuamoo Rd. and left into the park, then walk along the river and under the bridge.*

Lydgate State Park. This is by far the best family beach park on Kauai. The waters off the beach are protected by a hand-built breakwater creating two boulder-enclosed saltwater pools for safe swimming and snorkeling year-round. A recent dredging finds the pools in a recovery stage as sand had to be removed leaving mud offshore. But the numerous schools of fish are slowly returning. The smaller of the two pools is perfect for *keiki* (children). Behind the beach is Kamalani Playground, designed by the children of Kauai and built by the community. Children of all ages—that includes you—enjoy the swings, lava-tube slides, tree house, and more. Picnic tables abound in the park, and a large covered pavilion is available by permit for celebrations. The Kamalani Kai Bridge is a second playground—also built by the community—south of the original. (The two are united by a bike and pedestrian path that is part of the Nawiliwili-to-Anahola multiuse path project currently under construction.) ■ **TIP→** This park system is perennially popular; the quietest times to visit are early mornings and weekdays. If you want to witness a "baby luau," Lydgate State Park attracts them year-round, especially in summers. **Amenities:** lifeguards; parking; showers; toilets. **Best For:** partiers; walking; swimming; sunrise. ⊠ *Nalu Rd., just south of Wailua River, turn makai off Rte. 56 onto Lehu Dr. and left onto Nalu Rd.*

Kalapaki Beach. Five minutes south of the airport in Lihue, you'll find this wide, sandy-bottom beach fronting the Kauai Marriott. One of the big attractions is that this beach is almost always safe from rip currents and undertows because it's around the backside of a peninsula, in its own cove. There are tons of activities here, including all the usual water sports—beginning and intermediate surfing, body boarding, bodysurfing, and swimming—plus, there are two outrigger canoe clubs paddling in the bay and the Nawiliwili Yacht Club's boats sailing around the harbor. Kalapaki is the only place on Kauai where sailboats—in this case Hobie Cats—are available for rent (at Kauai Beach Boys, which fronts the beach next to Duke's Canoe Club restaurant). Visitors can also rent snorkel gear, surfboards, body boards, and kayaks from Kauai Beach Boys. A volleyball court on the beach is often used by a loosely organized group of local players; visitors are always welcome.

KAUAI'S BEST SWIMMING HOLES

You don't have to head to the beach to go swimming, and we're not talking chlorinated swimming pools, either. There are so many beaches and swimming holes around Kauai that you should never have to set foot in chlorine. But there's a difference between swimming in the ocean at the beach and swimming in these spots. These tend to be more remote, and—as the term *swimming hole* implies—they are enclosed. That doesn't mean they're safer than swimming in the ocean, with its possible rips and currents. Never dive—hidden boulders abound. Wear protective footwear—those boulders can have sharp edges. Stay away during or just after heavy rains and high surf, and do not take a shower under waterfalls, as tempting as it may sound, because you never know when a rock will come tumbling down.

Queen's Bath. Listen to us when we tell you not to attempt this in winter. This is one of those places where rogue waves like to roam; unfortunately, so do people. Several have drowned here during North Shore swells, so always check ocean conditions. During summer, this is an experience unlike many others around Kauai, as the winter surf recedes, revealing a lava shelf with two good-size holes for swimming— sometimes even snorkeling. Turtles cruise in and out, too, via an underwater entry. It's said that Queen Emma once bathed here; hence, the name. The trail down is short but steep; then there's a section of lava-rock scrambling before you get to the swimming holes. Over the years, the county has periodically closed access due to safety reasons and residents' complaints. Access is in tony Princeville, amid private residences, so be sure to park only in the designated spot. If it's full, do not park on the street, and do not park on anyone's lawn or driveway. ⊠ *In Princeville from Ka Haku Rd., turn makai on Punahele and right on Kapiolani.*

Uluwehi Falls. If you paddle upriver a couple of miles and hike a mile or so inland, you'll discover the 120-foot Uluwehi Falls, more commonly known as Secret Falls, with a big swimming area. Now, you could do this on your own—if you're familiar with the river and the trail; however, we recommend hiring one of the many Wailua River kayak guides so you don't get lost.

■TIP➔ Families prefer the stream end of the beach, whereas those seeking more solitude will prefer the cliff side of the beach. Duke's Canoe Club restaurant is one of only a couple of restaurants on the island actually on a beach; the restaurant's lower level is casual, even welcoming beach attire and sandy feet, perfect for lunch or an afternoon cocktail. **Amenities:** food and drink; parking; showers; toilets; water sports. **Best For:** swimming; surfing; partiers; walking. ⊠ *Off Wapaa Rd., which runs from Lihue to Nawiliwili.*

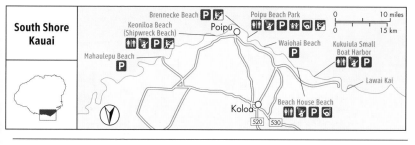

THE SOUTH SHORE

The South Shore's primary access road is Highway 520, a tree-lined, two-lane, windy road. As you drive along it, there's a sense of tunneling down a rabbit hole into another world, à la Alice. And the South Shore is certainly a wonderland. On average, it rains only 30 inches per year, so if you're looking for fun in the sun, this is a good place to start. The beaches with their powdery-fine sand are consistently good year-round, except during high surf, which, if it hits at all, will be in summer. If you want solitude, this isn't it; if you want excitement—well, as much excitement as quiet Kauai offers—this is the place for you.

The beaches in this section are listed from east to west.

Fodor's Choice ★ **Mahaulepu Beach.** This 2-mile stretch of coast with its sand dunes, limestone hills, sinkholes, and caves is unlike any other on Kauai. Remains of a large, ancient settlement, evidence of great battles, and the discovery of a now-underwater petroglyph field indicate that Hawaiians lived in this area as early as 700 AD. Mahaulepu's coastline is unprotected and rocky, which makes venturing into the ocean hazardous. There are three beach areas with bits of sandy-bottom swimming; however, we think the best way to experience Mahaulepu is simply to roam, especially at sunrise. ■**TIP**➔ Access to this beach is via private property. The owner allows access during daylight hours, but be sure to depart before sunset or risk getting locked in for the night. **Amenities:** parking. **Best For:** walking; solitude; sunrise. ⊠ *Poipu Rd., continue on Poipu Rd. past Hyatt (it turns into dirt road) to a T-intersection and turn makai; road ends at beach parking area, Poipu.*

Keoniloa Beach (*Shipwreck Beach*). Few—except the public relations specialists at the Grand Hyatt Kauai Resort and Spa, which backs the beach—refer to this beach by anything other than its common name: Shipwreck Beach. Its Hawaiian name means "long beach." Both make sense. It is a long stretch of crescent-shape beach punctuated by cliffs on both ends, and, yes, a ship once wrecked here. With its onshore break, the waters off Shipwreck are best for body boarding and bodysurfing; however, the beach itself is plenty big for sunbathing, sand-castle building, Frisbee, and other beach-related fun. Fishers pole fish from shore and off the cliff and sometimes pick *opihi* (limpets) off the rocks lining the foot of the cliffs. The eastern edge of the beach is the start of an interpretive dune walk (complimentary) held by the hotel staff; check with the concierge for dates and times. **Amenities:** food and drink; parking; showers; toilets.

In front of the Kauai Marriott, Kalapaki Beach is usually a safe bet for swimming and water sports.

Best for: surfing; walking; sunrise. ⊠ *Ainako Rd., continue on Poipu Rd. past Hyatt; turn makai onto Ainako Rd., Poipu.*

Brennecke Beach. There's little beach here on the eastern end of Poipu Beach Park, but Brennecke Beach is synonymous on the island with board surfing and bodysurfing, thanks to its shallow sandbar and reliable shore break. Because the beach is small and often congested, surfboards are prohibited near shore. The water on the rocky eastern edge of the beach is a good place to see the endangered green sea turtles noshing on plants growing on the rocks. **Amenities:** food and drink; parking. **Best For:** surfing; sunset. ⊠ *Hoone Rd., turn makai off Poipu Rd. onto Hoowili Rd., then left onto Hoone Rd.; beach is at intersection with Kuai Rd., Poipu.*

☺ ★ **Poipu Beach Park.** The most popular beach on the South Shore, and perhaps on all of Kauai, is Poipu Beach Park. The snorkeling's good, the body boarding's good, the surfing's good, the swimming's good, and the fact that the sun is almost always shining is good, too. The beach can be crowded at times, especially on weekends and holidays, but that just makes people-watching that much more fun. You'll see *keiki* (children) experiencing the ocean for the first time, snorkelers trying to walk with their flippers on, ukulele players, birthday party revelers, young and old, visitors and locals. Even the endangered Hawaiian monk seal often makes an appearance. **Amenities:** food and drink; lifeguards; parking; showers; toilets. **Best For:** swimming, snorkeling, partiers, walking. ⊠ *Hoone Rd., from Poipu Rd., turn right onto Hoone Rd., Poipu.*

Waiohai Beach. The first hotel built in Poipu in 1962 overlooked this beach, adjacent to Poipu Beach Park. Actually, there's little to distinguish

Seal-Spotting on the South Shore

When strolling on one of Kauai's lovely beaches, don't be surprised if you find yourself in the rare company of Hawaiian monk seals. These are among the most endangered of all marine mammals, with perhaps fewer than 1,200 remaining. They primarily inhabit the northwestern Hawaiian Islands, although more are showing their sweet faces on the main Hawaiian Islands, especially on Kauai. They're fond of hauling out on the beach for a long snooze in the sun, particularly after a night of gorging on fish. They need this time to rest and digest, safe from predators.

During the past several summers, female seals have birthed young on the beaches around Kauai, where they stay to nurse their pups for upward of six weeks. It seems the seals enjoy particular beaches for the same

reasons we do: the shallow, protected waters.

If you're lucky enough to see a monk seal, keep your distance and let it be. Although they may haul out near people, they still want and need their space. Stay several hundred feet away, and forget photos unless you've got a zoom lens. It's illegal to do anything that causes a monk seal to change its behavior, with penalties that include big fines and even jail time. In the water, seals may appear to want to play. It's their curious nature. Don't try to play with them. They are wild animals—mammals, in fact, with teeth.

If you have concerns about the health or safety of a seal, or just want more information, contact the **Hawaiian Monk Seal Conservation Hui** (☎ 808/651–7668 ⊕ www.kauaiseals. com).

where one starts and the other begins other than a crescent reef at the eastern end of Waiohai Beach. That crescent, however, is important. It creates a small, protected bay—good for snorkeling and beginning surfers. If you're a beginner, this is the spot. However, when a summer swell kicks up, the near-shore conditions become dangerous; offshore, there's a splendid surf break for experienced surfers. The beach itself is narrow and, like its neighbor, gets very crowded in summer. **Amenities:** parking. **Best For:** surfing; sunrise; sunset. ⊠ *Hoone Rd., from Poipu Rd., turn right onto Hoone Rd. Poipu.*

Beach House Beach. Don't pack the beach umbrella, beach mats, and cooler for this one—just your snorkel gear. The beach, named after the neighboring Beach House restaurant and on the road to Spouting Horn, is a small slip of sand during low tide and a rocky shoreline when it's high; however, it is conveniently located by the road's edge, and its rocky coastline and somewhat rocky bottom make it great for snorkeling. (As a rule, sandy-bottom beaches are not great for snorkeling. The rocks create safe hiding places and grow the food that fish and other marine life like to eat.) A sidewalk along the coastline on the restaurant side of the beach makes a great vantage point from which to peer into the water and look for *honu*, the Hawaiian green sea turtle. It's also a gathering spot to watch the sun set. ■ TIP➔ Make reservations for dinner at the Beach House days in advance and time it around sunset. **Amenities:**

The beach at Salt Pond Beach Park is worth a stop for its protected swimming cove.

parking; showers; toilets; water sports. **Best For:** snorkeling; surfing; sunset. ⊠ *Lawai Rd.,from Poipu Rd., turn onto Lawai Rd; park on street near restaurant or in public parking lot across from beach Poipu* .

🕓 **Kukuiula Small Boat Harbor.** This is a great beach to sit and people-watch as diving and fishing boats, kayakers, and canoe paddlers head out to sea. Shore and throw-net fishermen frequent this harbor as well. It's not a particularly large harbor, so it retains a quaint sense of charm, unlike Nawiliwili Harbor or Port Allen. The bay is a nice, protected area for limited swimming, but with all the boat traffic kicking up sand and clouding the water, it's probably not good for snorkeling. Outside the breakwater, there is a decent surf spot. **Amenities:** parking; showers; toilets. **Best For:** solitude; swimming; sunrise. ⊠ *Lawai Rd., from Poipu Rd., turn onto Lawai Rd.; it's about a mile up on the left. Watch for small green sign, Poipu* .

Fodor's Choice **Lawai Kai.** One of the most spectacular beaches on the South Shore is ★ inaccessible by land unless you tour the National Tropical Botanical Garden's Allerton Garden, which we highly recommend, or trespass behind locked fences, which we don't recommend. On the tour, you'll see the beach, but you won't lounge on it or frolic in the calm water behind the promontory on the eastern point of the beach. One way to legally access the beach on your own is by paddling a kayak 1 mile from Kukuiula Harbor. However, you have to rent the kayaks elsewhere and haul them on top of your car to the harbor. Also, the wind and waves usually run westward, making the in-trip a breeze but the return trip a workout against Mother Nature. Another way is to boulder-hop along the coast from Spouting Horn—a long trek over sharp lava rock that

SUN SAFETY ON KAUAI

Hawaii's weather—seemingly never-ending warm, sunny days with gentle trade winds—can be enjoyed year-round with good sun sense. Because of Hawaii's subtropical location, the length of daylight here changes little throughout the year. The sun is particularly strong, with a daily UV average of 14. Visitors should take extra precaution to avoid sunburns and long-term cancer risks due to sun exposure.

The Hawaii Dermatological Society recommends these sun safety tips:

■ Plan your beach, golf, hiking, and other outdoor activities for the early morning or late afternoon, avoiding the sun between 10 am and 4 pm, when it's the strongest.

■ Apply a broad-spectrum sunscreen with a sun protection factor (SPF) of at least 15. Hawaii lifeguards use sunscreens with an SPF of 30. Cover areas that are most prone to burning like your nose, shoulders, tops of feet, and ears. And don't forget to use sun-protection products on your lips.

■ Apply sunscreen at least 30 minutes before you plan to be outdoors and reapply every two hours, even on cloudy days. Clouds scatter sunlight, so you can still burn on an overcast day.

■ Wear light, protective clothing, such as a long-sleeve shirt and pants, broad-brimmed hat, and sunglasses.

■ Stay in the shade whenever possible—especially on the beach—by using an umbrella. Remember that sand and water can reflect up to 85% of the sun's damaging rays.

■ Children need extra protection from the sun. Apply sunscreen frequently and liberally on children over six months of age and minimize their time in the sun. Sunscreen is not recommended for children under six months.

we do not recommend. ■ TIP→ Do not attempt this beach in any manner during a south swell. **Amenities:** none. **Best For:** solitude; sunrise. ⊠ *For kayakers from Poipu Rd., turn onto Lawai Rd. and park at Kukuiula small boat harbor.*

THE WEST SIDE

The West Side of the island receives hardly enough rainfall year-round to water a cactus, and because it's also the leeward side, there are few tropical breezes. That translates to sunny and hot with long, languorous, and practically deserted beaches. You'd think the leeward waters—untouched by wind—would be calm, but there's no reef system, so the waters are not as inviting as one would like. ■ TIP→ The best place to gear up for the beaches on the West Side is on the South Shore or East Side. Although there's some catering to visitors here, it's not much.

Ⓒ **Salt Pond Beach Park.** A great family spot, Salt Pond Beach Park features a naturally made, shallow swimming pond behind a curling finger of rock where keiki splash and snorkel. This pool is generally safe except during a large south swell, which usually occurs in summer, if at all. The

The sunny South Shore beaches have some good surf breaks. Head to Poipu Beach for board rentals or lessons.

center and western edge of the beach is popular with body boarders and bodysurfers. On a cultural note, the flat stretch of land to the east of the beach is the last spot in Hawaii where ponds are used to harvest salt in the dry heat of summer. The beach park is popular with locals and can get crowded on weekends and holidays. **Amenities:** lifeguards; parking; showers; toilets. **Best For:** swimming; sunset; walking. ⊠ *Lolokai Rd., from Rte. 50 in Hanapepe, turn makai onto Lele Rd., then right onto Lolokai Rd. (Salt Pond Rd.), Hanapepe.*

Lucy Wright Beach Park. Named in honor of the first Native Hawaiian schoolteacher, this beach is on the western banks of the Waimea River. It is also where Captain James Cook first came ashore in the Hawaiian Islands in 1778. If that's not interesting enough, the sand here is not the white, powdery kind you see along the South Shore. It's a combination of pulverized, black lava rock and lighter-colored reef. In a way, it looks a bit like a mix of salt and pepper. Unfortunately, the intrigue of the beach doesn't extend to the waters, which are reddish and murky (thanks to river runoff) and choppy (thanks to an onshore break). Instead, check out the Waimea Landing State Recreation Pier, from which fishers drop their lines. It's located about 100 yards west of the river mouth. **Amenities:** parking; showers; toilets. **Best For:** walking; sunset; surfing. ⊠ *From Rte. 50 in Waimea, turn makai onto Pokile Rd., Waimea.*

Kekaha Beach Park. This is one of the premier spots on Kauai for sunset walks and the start of the state's longest beach. We don't recommend much water activity here without first talking to a lifeguard: The beach is exposed to open ocean and has an onshore break that can be hazardous any time of year. However, there are some excellent surf breaks—for experienced surfers only. Or, if you would like to run on a beach, this is the one—the hard-packed sand goes on for miles, all the way to Napali Coast, but you won't get past the Pacific Missile Range Facility and its post-9/11 restrictions. Another bonus for this beach is its relatively dry weather year-round. If it's raining where you are, try Kekaha Beach Park. Toilets here are the portable kind. **Amenities:** lifeguards; parking; showers; toilets. **Best For:** sunset; walking; surfing. ⊠ *From Rte. 50, drive to the west side of Kekaha and park across from the 27 mile marker.*

Fodor'sChoice
★
Polihale State Park. The longest stretch of beach in Hawaii starts in Kekaha and ends about 15 miles away at the start of Napali Coast. At the Napali end of the beach is the 5-mile-long, 140-acre Polihale State Park. In addition to being long, this beach is 300 feet wide in places and backed by sand dunes 50 to 100 feet tall. Polihale is a remote beach accessed via a rough, 5-mile haul-cane road (four-wheel drive preferred but not required) at the end of Route 50 in Kekaha. ■TIP➔ Be sure to start the day with a full tank of gas and a cooler filled with food and drink. Many locals wheel their four-wheel-drive vehicles up and over the sand dunes right onto the beach, but don't try this in a rental car. You're sure to get stuck and found in violation of your rental car agreement.

On weekends and holidays Polihale is a popular locals' camping location, but even on "busy" days this beach is never crowded. On days of high surf, only experts surf the waves. In general, the water here is extremely rough and not recommended for recreation; however, there's one small fringing reef, called Queen's Pond, where swimming is sometimes safe. Neighboring Polihale Beach is the Pacific Missile Range Facility (PMRF), operated by the U.S. Navy. Since September 11, 2001, access to the beaches fronting PMRF has been restricted. **Amenities:** parking; showers; toilets. **Best For:** walking; solitude; sunset. ⊠ *Rte. 50 ✢ Drive to end of Rte. 50 and continue on dirt road; several access points along the way.*

Water Sports and Tours

WORD OF MOUTH

"Please remember that the tour operators often (especially in the early season) cancel trips because of weather. So don't plan your trip for your last day."

—wbpiii

Updated by
David Simon

So, you've decided to vacation on an island. That means you're going to run into a little water at some time. Ancient Hawaiians are notorious water sports fanatics—they invented surfing, after all—and that proclivity hasn't strayed far from today's mind-set. Even if you're not into water sports or sports in general, there's a slim chance that you'll leave this island without getting out on the ocean, as Kauai's top attraction—Napali Coast—is something not to be missed.

For those who can't pack enough time snorkeling, fishing, Boogie boarding, or surfing into a vacation, Kauai has it all—everything except parasailing, that is, as it's illegal to do it here (though not on Maui, the Big Island, or Oahu). If you need to rent gear for any of these activities, you'll find plenty of places with large selections at reasonable prices. And no matter what part of the island you're staying on, you'll have several options for choice spots to enjoy playing in the water.

One thing to note, and we can't say this enough—the waters off the coast of Kauai have strong currents and can be unpredictable, so always err on the side of caution and know your limits. Follow the tagline repeated by the island's lifeguards—"When in doubt, don't go out."

BOAT TOURS

Deciding to see Napali Coast by boat is an easy decision. Choosing the outfitter to go with is not. There are numerous boat-tour operators to choose from, and, quite frankly, they all do a good job. Before you even start thinking about whom to go out with, answer these three questions: What kind of boat do I prefer? Where am I staying? Do I want to go in the morning or afternoon? Once you settle on these three, you can easily zero in on the tour outfitter.

First, the boat. The most important thing is to match your personality and that of your group with the personality of the boat. If you like thrills and adventure, the rubber, inflatable rafts—often called Zodi-acs, which Jacques Cousteau made famous and which the U.S. Coast Guard uses—will entice you. They're fast, sure to leave you drenched, and quite bouncy. If you prefer a smoother, more leisurely ride, then the large catamarans are the way to go. The next boat choice is size. Both the rafts and catamarans come in small and large. Again—think smaller, more adventurous; larger, more leisurely. ■ TIP→ Do not choose a smaller boat because you think there will be fewer people. There might be fewer people, but you'll be jammed together sitting atop strangers. If you prefer privacy over socializing, go with a larger boat, so you'll have more room to spread out. The smaller boats will also take you along the coast at a higher rate of speed, making photo opportunities a bit more challenging. One advantage to smaller boats, however, is that—depending on ocean conditions—some may slip into a sea cave or two. If that sounds interesting to you, call the outfitter and ask their policy on entering sea caves. Some won't, no matter the conditions, because they consider the caves sacred or because they don't want to cause any environmental damage.

There are three points boats leave from around the island (Hanalei, Port Allen, and Waimea), and all head to the same spot: Napali Coast. Here's the inside skinny on which is the best: If you're staying on the North Shore, choose to depart out of the North Shore. If you're stay-ing anywhere else, depart out of the West Side. It's that easy. Sure, the North Shore is closer to Napali Coast; however, you'll pay more for less overall time. The West Side boat operators may spend more time getting to Napali Coast; however, they'll spend about the same amount of time along Napali, plus you'll pay less. Finally, you'll also have to decide whether you want to go on a morning tour, which includes a deli lunch and a stop for snorkeling, or an afternoon tour, which does not stop to snorkel but does include a sunset over the ocean. The morning tours with snorkeling are more popular with families and those who love dolphins, which enjoy the "waves" created by the front of the cata-marans and might just escort you down the coast. The winter months will also be a good chance to spot some whales breaching. You don't have to be an expert snorkeler or even have any prior experience, but if it is your first time, note that although there will be some snorkeling instruction, there might not be much. Hawaiian spinner dolphins are so plentiful in the mornings that some tour companies guarantee you'll see them, though you won't get in the water and swim with them. The afternoon tours are more popular with nonsnorkelers—obviously—and photographers interested in capturing the setting sunlight on the coast. ■ TIP→ No matter which tour you select, book it online whenever possible. Most companies offer Web specials, usually around $10 to $20 off per person.

CATAMARAN TOURS

Blue Dolphin Charters. One of the best-known names in boat tours is now offering daily sport fishing trips for up to six passengers. The 40-foot *Que Sera* will head out where the fish are plentiful and the captain will share the catch at his discretion. Cost is $600, including all gear.

✉ *Port Allen Harbor, Eleele* ☎ *808/ 335–5553, 877/511–1311* ⊕ *www. kauaiboats.com.*

☾ **Capt. Andy's Sailing Adventures.** Departing from Port Allen and running two 55-foot sailing catamarans, Capt. Andy's runs the same five-hour snorkeling and four-hour sunset tours along Napali Coast as everyone else, though we're not crazy about its seating, which exists mostly in the cabin. It also operates a six-hour snorkel BBQ sail aboard a new addition—its *Southern Star* yacht—originally built for private charters. The new boat now operates as host for two of Capt. Andy's daily sailing trips for an upgraded feel. For a shorter adventure, they have a two-hour sunset sail, embarking out of Kukuiula Harbor in Poipu along the South Shore—with live Hawaiian music—on select days (check website for particulars). ■ **TIP→ If the winds and swells are up on the North Shore, this is usually a good choice—especially if you're prone to seasickness.** This is the only tour boat operator that allows infants on board—but only on the two-hour trip. Note, if you have reservations for the shorter tour, you'll check in at their Kukuiula Harbor office. Prices range from $69 to $159. ✉ *In Port Allen Marina Center,4353 Waialo Rd., Suite 1A–2A, Eleele* ✛ *Turn makai onto Rte. 541 off Rte. 50 at Eleele* ☎ *808/335–6833, 800/535–0830* ⊕ *www.napali.com.*

BEST BOAT TOURS
Best for snorkeling: Z-Tourz
Best for romance: Capt. Andy's Poipu Sail
Best for thrill seekers: Napali Explorer (Zodiac 1)
Best for mai tais: Blue Dolphin Charters
Best for pregnant women: Capt. Andy's
Best for charters: Captain Sundown
Best for price: Napali Riders

Captain Sundown. If you're staying on the North Shore, Captain Sundown is a worthy choice, especially for the nonadventurous. Get this: Captain Bob has been cruising Napali Coast since 1971—six days a week, sometimes twice a day. (And right alongside Captain Bob is his son Captain Larry.) To say he knows the area is a bit of an understatement. Here's the other good thing about this tour: they take only 15 to 17 passengers. Now, you'll definitely pay more, but it's worth it. The breathtaking views of the waterfall-laced mountains behind Hanalei and Haena start immediately, and then it's around Kee Beach and the magic of Napali Coast unfolds before you. All the while, the captains are trolling for fish, and if they catch any, guests get to reel 'em in. Afternoon sunset sails (seasonal) run three hours and check in around 3 pm—these are BYOB. Prices range from $144 to $199. During the winter months, Captain Bob moves his operation to Nawiliwili Harbor, where he runs four- to five-hour whale-watching tours. ✉ *Meet in Hanalei at Tahiti Nui parking lot, 5-5134 Kuhio Hwy., Hanalei* ☎ *808/826–5585* ⊕ *www.captainsundown.com.*

Catamaran Kahanu. This Hawaiian-owned-and-operated company has been in business since 1985 and runs a 40-foot power catamaran with 18-passenger seating. The five-hour tour includes snorkeling at Nualolo Kai, plus a deli lunch and soft drinks. The four-hour afternoon tour

Get out on the water and see the Napali Coast in style on a luxe cruising yacht.

includes a hot dinner and sunset. The boat is smaller than most and may feel a tad crowded, but the tour feels more personal, with a laid-back, *ohana* style. Saltwater runs through the veins of Captain Lani. Guests can witness the ancient cultural practice of coconut weaving or other Hawaiian craft demonstrations on board. There's no alcohol allowed. Prices range from $105 to $135. ⊠ *4353 Waialo Rd., Eleele* ✛ *From Rte. 50, turn left onto Rte. 541 at Eleele. Proceed just past Port Allen Marina Center; turn right at sign. Check-in booth on left* ☎ *808/645–6176, 888/213–7711* ✍ *catamarankahanu@gmail.com* ⊕ *www.catamarankahanu.com.*

HoloHolo Charters. Choose between the 50-foot catamaran called *Leila* for a morning snorkel sail to Napali Coast, or the 65-foot *Holo Holo* catamaran trip to the "forbidden island" of Niihau. Both boats have large cabins and little outside seating. Originators of the Niihau tour, HoloHolo Charters built their 65-foot powered catamaran with a wide beam to reduce side-to-side motion, and twin 425 HP turbo diesel engines specifically for the 17-mile channel crossing to Niihau. ■TIP➔ **It's the only outfitter running daily Niihau tours.** The Holo Holo also embarks on a daily sunset and sightseeing tour of the Napali Coast. Leila can hold 37 passengers, while her big brother can take a maximum of 49. Prices range from $99 to $179. ⊠ *Check in at Port Allen Marina Center, 4353 Waialo Rd., Eleele* ✛ *Turn makai onto Rte. 541 off Rte. 50, at Eleele* ☎ *808/335–0815, 800/848–6130* ⊕ *www. holoholocharters.com.*

★ **Kauai Sea Tours.** This company operates a 60-foot sailing catamaran designed almost identically to that of Blue Dolphin Charters—with all the same benefits—including great views and spacious seating. Snorkeling tours anchor near Makole (based on the captain's discretion). If snorkeling isn't your thing, try the four-hour sunset tour, with beer, wine, mai tais, pupus and a hot buffet dinner. Prices range from $115 to $149. ⊠ *Check in at Port Allen Marina Center, 4353 Waialo Rd., Eleele* ⟊ *Turn makai onto Rte. 541 off Rte. 50, at Eleele* ☎ *808/826–7254, 800/733–7997* ⊕ *www.kauaiseatours.com.*

Liko Kauai Cruises. There are many things to like about Liko Kauai Cruises. The 49-foot powered catamaran will enter sea caves, ocean conditions permitting. Sometimes, even Captain Liko himself—a bornand-bred West Side boy—still takes the captain's helm. We particularly like the layout of his boat—most of the seating is in the bow, so there's good visibility. A maximum of 32 passengers make each trip, which lasts five hours (an increase from the previous four-hour tours). Final destinations are dependent on the season, as is the afternoon tour, which typically operates just in the summer months. Trips depart out of Kikiaola Harbor in Waimea, a bit closer to the Napali Coast than those leaving from Port Allen. The rate is $140. ⊠ *4516 Alawai Rd., Waimea* ⟊ *Traveling west on Rte. 50, make the first turn mauka after crossing the bridge into Waimea town* ☎ *808/338–0333, 888/732–5456* ✍ *likokauai@msn.com* ⊕ *www.liko-kauai.com.*

Napali Catamaran. One of the few tour groups departing Hanalei, this company has been around since 1973. Once you're on board, it takes only five minutes before you're witnessing the magnificence of Napali Coast. Taking a maximum of 16 passengers, this 34-foot, powered catamaran is small enough—and with no mast, short enough—to dip into sea caves. In summer, they run two four-hour snorkeling tours per day, stopping at the best snorkeling site along Napali—Nualolo Kai. In winter, business slows as the surf picks up, and they run three-hour whalewatching tours, ocean conditions permitting. If it weren't for the bench seating bisecting the boat—meaning one group of passengers enjoys unobstructed views of the open ocean instead of Napali either on the way out or back—we'd really be happy. Rate is $160, on the high side for a four-hour tour. ⊠ *In Ching Young Village, 5-5190 Kuhio Hwy., Hanalei* ☎ *808/826–6853, 866/255–6853* ⊕ *www.napalicatamaran.com.*

RAFT TOURS

Capt. Andy's Rafting Expeditions. This company used to be known as Captain Zodiac; however, the outfit has changed hands over the years. It first started running Napali in 1974, and currently, Capt. Andy's (as in the sailing catamaran Capt. Andy's) is operating the business. Departing out of Kikiaola Harbor in Kekaha, this tour is much like the other raft tours, offering both snorkeling and beach-landing excursions. The rafts are on the smaller side—24 feet with a maximum of 14 passengers—and all seating is on the rubber hulls, so hang on. They operate three different rafts, so there's a good chance of availability. Price is $185 in summer; $159 in winter, including snorkeling at Nualolo Kai (ocean conditions permitting), sightseeing along Napali Coast, a hiking tour through an ancient Hawaiian fishing village, and a hot buffet lunch on the beach. You're closer to the water on the Zodiacs, so you'll have great views of humpbacks, spinner dolphins, sea turtles, and other

DOES RAIN MEAN CANCELLATION?

If it's raining where you're staying, that doesn't mean it's raining over the water, so don't shy away from a boat tour. Besides, it's not the rain that should concern you—it's the wind. Especially from due north and south, wind creates surface chop and makes for rough riding. Larger craft are designed to handle winter's ocean swells, however, so unless monster waves are out there, your tour should depart without a hitch. If the water is too rough, your boat captain may reroute to calmer waters. It's a tough call to make, but your comfort and safety are always the foremost factor. ■TIP→ In winter months, North Shore departures are canceled much more often than those departing the West Side. This is because the boats are smaller and the waves are bigger on this side of the island. If you want the closest thing to a guarantee of seeing Napali Coast in winter, choose a West Side outfitter. Oh, and even if your tour boat says it cruises the "entire Napali," keep in mind that "ocean conditions permitting" is always implied.

wildlife. ⊠ *Traveling west on Hwy. 50, head approximately 1 mile past Waimea, turn makai into Kikiaola Small Boat Harbor (blue and white sign). Parking lot on right* ☎ *808/335–6833, 800/535–0830* ⊕ *www. napali.com.*

Kauai Sea Tours. This company holds a special permit from the state to land at Nualolo Kai along Napali Coast, ocean conditions permitting. Here, you'll enjoy a picnic lunch, as well as an archaeological tour of an ancient Hawaiian fishing village, ocean conditions permitting. Kauai Sea Tours operates four 24-foot inflatable rafts—maximum occupancy 14. These are small enough for checking out the insides of sea caves and the undersides of waterfalls. Four different tours are available, including whale watching, depending on the season. Prices range from $79 to $155. ⊠ *4353 Waialo Rd., Unit 2B, Eleele* ⊹ *Turn makai onto Rte. 541 off Rte. 50, at Eleele. Check in at Port Allen Marina Center* ☎ *808/826–7254, 800/733–7997* ⊕ *www.kauaiseatours.com.*

Fodor's Choice
★

Napali Explorer. Owned by a couple of women, these tours operate out of Waimea, a tad closer to Napali Coast than most of the other West Side catamaran tours. Departing out of the West Side, the company runs two different sizes of inflatable rubber raft: a 48-foot, 36-passenger craft with an onboard toilet, freshwater shower, shade canopy, and seating in the stern (which is surprisingly smooth and comfortable) and bow (which is where the fun is); and a 26-foot, 14-passenger craft for the all-out fun and thrills of a white-knuckle ride in the bow. The smaller vessel stops at Nualolo Kai and ties up on shore for a tour of the ancient fishing village. Though they used to operate out of Hanalei Bay during the summer, the company is now strictly a West Side operation. Rates are $105 to $149, including snorkeling. Charters are available. ⊠ *9643 Kaumalii Hwy., Waimea* ⊠ *Hanalei* ⊹ *Follow Rte. 50 west to Waimea; office is mauka across from the Shrimp Station* ☎ *808/338–9999, 877/335–9909* ⊕ *www.napaliexplorer.com.*

Napali Riders. This tour-boat outfitter distinguishes itself in two ways. First, it cruises the entire Napali Coast, clear to Kee Beach and back. Second, it has a reasonable price, because it's a no-frills tour—no lunch provided, just beverages and snacks. The company runs four-hour snorkeling trips out of Kiki-aola Harbor in Waimea on a 30-foot inflatable raft with a 28-passenger maximum—that's fewer than they used to take, but can still be a bit cramped. The cost is $129. ⊠ *9600 Kaumualii Hwy., Waimea ✛ Turn makai approximately 1 mile after crossing Waimea River; across from Rte. 550* ☎ *808/742–6331* ⊕ *www.napaliriders.com.*

<aside>
UP FOR A DINNER CRUISE?

If you're thinking of a romantic dinner cruise, you're on the wrong island. Kauai's waters are just not conducive to such. So, even though you'll see some boat companies advertising "dinner cruises," the only difference between their snorkeling cruise and this is that there is no snorkeling, of course, and instead of deli sandwiches, there might be kalua pig, teriyaki chicken, or something similar. But the sunset view from the water, lighting up the sky and the coastline, is no less spectacular.
</aside>

★ **Z-Tourz.** What we like about Z-Tourz is that it is the only boat company to make snorkeling its priority. As such, it focuses on the South Shore's abundant offshore reefs, stopping at two locations. If you want to see Napali, this boat is not for you; if you want to snorkel with the myriad of Hawaii's tropical reef fish and turtles (pretty much guaranteed), this is your boat. Z-Tourz runs daily three-hour tours on a 26-foot rigid-hull inflatable (think Zodiac) with a maximum of 16 passengers. These snorkel tours are guided, so someone actually identifies what you're seeing. Rate is $94, which includes lunch and snorkel gear. Check in at the business center then ride to Kukuiula Harbor in Poipu. ⊠ *3417 Poipu Rd., Suite 112, Poipu* ☎ *808/742–7422, 888/998–6879* ⊕ *www.ztourz.com.*

RIVERBOAT TOURS TO FERN GROTTO

Smith's Motor Boat Services. This 2-mile, upriver trip culminates at a yawning lava tube that is covered with enormous fishtail ferns. During the boat ride, guitar and ukulele players regale you with Hawaiian melodies and tell the history of the river. It's a kitschy bit of Hawaiiana, worth the little money ($20) and short time required. Flat-bottom, 150-passenger riverboats (that rarely fill up) depart from Wailua Marina at the mouth of the Wailua River. ■TIP➔ It's extremely rare, but occasionally after heavy rains the tour doesn't disembark at the grotto; if you're traveling in winter, ask beforehand. Round-trip excursions take 1½ hours, including time to walk around the grotto and environs. Tours run at 9:30, 11, 2, and 3:30 daily. Reservations are not required. Contact Smith's Motor Boat Services for more information. ⊠ *5971 Kuhio Hwy., Kapaa* ☎ *808/821–6892* ⊕ *www.smithskauai.com.*

BODY BOARDING AND BODYSURFING

The most natural form of wave riding is bodysurfing, a popular sport on Kauai because there are many shore breaks around the island. Wave riders of this style stand waist-deep in the water, facing shore, and swim madly as a wave picks them up and breaks. It's great fun and requires no special skills and absolutely no equipment other than a swimsuit. The next step up is body boarding, also called Boogie boarding. In this case, wave riders lie with their upper body on a foam board about half the length of a traditional surfboard and kick as the wave propels them toward shore. Again, this is easy to pick up, and there are many places around Kauai to practice. The locals wear short-finned flippers to help them catch waves, although they are not necessary for and even hamper beginners. It's worth spending a few minutes watching these experts as they spin, twirl, and flip—that's right—while they slip down the face of the wave. Of course, all beach safety precautions apply, and just because you see wave riders of any kind in the water doesn't mean the water is safe for everyone. Any snorkeling-gear outfitter also rents body boards.

Some of our favorite bodysurfing and body-boarding beaches are **Brennecke, Wailua, Kealia, Kalihiwai,** and **Hanalei.**

DEEP-SEA FISHING

Simply step aboard and cast your line for mahimahi, ahi, ono, and marlin. That's about how quickly the fishing—mostly trolling with lures—begins on Kauai. The water gets deep quickly here, so there's less cruising time to fishing grounds. Of course, your captain may elect to cruise to a hot location where he's had good luck lately.

There are oodles of charter fishermen around; most depart from Nawiliwili Harbor in Lihue, and most use lures instead of live bait. Inquire about each boat's "fish policy," that is, what happens to the fish if any are caught. Some boats keep all; others will give you enough for a meal or two, even doing the cleaning themselves. On shared charters, ask about the maximum passenger count and about the fishing rotation; you'll want to make sure everyone gets a fair shot at reeling in the big one. Another option is to book a private charter. Shared and private charters run four, six, and eight hours in length.

BOATS AND CHARTERS

Captain Don's Sport Fishing & Ocean Adventure. Captain Don is very flexible and treats everyone like family—he'll stop to snorkel or whale watch if that's what the group (four to six) wants. Saltwater fly-fishermen (bring your own gear) are welcome. He'll even fish for bait and let you keep part of whatever you catch. The *June Louise* is a 34-foot twin diesel. Rates start at $140 for shared, $595 for private charters. ⊠ *Nawiliwili Boat Harbor, Slip 313* ☎ *808/639–3012* ⊕ *www.captaindonsfishing.com.*

Explore Kauai Sportfishing. If you're staying on the West Side, you'll be glad to know that Napali Explorer (of the longtime rafting tour business) is now running fishing trips out of Port Allen under the name Explore Kauai Sportfishing. It offers shared and exclusive charters of

CLOSE UP

Niihau: The Forbidden Isle

Seventeen miles from Kauai, across the Kaulakahi Channel, sits the privately owned island of Niihau. It's known as the Forbidden Isle, because access is limited to the Robinson family, who owns it, and the 200 or so Native Hawaiians who were born there.

Niihau was bought from King Kamehameha in 1864 by a Scottish widow, Eliza Sinclair. Sinclair was introduced to the island after an unusually wet winter; she saw nothing but green pastures and thought it would be an ideal place to raise cattle. The cost was $10,000. It was a real deal, or so Sinclair thought.

Unfortunately, Niihau's usual rainfall is about 12 inches a year, and the land soon returned to its normal, desert-like state. Regardless, Sinclair did not abandon her venture, and today the island and ranching operation are owned by Bruce Robinson, Eliza Sinclair's great-great-grandson.

Visits to the island are restricted to custom hunting expeditions and flight-seeing tours through Niihau Helicopter. Tours depart from Kaumakani and avoid the western coastline, especially the village of Puuwai. There's a five-passenger minimum for each flight, and reservations are essential. A picnic lunch on a secluded Niihau beach is included, with time for swimming, beachcombing, and snorkeling. The half-day tour is $385 per person.

For more information contact **Niihau Tours** (✉ Box 690370, Makaweli ☎ 808/335–3500 or 877/441–3500 ⊕ www.niihau.us).

4

four, six, and eight hours in a 41-foot Concord called *Happy Times*. The shared tours max out at six fishermen, and a portion of the catch is shared with all. The boat is also used for specialty charters—that is, film crews, surveys, burials, and even Niihau fishing. Rates range from $130 to $179 per person. ✉ *Check in at Port Allen Small Boat Harbor, Waialo Rd., Eleele* ☎ *808/338–9999, 877/335–9909* ⊕ *www.napali-explorer.com.*

Hana Paa. The advantage with Hana Paa is that it takes fewer people (minimum two, maximum four for a nonprivate excursion), but you pay for it. Rates start at $310 for shared, $600 for private charters, which can accommodate up to six people. The company's fish policy is flexible, and the boat is roomy. The *Maka Hou II* is a 38-foot Bertram. ✉ *Nawiliwili Boat Harbor* ☎ *808/823–6031, 866/776–3474* ⊕ *www.fishkauai.com.*

Kai Bear. The father of this father-and-son duo has it figured out: He lets the son run the business and do all the work. Or so he says. Fish policy: Share the catch. Rates start at $159 for a four-hour, shared charter (six fishermen max) and run all the way to $2,000 for an eight-hour, keep-all-the-fish-you-want exclusive charter. What's particularly nice about this company are the boats: the 38-foot Bertram *Kai Bear* and the 42-foot Bertram *Grander* is very roomy. ✉ *Nawiliwili Small Boat Harbor* ☎ *808/652–4556* ⊕ *www.kaibear.com.*

KAYAKING

Kauai is the only Hawaiian island with navigable rivers. As the oldest inhabited island in the chain, Kauai has had more time for wind and water erosion to deepen and widen cracks into streams and streams into rivers. Because this is a small island, the rivers aren't long, and there are no rapids; that makes them perfectly safe for kayakers of all levels, even beginners.

For more advanced paddlers, there aren't many places in the world more beautiful for sea kayaking than Napali Coast. If this is your draw to Kauai, plan your vacation for the summer months, when the seas are at their calmest. ■TIP➔ Tour and kayak-rental reservations are recommended at least two weeks in advance during peak summer and holiday seasons. In general, tours and rentals are available year-round, Monday through Saturday. Pack a swimsuit, sunscreen, a hat, bug repellent, water shoes (sport sandals, aqua socks, old tennis shoes), and motion sickness medication if you're planning on sea kayaking.

RIVER KAYAKING

Tour outfitters operate on the Huleia, Wailua, and Hanalei rivers with guided tours that combine hiking to waterfalls, as in the case of the first two, and snorkeling, as in the case of the third. Another option is renting kayaks and heading out on your own. Each has its advantages and disadvantages, but it boils down as follows:

If you want to swim at the base of a remote 100-foot waterfall, sign up for a five-hour kayak (4-mile round-trip) and hiking (2-mile round-trip) tour of the **Wailua River.** It includes a dramatic waterfall that is best accessed with the aid of a guide, so you don't get lost. ■TIP➔ Remember—it's dangerous to swim under waterfalls no matter how good a water massage may sound. Rocks and logs are known to plunge down, especially after heavy rains.

If you want to kayak on your own, choose the **Hanalei River.** It's most scenic from the kayak itself—there are no trails to hike to hidden waterfalls. And better yet, a rental company is right on the river—no hauling kayaks on top of your car.

If you're not sure of your kayaking abilities, head to the **Huleia River;** 3½-hour tours include easy paddling upriver, a nature walk through a rain forest with a cascading waterfall, a rope swing for playing Tarzan and Jane, and a ride back downriver—into the wind—on a motorized, double-hull canoe.

As for the kayaks themselves, most companies use the two-person sit-on-top style that is quite buoyant—no Eskimo rolls required. The only possible danger comes in the form of communication. The kayaks seat two people, which means you'll share the work (good) with a guide, or your spouse, child, parent, or friend (the potential danger part). On the river, the two-person kayaks are known as "divorce boats." Counseling is not included in the tour price.

SEA KAYAKING

In its second year and second issue, *National Geographic Adventure* ranked kayaking Napali Coast second on its list of America's Best 100 Adventures, right behind rafting the Colorado River through the Grand Canyon. That pretty much says it all. It's the adventure of a lifetime in one day, involving eight hours of paddling. Although it's good to have some kayaking experience,

WORD OF MOUTH

"My husband and I kayaked the Wailua River and did the one-mile hike to the Uluwehi Falls (aka Secret Falls), and I highly recommend it. This is the only kayaking we have ever done. We were in okay shape, and did not have much trouble." —jcb

feel comfortable on the water, and be reasonably fit, it doesn't require the preparation, stamina, or fortitude of, say, climbing Mt. Everest. Tours run May through September, ocean conditions permitting. In the winter months sea-kayaking tours operate on the South Shore—beautiful, but not Napali.

EQUIPMENT AND TOURS

Kayak Kauai. Based in Hanalei, this company offers guided tours on the Hanalei and Wailua rivers, and along Napali Coast. It has a great shop right on the Hanalei River for kayak rentals and camping gear. The guided Hanalei River Kayak and Snorkel Tour starts at the shop and heads downriver, so there's not much to see of the scenic river valley. (For that, rent a kayak on your own.) Instead, this three-hour tour paddles down to the river mouth, where the river meets the sea. Then, it's a short paddle around a point to snorkel at either Princeville Hotel Beach or, ocean conditions permitting, a bit farther at Hideaways Beach. This is a great choice if you want to try your paddle at a bit of ocean kayaking.

A second location in Kapaa is the base for Wailua River guided tours and kayak rentals. It's not right on the river, however, so shuttling is involved. For rentals, the company provides the hauling gear necessary for your rental car. Guided tours range from $60 to $214. Kayak rentals range from $28 to $75, depending on the river, depending on kayak size (single or double). ⌧ *Hanalei: 1 mile past Hanalei bridge, on makai side, 5-5070 Kuhio Hwy.* ⌧ *Kapaa: south end of Coconut Marketplace, 4-484 Kuhio Hwy.* ☎ *808/826–9844, 800/437–3507* ⊕ *www.kayakkauai.com.*

Kayak Wailua. We can't quite figure out how this family-run business offers pretty much the same Wailua River kayaking tour as everyone else—except for lunch and beverages, which are BYO—for half the price, but it does. They say it's because they don't discount and don't offer commission to activities and concierge desks. Their 4½-hour kayak, hike, and waterfall swim costs $39.95, and their three-hour kayak-to-a-swimming-hole costs $34.95. We say fork over the extra $5 for the longer tour and hike to the beautiful 150-foot Secret Falls. Six tours a day are offered, beginning at 8 am and running on each hour until 1 pm. With the number of boats going out, large groups can be accommodated. ⌧ *4565 Haleilio Rd., behind the old Coco Palms hotel, Kapaa* ☎ *808/822–3388* ⊕ *www.kayakwailua.com.*

KAUAI'S TOP WATER ACTIVITIES

Tour company/Outfitter	Length	am/pm	Departure Point	Adult/Kid Price	Kids' Ages	Snack or Meal	Alcoholic Beverages Included	Boat Type	Capacity	Worth Noting
Snorkel Cruise										
Captain Sundown	6 hrs.	am	North Shore	$195	NA	Meal	No	Cat	17	Departs out of Hanalei Bay; exquisite scenery at very start
Napali Explorer	4–5 hrs.	am	West Side	$149/$99	5–12	Meal	No	Inflatable	35	Departs out of West Side, so it's closer to the Napali Coast
Z-Tourz	3 hrs.	am	South Shore	$94/$84	5–12	Meal	No	Inflatable	16	Provides all snorkel gear, including wetsuits
Niihau Cruise										
Blue Dolphin Charters	7 hrs.	am	West Side	$196/$149	5–11	Meal	Yes	Cat	49	Offers upgrade to scuba
HoloHolo Charters	7 hrs.	am	West Side	$179/$129	6–12	Meal	Yes	Cat	49	Fast, smooth boat built for open ocean; runs 7 days a week
Kayak										
Ocean										
Napali Kayak	9 hrs.	am	North Shore	$200	NA	Meal	NA	NA	NA	Owners are long-term Napali guides
Wailua River										
Outfitters Kauai	5 hrs.	am/pm	East Side	$102/$82	5–14	Meal	NA	NA	NA	Top kayak equipment
Hanalei River										
Kayak Kauai	3 hrs.	am/pm	North Shore	$60/$45	4–11	Water	NA	NA	NA	Only guides on Hanalei River

Fodor's Choice
★ **Napali Kayak.** A couple of longtime guides ventured out on their own a few years back to create this company, which focuses solely on sea kayaking—Napali Coast in summer, as the name implies, and the South Shore in winter (during peak times only). These guys are highly experienced and still highly enthusiastic about their livelihood. So much so, that REI Adventures hires them to run their multiday, multisport tours. Now, that's a feather in their cap, we'd say. Prices start at $200. You can also rent kayaks; price range from $25 to $75. If you want to try camping on your own at Kalalau (you'll need permits), Napali Kayak will provide kayaks outfitted with dry bags, extra paddles and seat backs, while also offering transportation drop-off and pickup. ✉ *5-5075 Kuhio Hwy., next to Postcards Café, Hanalei* ☎ *808/826–6900, 866/977–6900* ⊕ *www.napalikayak.com.*

> **HAWAII STATE SPORT: CANOE PADDLING**
>
> In summer, it's not unusual to see Hawaii's state sport in action: outrigger canoe racing. These are the same styles of canoes ancient Hawaiians paddled in races that pitted one chief's warriors against another's. Summer is regatta season, and the half dozen or more canoe clubs around the island gather to race in ¼-mile, ½-mile, and longer races. You can catch the hundreds of paddlers lining the beaches and cheering on their clubs, oftentimes in Hanalei, Kalapaki, and Waimea Bay, as well as the Wailua River.

4

☺ **Outfitters Kauai.** This well-established tour outfitter operates year-round river-kayak tours on the Huleia and Wailua rivers, as well as sea-kayaking tours along Napali Coast in summer and the South Shore in winter. Outfitters Kauai's specialty, however, is the Kipu Safari. This all-day adventure starts with kayaking up the Huleia River and includes a rope swing over a swimming hole, a wagon ride through a working cattle ranch, a picnic lunch by a private waterfall, hiking, and two "zips" across the rain-forest canopy (strap on a harness, clip into a cable, and zip over a quarter of a mile). They then offer a one-of-a-kind Waterzip Zipline at their mountain stream-fed blue pool. The day ends with a ride on a motorized double-hull canoe. It's a great tour for the family, because no one ever gets bored. The Kipu Safari costs $182; other guided tours range from $102 to $229. ✉ *2827-A Poipu Rd., Poipu* ☎ *808/742–9667, 888/742–9887* ⊕ *www.outfitterskauai.com.*

Wailua Kayak & Canoe. This is the only purveyor of kayak rentals on the Wailua River, which means no hauling your kayak on top of your car (a definite plus). Rates are $45 for a single, $75 for a double, for either a morning or afternoon. Guided tours are also available with rates ranging from $55 to $90. This outfitter promotes itself as "Native Hawaiian owned and operated." ✉ *169 Wailua Rd., across from Wailua Beach, turn mauka at Kuamoo Rd. and take first left, Kapaa* ☎ *808/821–1188* ⊕ *www.wailuariverkayaking.com.*

KITEBOARDING

Several years ago, the latest wave-riding craze to hit the Islands was kiteboarding, and the sport is still going strong. As the name implies, there's a kite and a board involved. The board you strap on your feet; the kite is attached to a harness around your waist. Steering is accomplished with a rod that's attached to the harness and the kite. Depending on conditions and the desires of the kiteboarder, the kite is played out some 30 to 100 feet in the air. The result is a cross between waterskiing—without the boat—and windsurfing. Speeds are fast and aerobatic maneuvers are involved. Unfortunately, neither lessons nor rental gear are available for the sport on Kauai (Maui is a better bet), so if you aren't a seasoned kiteboarder already, you'll have to be content with watching the pros—who can put on a pretty spectacular show. The most popular year-round spots for kiteboarding are **Kapaa Beach Park, Anini Beach Park,** and **Mahaulepu Beach.** ■TIP→ Many visitors come to Kauai dreaming of parasailing. If that's you, make a stop at Maui or the Big Island. There's no parasailing on Kauai.

SCUBA DIVING

The majority of scuba diving on Kauai occurs on the South Shore. Boat and shore dives are available, although boat sites surpass the shore sites for a couple of reasons. First, they're deeper and exhibit the complete symbiotic relationship of a reef system, and second, the visibility is better a little farther offshore.

The dive operators on Kauai offer a full range of services, including certification dives, referral dives, boat dives, shore dives, night dives, and drift dives. ■TIP→ As for certification, we recommend completing your confined-water training and classroom testing before arriving on the island. That way, you'll spend less time training and more time diving.

BEST SPOTS

The best and safest scuba-diving sites are accessed by boat on the South Shore of the island, right off the shores of Poipu. The captain selects the actual site based on ocean conditions of the day. Beginners may prefer shore dives, which are best at **Koloa Landing** on the South Shore year-round and **Makua (Tunnels) Beach** on the North Shore in the calm summer months. Keep in mind, though, that you'll have to haul your gear a ways down the beach.

For the advanced diver, the island of Niihau—across an open ocean channel in deep and crystal clear waters—beckons and rewards, usually with some big fish. Seasport Divers, Fathom Five, and Bubbles Below venture the 17 miles across the channel in summer when the crossing is smoothest. Divers can expect deep dives, walls, and strong currents at Niihau, where conditions can change rapidly. To make the long journey worthwhile, three dives and Nitrox are included.

DID YOU KNOW?

You'll find some super river kayaking on Kauai, as here on the Kalihiwai River.

SCUBA Q&A

Q: Do I have to be certified to go scuba diving?

A: Absolutely not. You can try Discover Scuba, which allows you to dive up to 40 feet after an introductory lesson in a pool. Most dive outfitters on Kauai offer this introductory program.

Q: Can I dive if I have asthma?

A: Only if your doctor signs a medical release—the original of which you must present to your dive outfitter.

Q: Can I get certified on Kauai?

A: Yes. Start to finish, it'll take three days. Or, you can complete your classroom and confined-water training at home and just do your checkout dives on Kauai.

Q: How old do you have to be to learn how to dive?

A: Most certifying agencies require that you be at least 12 years old (with PADI it's 10) when you start your scuba-diving course. You will normally receive a junior certification, which can be upgraded to a full certification when you are 15 years old.

Q: Can I wear contact lenses or glasses while diving?

A: You can either wear contact lenses with a regular mask or opt for a prescription mask—just let your dive outfitter know in advance.

Q: What if I forget my certification card?

A: Let your dive outfitter know immediately; with advance notice, they can usually dig up your certification information online.

EQUIPMENT, LESSONS, AND TOURS

Bubbles Below. Marine ecology is the emphasis here aboard the 36-foot, eight-passenger Kai Manu. This company discovered some pristine dive sites on the West Side of the island where white-tip reef sharks are common—and other divers are not. Thanks to the addition of a 32-foot powered catamaran—the six-passenger *Dive Rocket*—the group also runs Niihau, Napali, and North Shore dives year-round (depending on ocean conditions, of course). They're still known for their South Shore trips and lead dives on the East Side walls as well, so they truly do circumnavigate the island. A bonus on these tours is the pizza and wide variety of other grinds served between dives. Open-water certification dives, check-out dives, and intro shore dives are available upon request. There's a charge of $130 for a standard two-tank boat dive and up to $30 extra for rental gear, though different tours can be up to $310. ⊠ *Port Allen Small Boat Harbor, Eleele* ✦ *Turn makai onto Rte. 541 from Rte. 50 in Eleele* ☎ *808/332–7333, 866/524–6268* ⊕ *www.bubblesbelowkauai.com.*

Kauai Down Under Scuba. Though this company is now offering boat diving, it definitely specializes in shore diving, typically at Koloa Landing (year-round) and Tunnels (summers). They're not only geared toward beginning divers—for whom they provide a very thorough and gentle certification program as well as the Discover Scuba program—but also offer night dives and scooter (think James Bond) dives. Their main emphasis is a detailed review of marine biology, such as pointing out rare dragon eel and harlequin shrimp tucked away in pockets of coral. ■ TIP→ Hands down, we recommend Kauai Down Under Scuba for beginners, certification (all levels), and refresher dives. One reason is that their instructor-to-student ratio never exceeds 1:4—that's true of all their dive groups. Rates range from $79 for a one-tank certified dive to $450 for certification—all dive gear included. ⊠ *Location dependent on beach they are diving at that day, Koloa* ☎ *877/441–3483, 808/742–9534* ⊕ *www.kauaidownunderscuba.com.*

Fodor's Choice ★ **Ocean Quest Watersports/Fathom Five.** A few years ago, Fathom Five, the South Shore boat-diving specialist, teamed up with Ocean Quest Watersports, a separate company specializing in shore dives at Tunnels on the North Shore. Today, they offer it all: boat dives, shore dives, night dives, certification dives. They're pretty much doing what everyone else is with a couple of twists. First, they offer a three-tank premium charter for those really serious about diving. Second, they operate a Nitrox continuous-flow mixing system, so you can decide the mix rate. Third, they tag on a twilight dive to the standard, one-tank night dive, making the outing worth the effort. Fourth, their shore diving isn't an afterthought. Finally, we think their dive masters are pretty darn good, too. They even dive Niihau in the summer aboard their 35-foot Force. Prices start at $75 for a one-tank shore dive and top out at $495 for full certification. The standard two-tank boat dive runs $125 plus $40 for gear rental, if needed. ■ TIP→ In summer, book well in advance. ⊠ *3450 Poipu Rd., just south of Koloa* ☎ *808/742–6991, 800/972–3078* ⊕ *www.fathomfive.com.*

Seasport Divers. Rated highly by readers of *Scuba Diving* magazine, Seasport Divers' 48-foot *Anela Kai* tops the chart for dive-boat luxury. But owner Marvin Otsuji didn't stop with that. In 2006, he added a second boat—a 32-foot catamaran—that's outfitted for diving, but we like it as an all-around charter. The company does a brisk business, which means it won't cancel at the last minute because of a lack of reservations, like some other companies, although they may book up to 18 people per boat. ■ TIP→ There are slightly more challenging trips in the morning; mellower dive sites are in the afternoon. The company also runs a good-size dive shop for purchases and rentals, as well as a classroom for certification. Niihau trips are available in summer. All trips leave from Kukuiula Harbor in Poipu. Rates start at $125 for a two-tank boat dive; rental gear is $25 extra. ⊠ *Check-in office: 2827 Poipu Rd., just north of Lawai Rd. turn off to Spouting Horn. Look for yellow submarine in parking lot, Poipu* ☎ *808/742–9303, 800/685–5889* ⊕ *www.seasportdivers.com.*

SNORKELING

Generally speaking, the calmest water and best snorkeling can be found on Kauai's North Shore in summer and South Shore in winter. The East Side, known as the windward side, has year-round, prevalent northeast trade winds that make snorkeling unpredictable, although there are some good pockets. The best snorkeling on the West Side is accessible only by boat.

A word on feeding fish: Don't. As Captain Ted with HoloHolo Charters says, fish have survived and populated reefs for much longer than we have been donning goggles and staring at them. They will continue to do so without our intervention. Besides, fish food messes up the reef and—one thing always leads to another—can eliminate a once-pristine reef environment. As for gear, if you're snorkeling with one of the Napali boat-tour outfitters, they'll provide it. However, depending on the company, it might not be the latest or greatest. If you have your own, bring it. On the other hand, if you're going out with SeaFun or Z-Tourz *(see Boat Tours)*, the gear is top-notch. If you need to rent, hit one of the "snorkel-and-surf" shops such as Snorkel Bob's in Koloa and Kapaa, Nukumoi in Poipu, or Seasport in Poipu and Kapaa, or shop Wal-Mart or Kmart if you want to drag it home. Typically, though, rental gear will be better quality than that found at Wal-Mart or Kmart. ■TIP→ If you wear glasses, you can rent prescription masks at the rental shops—just don't expect them to match your prescription exactly.

BEST SPOTS

Just because we say these are good places to snorkel doesn't mean that the exact moment you arrive, the fish will flock—they are wild, after all.

The beaches here are listed in clockwise fashion starting on the North Shore.

Kee Beach. Although it can get quite crowded, Kee Beach is quite often a good snorkeling destination. Just be sure to come during the off-hours, say early in the morning or later in the afternoon. ■TIP→ Snorkeling here in winter can be hazardous. Summer is the best and safest time, although you should never swim beyond the reef. During peak times, a parking lot is available back down the road away from the beach. ⊠ *At end of Rte. 560, Haena.*

★ **Tunnels (Makua).** The search for Tunnels (Makua) is as tricky as the snorkeling. Park at Haena Beach Park and walk east—away from Napali Coast—until you see a sand channel entrance in the water, almost at the point. Once you get here, the reward is fantastic. The name of this beach comes from the many underwater lava tubes, which always attract marine life. The shore is mostly beach rock interrupted by three sand channels. You'll want to enter and exit at one of these channels (or risk stepping on a sea urchin or scraping your stomach on the reef). Follow the sand channel to a drop-off; the snorkeling along here is always full of nice surprises. Expect a current running east to west. Snorkeling here in winter can be hazardous; summer is the best and safest time for snorkeling. ⊠ *Haena Beach Park. Near end of Rte. 560, across from lava-tube sea caves, after stream crossing.*

☾ **Lydgate Beach Park.** Lydgate Beach Park is the absolute safest place to snorkel on Kauai. With its lava-rock wall creating a protected swimming pool, this is the perfect spot for beginners, young and old. The fish are so tame here it's almost like swimming in a saltwater aquarium. There is also a playground for children, plenty of parking and

Continued on page 126

SNORKELING IN HAWAII

The waters surrounding the Hawaiian Islands are filled with life—from giant manta rays cruising off the Big Island's Kona Coast to humpback whales giving birth in Maui's Maalaea Bay. Dip your head beneath the surface to experience a spectacularly colorful world: pairs of milletseed butterflyfish dart back and forth, redlipped parrotfish snack on coral algae, and spotted eagle rays flap past like silent spaceships. Sea turtles bask at the surface while tiny wrasses give them the equivalent of a shave and a haircut. The water quality is typically outstanding; many sites afford 30-foot-plus visibility. On snorkel cruises, you can often stare from the boat rail right down to the bottom.

Certainly few destinations are as accommodating to every level of snorkeler as Hawaii. Beginners can tromp in from sandy beaches while more advanced divers descend to shipwrecks, reefs, craters, and sea arches just offshore. Because of Hawaii's extreme isolation, the island chain has fewer fish species than Fiji or the Caribbean—but many of the fish that are here exist nowhere else. The Hawaiian waters are home to the highest percentage of endemic fish in the world.

The key to enjoying the underwater world is slowing down. Look carefully. Listen. You might hear the strange crackling sound of shrimp tunneling through coral, or you may hear whales singing to one another during winter. A shy octopus may drift along the ocean's floor beneath you. If you're hooked, pick up a waterproof fishkey from Long's Drugs. You can brag later that you've looked the Hawaiian turkeyfish in the eye.

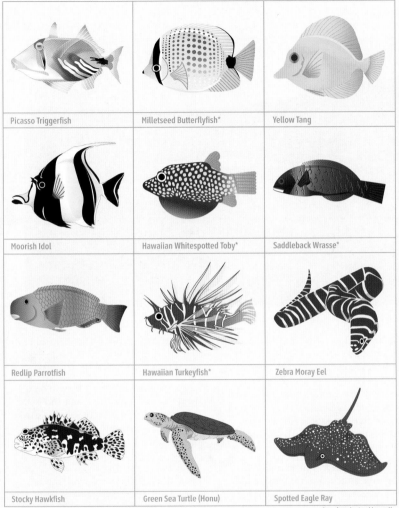

Picasso Triggerfish

Milletseed Butterflyfish*

Yellow Tang

Moorish Idol

Hawaiian Whitespotted Toby*

Saddleback Wrasse*

Redlip Parrotfish

Hawaiian Turkeyfish*

Zebra Moray Eel

Stocky Hawkfish

Green Sea Turtle (Honu)

Spotted Eagle Ray

*endemic to Hawaii

4

IN FOCUS SNORKELING IN HAWAII

POLYNESIA'S FIRST CELESTIAL NAVIGATORS: HONU

Honu is the Hawaiian name for two native sea turtles, the hawksbill and the green sea turtle. Little is known about these dinosaur-age marine reptiles, though snorkelers regularly see them foraging for *limu* (seaweed) and the occasional jellyfish in Hawaiian waters. Most female honu nest in the uninhabited Northwestern Hawaiian Islands, but a few sociable ladies nest on Maui and Big Island beaches. Scientists suspect that they navigate the seas via magnetism—sensing the earth's poles. Amazingly, they will journey up to 800 miles to nest—it's believed that they return to their own birth sites. After about 60 days of incubation, nestlings emerge from the sand at night and find their way back to the sea by the light of the stars.

SNORKELING

Many of Hawaii's reefs are accessible from shore.

The basics: Sure, you can take a deep breath, hold your nose, squint your eyes, and stick your face in the water in an attempt to view submerged habitats . . . but why not protect your eyes, retain your ability to breathe, and keep your hands free to paddle about when exploring underwater? That's what snorkeling is all about.

Equipment needed: A mask, snorkel (the tube attached to the mask), and fins. In deeper waters (any depth over your head), life jackets are advised.

Steps to success: If you've never snorkeled before, it's natural to feel a bit awkward at first, so don't sweat it. Breathing through a mask and tube, and wearing a pair of fins take getting used to. Like any activity, you build confidence and comfort through practice.

If you're new to snorkeling, begin by submerging your face in shallow water or a swimming pool and breathing calmly through the snorkel while gazing through the mask.

Next you need to learn how to clear water out of your mask and snorkel, an essential skill since splashes can send water into tube openings and masks can leak. Some snorkels have built-in drainage valves, but if a tube clogs, you can force water up and out by exhaling through your mouth. Clearing a mask is similar: lift your head from water while pulling forward on mask to drain. Some masks have built-in purge valves, but those without can be cleared underwater by pressing the top to the forehead and blowing out your nose (charming, isn't it?), allowing air to bubble into the mask, pushing water out the bottom. If it sounds hard, it really isn't. Just try it a few times and you'll soon feel like a pro.

4

Now your goal is to get friendly with fins—you want them to be snug but not too tight—and learn how to propel yourself with them. Fins won't help you float, but they will give you a leg up, so to speak, on smoothly moving through the water or treading water (even when upright) with less effort.

Flutter stroking is the most efficient underwater kick, and the farther your foot bends forward the more leg power you'll be able to transfer to the water and the farther you'll travel with each stroke. Flutter kicking movements involve alternately separating the legs and then drawing them back together. When your legs separate, the leg surface encounters drag from the water, slowing you down. When your legs are drawn back together, they produce a force pushing you forward. If your kick creates more forward force than it causes drag, you'll move ahead.

Submerge your fins to avoid fatigue rather than having them flailing above the water when you kick, and keep your arms at your side to reduce drag. You are in the water—stretched out, face down, and snorkeling happily away—but that doesn't mean you can't hold your breath and go deeper in the water for a closer look at some fish or whatever catches your attention. Just remember that when you do this, your snorkel will be submerged, too, so you won't be breathing (you'll be holding your breath). You can dive head-first, but going feet-first is easier and less scary for most folks, taking less momentum. Before full immersion, take several long, deep breaths to clear carbon dioxide from your lungs.

If your legs tire, flip onto your back and tread water with inverted fin motions while resting. If your mask fogs, wash condensation from lens and clear water from mask.

TIPS FOR SAFE SNORKELING

- Snorkel with a buddy and stay together.

- Plan your entry and exit points prior to getting in the water.

- Swim into the current on entering and then ride the current back to your exit point.

- Carry your flippers into the water and then put them on, as it's difficult to walk in them.

- Make sure your mask fits properly and is not too loose.

- Pop your head above the water periodically to ensure you aren't drifting too far out, or too close to rocks.

- Think of the water as someone else's home—don't take anything that doesn't belong to you, or leave any trash behind.

- Don't touch any sea creatures; they may sting.

- Wear a T-shirt over your swimsuit to help protect you from being fried by the sun.

- When in doubt, don't go without a snorkeling professional; try a guided tour.

Green sea turtle (Honu)

full-service restrooms with showers. ✉ *4470 Nalu Rd., just south of Wailua River, turn makai off Rte. 56 onto Lehu Dr. and left onto Nalu Rd., Kapaa.*

Poipu Beach Park. You'll generally find good year-round snorkeling at Poipu Beach Park, except during summer's south swells (which are not nearly as frequent as winter's north swells). The best snorkeling fronts the Marriott Waiohai Beach Club. Stay inside the crescent created by the sandbar and rocky point. The current runs east to west. ✉ *Hoone Rd. From Poipu Rd., turn right onto Hoone Rd.*

Beach House (*Lawai Beach*). Don't pack the beach umbrella, beach mats, or cooler for snorkeling at Beach House. Just bring your snorkeling gear. The beach—named after its neighbor the Beach House restaurant—is on the road to Spouting Horn. It's a small slip of sand during low tide and a rocky shoreline during high tide. However, it's right by the road's edge, and its rocky coastline and somewhat rocky bottom make it great for snorkeling. Enter and exit in the sand channel (not over the rocky reef) that lines up with the Lawai Beach Resort's center atrium. Stay within the rocky points anchoring each end of the beach. The current runs east to west. ✉ *5017 Lawai Rd., makai side of Lawai Rd. Park on road in front of Lawai Beach Resort, Koloa.*

Fodor'sChoice
★
Niihau. With little river runoff and hardly any boat traffic, the waters off the island of Niihau are some of the clearest in all Hawaii, and that's good for snorkeling. Like Nualolo Kai, the only way to snorkel here is to sign on with one of the two tour boats venturing across a sometimes rough open ocean channel: Blue Dolphin Charters and HoloHolo (⇨ *see Boat Tours*).

★ **Nualolo Kai.** Nualolo Kai was once an ancient Hawaiian fishpond and is now home to the best snorkeling along Napali Coast (and perhaps on all of Kauai). The only way to access it is by boat, and only a few Napali snorkeling-tour operators are permitted to do so. We recommend Napali Explorer and Kauai Sea Tours (⇨ *see Boat Tours*).

TOURS

☼ **SeaFun Kauai.** This guided snorkeling tour, for beginners and intermediates alike, is led by a marine expert, so there's instruction plus the guide actually gets into the water with you and identifies marine life. You're guaranteed to spot tons of critters you'd never see on your own. This is a land-based operation and the only one of its kind on Kauai. (Don't think those snorkeling cruises are guided snorkeling tours—they rarely are. A member of the boat's crew serves as lifeguard not a marine-life *guide*.) A half-day tour includes all your snorkeling gear—and a wet suit to keep you warm—and stops at one or two snorkeling locations, chosen based on ocean conditions. They will come pick up customers at some of the resorts, so inquire within. The cost is $80. ✉ *3-2087 Kaumualii Hwy. Check in at Kilohana Plantation in Puhi,*

If you manage to get up close and personal with a Hawaiian monk seal, consider yourself lucky—it's an endangered species.

next to Kauai Community College ☎ 808/245–6400, 800/452–1113 ⊕ www.alohakauaitours.com.

STAND-UP PADDLING

Unlike kiteboarding, this is a new sport that even a novice can pick up—*and* have fun doing. Technically, it's not really a new sport but a reinvigorated one from the 1950s. Beginners start with a heftier surfboard and a longer-than-normal canoe paddle. And, just as the name implies, stand-up paddlers stand on their surfboards and paddle out from the beach—no timing a wave and doing a push-up to stand. The perfect place to learn is a river (think **Hanalei** or **Wailua**) or a calm lagoon (try **Anini** or **Kalapaki**). But this sport isn't just for beginners. Tried-and-true surfers turn to it when the waves are not quite right for their preferred sport, because it gives them another reason to be on the water. Stand-up paddlers catch waves earlier and ride them longer than long-board surfers. In the past couple of years, professional stand-up paddling competitions have popped up, and surf shops and instructors have adapted to its quick rise in popularity.

EQUIPMENT AND LESSONS

Not all surf instructors teach stand-up paddling, but more and more are, like Blue Seas Surf School and Titus Kinimaka Hawaiian School of Surfing (⇨ *see Surfing*).

Back Door Surf Co. Along with its sister store across the street—Hanalei Surf Shop—Back Door Surf Co. provides just about all the rentals

TIPS ON SAFE SNORKELING

Mike Hopkins with SeaFun Kauai, a guided walk-in snorkeling tour operator, suggests these tips for safe snorkeling:

■ Snorkel with a buddy and stay together.

■ Choose a location where lifeguards are present.

■ Ask the lifeguard about conditions.

■ Plan your entry and exit points.

■ Swim into the current on entering and then ride the current back to your exit point.

■ Look up periodically to gauge your location with a reference point on land.

■ When in doubt, try a guided tour.

necessary for a fun day at Hanalei Bay and houses the company's full inventory of stand-up paddleboards, available for single-day or longer rental periods. ⊠ *5-5190 Kuhio Hwy., Ching Young Village, Hanalei* ☎ *808/826–1900* ⊕ *www.hanaleisurf.com.*

Hawaiian Surfing Adventures. This Hanalei location has a wide variety of stand-up boards and paddles for rent, with a few options depending on your schedule. A 2.5-hour rental is $30, 4.5 hours goes for $40, and $50 gets you a full day's use. Check in at the storefront and then head down to the beach where your gear will be waiting. Lessons are also available on the scenic Hanalei River or in Hanalei Bay, and include one hour of instruction and two hours to practice with the board (lessons range from $55 to $75, depending on group size). The company also offers surfboard rentals and surfing lessons. ⊠ *5134 Kuhio Hwy., Hanalei* ✛ *From Princeville, look mauka for a dark green building when entering Hanalei town* ☎ *808/482–0749* ⊕ *www.hawaiiansurfingadventures.com.*

Kauai Beach Boys. This outfitter is located right on the beach at Kalapaki, so there's no hauling your gear on your car. The rates are reasonable ($25 an hour, $60 for the day) and the convenience is essential. ⊠ *Kalapaki Beach* ☎ *808/246–6333.*

SURFING

Good ol' stand-up surfing is alive and well on Kauai, especially in winter's high-surf season on the North Shore. If you're new to the sport, we highly recommend taking a lesson. Not only will this ensure you're up and riding waves in no time, but instructors will provide the right board for your experience and size, help you time a wave, and give you a push to get your momentum going. ■TIP→ You don't need to be in top physical shape to take a lesson. Because your instructor helps push you into the wave, you won't wear yourself out paddling. If you're experienced and want to hit the waves on your own, most surf shops rent boards for all levels, from beginners to advanced.

Winter brings big surf to Kauai's North Shore. You can see some of the sport's biggest celebrities catching waves at Haena and Hanalei Bay.

BEST SPOTS

Perennial-favorite beginning surf spots include **Poipu Beach** (the area fronting the Marriott Waiohai Beach Club); **Hanalei Bay** (the area next to the Hanalei Pier); and the stream end of **Kalapaki Beach**. More advanced surfers move down the beach in Hanalei to an area fronting a grove of pine trees known as **Pine Trees**. When the trade winds die, the north ends of **Wailua** and **Kealia** beaches are teeming with surfers. Breaks off **Poipu** and **Beach House/Lawai Beach** attract intermediates year-round. During high surf, the break on the cliff side of **Kalihiwai** is for experts only. Advanced riders will head to Polihale to face the heavy West Side waves when conditions are right.

LESSONS

Blue Seas Surf School. Surfer and instructor Charlie Smith specializes in beginners (especially children) and will go anywhere on the island to find just the right surf. His soft-top longboards are very stable, making it easier to stand up. He specializes in one-on-one or family lessons, so personal interaction is a priority. He has also added stand-up paddling to his operation. Rates start at $65 for a 1½-hour lesson. (Transportation provided, if needed.) ⊠ *Marriott's Waiohai Beach Club, 2249 Poipu Rd., Koloa* ☎ *808/634–6979* ⊕ *www.blueseassurfingschool.com.*

Margo Oberg Surfing School. Seven-time world surfing champion and hall of famer Margo Oberg runs a surf school that meets on the beach in front of the Sheraton Kauaii in Poipu. Lessons are $68 for two hours, though Margo's staff teaches more than she does these days. ⊠ *2440 Hoonani Rd., Koloa* ☎ *808/332–6100* ⊕ *www.surfonkauai.com.*

WANT TO GO SURFING?

Thinking about taking surf lessons? These are a few good questions to ask your potential surf instructor:

■ What equipment do you provide? (If you're a beginner, you'll want to hear about their soft-top beginner boards. You'll also want to know if they'll provide rash guards and aqua socks.)

■ Who will be my instructor? (It's not always the name on the company logo. Ask about your instructor's qualifications.)

■ How do you select the location? (Ideally, you'll be assured that they pick the location because of its gentle waves, sandy beach bottom, and good year-round conditions.)

■ What if the waves are too big? (Under the best circumstances, they'll select another location or reschedule for another day.)

■ How many students do you take at a time? (Don't book if it's more than four students per instructor. You'll definitely want some personal attention.)

■ Are you CPR- and lifeguard-certified? (It's good to know your instructor will be able to help if you get into trouble.)

Nukumoi Surf Co. The parents of Kauai-grown and world-famous Rochelle Ballard own this surf shop. Not that the instructors who teach surfing here these days taught Rochelle, but they are die-hard surfers, even if they never made the international scene. Lessons run $75 for two hours with no more than four students per instructor. Their primary surf spot is the beach fronting the Sheraton. Nukumoi also does stand-up rentals ($25/hour; $100/day; $300/week). ⊠ *2100 Hoone Rd., across from Poipu Beach Park Koloa* ☎ *808/742–8019* ⊕ *www.nukumoisurf.com.*

Titus Kinimaka Hawaiian School of Surfing. Famed as a pioneer of big-wave surfing, this Hawaiian believes in giving back to his sport. Beginning, intermediate, and advanced lessons are available. If you want to learn to surf from a living legend, this is the man. ■TIP➜ He employs other instructors, so if you want Titus, be sure to ask for him. (And good luck, because if the waves are going off, he'll be surfing, not teaching.) Rates are $55 for a 90-minute group lesson; $65 for a 90-minute group stand-up paddle lesson. Customers are also able to use the board for a while after the lesson is complete. ⊠ *Meets at Quicksilver shop in Hanalei, 5-5088 Kuhio Hwy., 1A, Hanalei* ☎ *808/652–1116.*

EQUIPMENT

Hanalei Surf Company. You can rent boards here and shop for rash guards, wet suits, and some hip surf-inspired apparel. ⊠ *Mauka at Hanalei Center, 5-5161 Kuhio Hwy., Hanalei* ☎ *808/826–9000.*

Nukumoi Surf Co. If you're looking for convenience, this is the spot. No toting boards on your car, because this shop is located right across from the beach. ⊠ *2100 Hoone Rd., across from Poipu Beach Park, Koloa* ☎ *808/742–8019.*

Humpback whales arrive at Kauai in December and stick around until early April. Head out on a boat tour for a chance to see these majestic creatures breach.

Progressive Expressions. This full-service shop has a choice of rental boards and a whole lotta shopping. ✉ *5428 Koloa Rd., Koloa* ☎ *808/742–6041.*

Tamba Surf Company. This is your best bet for surf rentals on the East Side and the biggest name in local surf apparel. ✉ *4-1543 Kuhio Hwy., mauka on north end of Hwy. 56 in Kapaa, across from Scotty's Beachside BBQ, Kapaa* ☎ 808/823–6942 ⊕ *www.tambasurfcompany.com.*

WHALE WATCHING

Every winter North Pacific humpback whales swim some 3,000 miles over 30 days, give or take a few, from Alaska to Hawaii. Whales arrive as early as November and sometimes stay through April, though they seem to be most populous in February and March. They come to Hawaii to breed, calve, and nurse their young.

TOURS

Of course, nothing beats seeing a whale up close. During the season, any boat on the water is looking for whales; they're hard to avoid, whether the tour is labeled "whale watching" or not. Consider the whales a lucky-strike extra to any boating event that may interest you. If whales are definitely your thing, though, you can narrow down your tour boat decision by asking a few whale-related questions like whether there's a hydrophone on board, how long the captain has been running tours in Hawaii, and if anyone on the crew is a marine biologist or trained naturalist.

Several boat operators will add two-hour, afternoon whale-watching tours during the season that run on the South Shore (not Napali). Operators include **Blue Dolphin, Catamaran Kahanu, HoloHolo,** and **Napali Explorer** (⇨ *see Boat Tours*). Trying one of these excursions is a good option for those who have no interest in snorkeling or sightseeing along Napali Coast, although keep in mind, the longer you're on the water, the more likely you'll be to see the humpbacks.

One of the more unique ways to, *possibly,* see some whales is atop a kayak. For such an encounter, try **Outfitters Kauai**'s South Shore kayak trip (⇨ *see Kayaking Tours*). There are a few lookout spots around the island with good land-based viewing: Kilauea Lighthouse on the North Shore, the Kapaa Scenic Overlook just north of Kapaa town on the East Side, and the cliffs to the east of Keoniloa (Shipwreck) Beach on the South Shore.

Golf, Hiking, and Outdoor Activities

WORD OF MOUTH

"I'm a nature lover, so for me, Kauai is paradise. I can't imagine a place with more beauty—and with so much variety in such a relatively small area. You don't need to risk your life or be an experienced hiker in order to be rewarded with breathtaking views in Kauai."

—Songdoc

Updated by
David Simon

For those of you who love ocean sports but need a little break from all that sun, sand, and salt, there are plenty of options on Kauai to keep you busy on the ground. You can hike the island's many trails, or consider taking your vacation into flight with a treetop zipline. You can have a back-country adventure in a four-wheel drive, or relax in an inner tube floating down the cane-field irrigation canals.

Before booking tours, check with your concierge to find out what the forecast is for water and weather conditions. ■TIP➔ Don't rely on the Weather Channel for accurate weather reports, as they're often reporting Oahu weather. If you happen to arrive during a North Shore lull in the surf, you'll want to plan to be on the ocean in a kayak or snorkeling on the reef. If it's raining, ATV tours are the activity of choice.

For the golfer in the family, Kauai's spectacular courses are rated among the most scenic, as well as the most technical. Princeville Golf Course has garnered accolades from three national publications, and Poipu Bay Golf Course hosted the prestigious season-end PGA Grand Slam of Golf for 13 years, although Tiger (he won a record five-straight tournaments) and company are, unfortunately, now heading elsewhere for this tourney.

One of the most popular Kauai experiences is to see the island from the air. In an hour, you can see waterfalls, craters, and other places that are inaccessible even by hiking trails (some say that 70% or more of the island is inaccessible). The majority of flights depart from the Lihue airport and follow a clockwise pattern around the island. ■TIP➔ If you plan to take an aerial tour, it's a good idea to fly when you first arrive, rather than saving it for the end of your trip. It will help you visualize what's where on the island, and it may help you decide what you want to see from a closer vantage point during your stay. Many companies advertise a low-price 30- or 40-minute tour, which they rarely fly, so don't expect to book a flight at the advertised rate. The most popular flight is 60 minutes long, and some companies offer DVDs for an additional charge, so there's no need to spend your time in the air snapping pictures.

AERIAL TOURS

If you only drive around Kauai in your rental car, you will not see *all* of Kauai. There is truly only one way to see it all, and that's by air. Helicopter tours are the favorite way to get a bird's-eye view of Kauai—they fly at lower altitudes, hover above waterfalls, and wiggle their way into areas that a fixed-wing aircraft cannot. That said, if you've already tried the helitour, how about flying in the open cockpit of a biplane—à la the Red Baron?

Air Tour Kauai. This company, which is operated by the same group that runs Skydive Kauai, can hold up to six people in its Cessna 207 plane. The flights take off from the less-crowded Port Allen Airport and will last 65 to 70 minutes. The price is $125 per person. ⊠ *Port Allen Airport, Hanapepe* ☎ *808/639–3446* ⊕ *airtourkauai.com.*

★ **Blue Hawaiian Helicopters.** This multi-island operator flies the latest in helicopter technology, the Eco-Star, costing $1.8 million. It has 23% more interior space for its six passengers, has unparalleled viewing, and offers a few extra safety features. As the name implies, the helicopter is also a bit more environmentally friendly, with a 50% noise-reduction rate. Flights run a tad shorter than others (50 to 55 minutes instead of the 55 to 65 minutes that other companies tout), but the flight feels very complete. The rate is $240 and includes taxes and fuel surcharge. A DVD of your actual tour is available for an additional $25. ⊠ *Harbor Mall, 3501 Rice St., 107A, Nawiliwili* ☎ *808/245–5800, 800/745–2583* ⊕ *www.bluehawaiian.com.*

Inter-Island Helicopters. This company flies four-seater Hughes 500 helicopters *with the doors off.* It can get chilly at higher elevations, so bring a sweater and wear long pants. Tours depart from Hanapepe's Port Allen Airport, so if you're staying on the West Side, this is a good bet. Prices range from $260 to $310 per person. ⊠ *3441 Kuiloko Road, Hanapepe* ✛ *From Rte. 50, turn makai onto Rte. 543 in Hanapepe* ☎ *808/335–5009, 800/656–5009* ⊕ *www.interislandhelicopters.com.*

Fodor's Choice ★ **Jack Harter Helicopters.** Jack Harter was the first company to offer helicopter tours on Kauai. The company flies the six-passenger ASTAR helicopter with floor-to-ceiling windows, and the four-person Hughes 500, which is flown with no doors. The doorless ride can get windy, but it's the best bet for taking reflection-free photos. Pilots provide information on the Garden Island's history and geography through two-way intercoms. The company flies out of Lihue and has a second office at the Kauai Marriott. Tours are 60 to 65 minutes and 90 to 95 minutes and cost $259 to $384, including taxes and fuel surcharge. ✉ *4231 Ahukini Rd.* ☏ *808/245–3774, 888/245–2001* ⊕ *www.helicopters-kauai.com.*

Safari Helicopters. This company flies the "Super" ASTAR helicopter, which offers floor-to-ceiling windows on its doors, four roof windows, and Bose X-Generation headphones. Two-way microphones allow passengers to converse with the pilot. A major perk Safari can offer is its 90-minute "eco-tour," which adds a landing in Olokele Canyon. Passengers will then be met by Keith Robinson of THE Robinson family, who will provide a brief tour of the Kauai Wildlife Refuge, with endangered, endemic plants. The once daily tour goes out Monday through Friday at 3:30 pm. Flight prices range from $224 to $304, including taxes and fuel surcharge; a DVD is $40 extra. ✉ *3225 Akahi St.* ☏ *808/246–0136, 800/326–3356* ⊕ *www.safarihelicopters.com.*

Sunshine Helicopter Tours. If the name of this company sounds familiar, it may be because its pilots fly on all the main Hawaiian Islands. On Kauai, Sunshine Helicopters departs out of two different locations: Lihue and Princeville. They fly the six-passenger FX STAR and super roomy six-passenger WhisperSTAR birds. Prices for the 45–55 minute Lihue flights range from $244 to $294, including tax and fuel surcharges. The 40–50 minute Princeville flights will run from $289 to $364. ■ TIP→ Discounts can be substantial by booking online and taking advantage of the "early-bird" seating during off hours. ✉ *3416 Rice Street, #203* ✉ *3441 Kuiloko Rd., Port Allen Airport, Hanapepe* ✉ *Princeville Airport, Princeville* ☏ *808/240–2577, 888/245–4354* ⊕ *www. sunshinehelicopters.com.*

Tropical Bi-planes. This company flies both a bright-red Waco biplane, built in 2002 and based on a 1936 design, and a Cessna 182 Skylane. The biplane can carry two passengers, the Cessna holds three. ■ TIP→ If a couple takes two seats in the Cessna, they will not sell the third seat, as to keep it a personal experience. An open cockpit and staggered wing design mean there's nothing between you and the sights. You will be seeing the sights at an altitude of 1,500 feet at about 85 mph. Biplane tours range from $210 to $410 per couple, depending on length. Cessna tours cost $125 per person for the one-hour flight. ✉ *Lihue Airport Commuter Terminal, 3901 Mokulele Loop* ☏ *808/246–9123, 888/280–9123* ⊕ *www.tropicalbiplanes.com.*

ATV TOURS

Although all the beaches on the island are public, much of the interior land—once sugar and pineapple plantations—is privately owned. This is really a shame, because the valleys and mountains that make up the vast interior of the island easily rival the beaches in sheer beauty. The good news is some tour operators have agreements with landowners that make exploration possible, albeit a bit bumpy, and unless you have back troubles, that's half the fun. ■ TIP→ If it looks like rain, book an ATV tour ASAP. That's the thing about these tours: the muddier, the better.

★ **Kauai ATV Tours.** This is *the* thing to do when it rains on Kauai. Consider it an extreme mud bath. Kauai ATV in Koloa is the originator of the island's all-terrain-vehicle tours. Its $125 three-hour Koloa tour takes you through a private sugar plantation and historic cane-haul tunnel. The $155 four-hour waterfall tour visits secluded waterfalls and includes a picnic lunch. This popular option includes a hike through a bamboo forest and a swim in a freshwater pool at the base of the falls—to rinse off all that mud. You must be 16 or older to operate your own ATV, but Kauai ATV also offers its four-passenger "Ohana Bug" and two-passenger "Mud Bugs" to accommodate families with kids ages five and older. There are price breaks ($105 for the three-hour tour, $135 for the four-hour) for passengers. ✉ *3477A Weliweli Rd., Koloa* ☎ *808/742–2734, 877/707–7088* ⊕ *www.kauaiatv.com.*

Kipu Ranch Adventures. This 3,000-acre property extends from the Huleia River to the top of Mt. Haupu. *Jurassic Park, Indiana Jones,* and *Mighty Joe Young* were filmed here, and you'll see the locations for all of them on the $125 three-hour Ranch Tour. The $150 four-hour Waterfall Tour includes a visit to two waterfalls and a picnic lunch. Kipu Ranch was once a sugar plantation, but today it is a working cattle ranch, so you'll be in the company of bovines as well as pheasants, wild boars, and peacocks. ✉ *235 Kipu Rd. Take Puhi Bypass Rd. off Hwy. 50 and turn right onto Kipu Rd.* ☎ *808/246–9288* ⊕ *www.kiputours.com.*

BIKING

Kauai is a labyrinth of cane-haul roads, which are fun for exploring on two wheels. The challenge is finding roads where biking is allowed and then not getting lost in the maze. Maybe that explains why Kauai is not a hub for the sport . . . yet. Still, there are some epic rides for those who are interested—both the adrenaline-rush and the mellower beach-cruiser kind. If you want to grind out some mileage, the main highway that skirts the coastal areas is generally safe, though there are only a few designated bike lanes. It's hilly, but you'll find that keeping your eyes on the road and not the scenery is the biggest challenge. "Cruisers" should head to Kapaa. A new section of Ke Ala Hele Makalae, a pedestrian trail that runs along the East Side of Kauai, was completed in the summer of 2009, totaling 6½ miles of completed path. You can rent bikes (with helmets) from the activities desks of certain hotels, but these are not the best quality. You're better off renting from Kauai Cycle in Kapaa, Outfitters Kauai in Poipu, or Pedal 'n' Paddle in Hanalei.

★ **Ke Ala Hele Makalae** (*Nawiliwili to Anahola Bike/Pedestrian Path*). For the cruiser, this path follows the coastline on Kauai's East Side. Eventually, it will run some 20 miles and offer scenic views, picnic pavilions, and restroom facilities along the way—all in compliance with the Americans with Disabilities Act. For now, there are 2.5 miles of path in Lydgate Beach Park to secluded Kuna Bay (aka Donkey Beach). The easiest way to access the completed sections of the path is from Kealia Beach. Park here and head north into rural lands with spectacular coastline vistas or head south into Kapaa for a more inter-active experience. ⊠ *Trailhead is 1 mile north of Kapaa; park at north end of Kealia Beach.*

Moalepe Trail. This trail is perfect for intermediate to advanced riders. The first 2 miles of this 5-mile, double-track road winds through pastureland. The real challenge begins when you reach the steep and rutted switchbacks, which during a rainy spell can be hazardous to attempt. Moalepe dead-ends at the Kuilau Trail. If you choose to continue down the Kuilau Trail, it will end at the Keahua Arboretum stream. ⊠ *From Kuhio Hwy. in Kapaa, drive mauka on Kuamoo Rd. for 3 miles and turn right onto Kamalu Rd. It dead-ends at Olohena Rd. Turn left and follow until the road veers sharply to the right. The trailhead will be right in front of you.*

Powerline Trail. Advanced riders like this trail. It's actually a service road for the electric company that splits the island. It's 13 miles in length; the first 5 miles goes from 620 feet in elevation to almost 2,000. The remaining 8 miles descends gradually over a variety of terrain, some technical. Some sections will require carrying your bike. The views will stay with you forever. Trailhead is *mauka* just past the stream crossing at Keahua Arboretum, or at the end of the appropriately named Powerline Road in Princeville, past Princeville Ranch Stables. ■ TIP→ When it's wet—in summer or winter—this trail is a mess. Check with a knowledgeable bike shop for trail conditions first and be prepared to improvise.

Spalding Monument Loop. For the novice rider, this loop offers a good workout and a summit ocean view that is not overly strenuous to reach. If you pick up a bike at Kauai Cycle in Kapaa, you can ride a mile up Ke Ala Hele Makalae path to reach the head of the loop, and even make a snack stop at the Kealia Store without a detour. From Kealia Store, ride up a gradual incline 2 miles through horse pastures to Spalding Monument, named for a former plantation owner, although there is no longer any signage. Palms circle the lava-rock wall, where you can picnic while enjoying a 180-degree ocean view. Behind you is the glorious mountain backdrop of Kalalea. Follow the paved road north toward Kalalea for 2 more miles. Turn right at the highway, and it's another 2 miles south to a parking lot for Donkey Beach on the ocean side. The lot is not far from mile marker 12 and sits on the top of a hill. Follow the path down to the beach and turn right on Ke Ala Hele Makalae, following what was once an old cane-haul road that heads right back into Kapaa town. ⊠ *The loop begins at the Kealia Store, past mile marker 10 on the mauka side of the road.*

Wailua Forest Management Road. For the novice mountain biker, this is an easy ride, and it's also easy to find. From Route 56 in Wailua, turn mauka on Kuamoo Road and continue 6 miles to the picnic area, known as Keahua Arboretum; park here. The potholed four-wheel-drive road includes some stream crossings—⚠ stay away during heavy rains because the streams flood—and continues for 2 miles to a T-stop, where you should turn right. Stay on the road for about 3 miles until you reach a gate; this is the spot where the gates in the movie *Jurassic Park* were

Continued on page 142

HAWAII'S PLANTS 101

Hawaii is a bounty of rainbow-colored flowers and plants. The evening air is scented with their fragrance. Just look at the front yard of almost any home, travel any road, or visit any local park and you'll see a spectacular array of colored blossoms and leaves. What most visitors don't know is that many of the plants they are seeing are not native to Hawaii; rather, they were introduced during the last two centuries as ornamental plants, or for timber, shade, or fruit.

Hawaii boasts nearly every climate on the planet, excluding the two most extreme: arctic tundra and arid desert. The Islands have wine-growing regions, cactus-speckled ranchlands, icy mountaintops, and the rainiest forests on earth.

Plants introduced from around the world thrive here. The lush lowland valleys along the windward coasts are predominantly populated by non-native trees including yellow- and red-fruited **guava**, silvery-leafed **kukui**, and orange-flowered **tulip trees**.

The colorful **plumeria flower**, very fragrant and commonly used in lei making, and the giant multicolored **hibiscus flower** are both used by many women as hair adornments, and are two of the most common plants found around homes and hotels. The umbrella-like **monkeypod tree** from Central America provides shade in many of Hawaii's parks including Kapiolani Park in Honolulu. Hawaii's largest tree, found in Lahaina, Maui, is a giant **banyan tree.** Its canopy and massive support roots cover about two-thirds of an acre. The native **ohia tree**, with its brilliant red brush-like flowers, and the **hapuu**, a giant tree fern, are common in Hawaii's forests and are also used ornamentally in gardens.

Bougainvillea

Guava

Monkeypod

Banyan

Ohia Lehua*

Tulip Tree

Plumeria

Pandanus

Hibiscus

Anthurium

Kukui

Hapuu

*endemic to Hawaii

DID YOU KNOW?

More than 2,200 plant species are found in the Hawaiian Islands, but only about 1,000 are native. Of these, 320 are so rare, they are endangered. Hawaii's endemic plants evolved from ancestral seeds arriving in the Islands over thousands of years as baggage with birds, floating on ocean currents, or drifting on winds from continents thousands of miles away. Once here, these plants evolved in isolation, creating many new species known nowhere else in the world.

One of the most visited sites on Kauai is Waimea Canyon. Make sure to stop at Puu ka Pele and Puu Hinahina lookouts.

filmed, though it looks nothing like the movie. Go around the gate and down the road for another mile to a confluence of streams at the base of Mt. Waialeale. Be sure to bring your camera. ⊠ *Kuamoo Rd., Kapaa.*

Waimea Canyon Road. For those wanting a very challenging road workout, climb this road, also known as Route 550. After a 3,000-foot climb, the road tops out at mile marker 12 adjacent to Waimea Canyon, which will pop in and out of view on your right as you ascend. From here it continues several miles (mostly level) past the Kokee Museum and ends at the Kalalau Lookout. It's paved the entire way, uphill 100%, and curvy. △ There's not much of a shoulder on either road— sometimes none—so be extra cautious. The road gets busier as the day wears on, so you may want to consider a sunrise ride. A slightly more moderate uphill climb is Kokee Road, Route 552, from Kekaha, which intersects with Route 550. By the way, bikes aren't allowed on the hiking trails in and around Waimea Canyon and Kokee State Park, but there are miles of wonderful 4WD roads perfect for mountain biking. Check at Kokee Lodge for a map and conditions. ⊠ *Road turns mauka off Rte. 50, just after grocery store in downtown Waimea.*

EQUIPMENT AND TOURS

★ **Kauai Cycle.** This reliable, full-service bike shop rents, sells, and repairs bikes. Cruisers, mountain bikes (front- and full-suspension), and road bikes are available for $20 to $45 per day and $110 to $250 per week with directions to trails. The Ke Ala Hele Makalae is right out their back door. ⊠ *934 Kuhio Hwy., across from Taco Bell, Kapaa* ☎ *808/821–2115* ⊕ *www.kauaicycle.com.*

Outfitters Kauai. Hybrid "comfort" and mountain bikes (both full-suspension and hardtails), as well as road bikes, are available at this shop in Poipu. You can ride right out the door to tour Poipu, or get information on how to do a self-guided tour of Kokee State Park and Waimea Canyon. The company also leads sunrise and evening coasting tours (under the name **Bicycle Downhill**) from Waimea Canyon past the island's West Side beaches. Rentals cost $25 to $45 per day. Tours cost $102 plus tax. Stand-up paddle tours are also available. ⊠ *2827-A Poipu Rd., Poipu* ⊕ *Follow Poipu Rd. south from Koloa town; shop is on right before turnoff to Spouting Horn* ☎ *808/742–9667, 888/742–9887* ⊕ *www. outfitterskauai.com.*

★ **Pedal 'n' Paddle.** This company rents old-fashioned, single-speed beach cruisers and hybrid road bikes for $15 to $20 per day; $60 to $80 per week, with a discount for more than one week's use. In the heart of Hanalei, this is a great way to cruise the town; the more ambitious cyclist can head to the end of the road. Be careful, though, because there are no bike lanes on the twisting and turning road to Kee. ⊠ *Ching Young Village, Rte. 560, Hanalei* ☎ *808/826–9069* ⊕ *www.pedalnpaddle.com.*

GOLF

For golfers, the Garden Isle might as well be known as the Robert Trent Jones Jr. Isle. Four of the island's nine courses, including Poipu Bay—onetime home of the PGA Grand Slam of Golf—are the work of Jones, who maintains a home at Princeville. Combine these four courses with those from Jack Nicklaus, Robin Nelson, and local legend Toyo Shirai, and you'll see that golf sets Kauai apart from the other Islands as much as the Pacific Ocean does. ■TIP➔ Afternoon tee times can save you big bucks.

Kauai Lagoons Golf Club. With the development of the Kauai Lagoons Resort, the golf club is getting a face-lift, albeit a slow one due to the economy. Yes, Jack is back. When Nicklaus is done with this course, 27 championship-style holes (the links-style course is gone) will await golfers. For now, 18 holes are playable including a half mile of ocean-hugging holes redesigned to take advantage of the obvious visual splendor of Kalapaki Bay. Number 18 is the island green named "The Bear" for its challenging play into the trade winds. ⊠ *3351 Hoolaulea Way* ☎ *808/241–6000, 800/634–6400* ⊕ *www.kauailagoonsgolf.com* 🏌 *18 holes. 6977 yds. Par 72. Greens fee: $155–195* ⌒ *Facilities: Driving range, putting green, golf carts, rental clubs, lessons.*

Kauai Mini Golf. The only miniature golf course on the island, Kauai Mini Golf is also a full botanical garden. The 18-hole course was designed to be challenging, beautiful, and family-friendly. Replacing the typical clown's nose and spinning wheels are some water features and tropical tunnels. Surrounding each hole is flora and plant life that walks players through different eras of Hawaiian history. A gift shop with local products and a concessions counter make it a fun activity for any time of day. Open Tuesday through Sunday from 11 am to 9 pm.

Our top choice for playing golf on the East Side of Kauai is here, at the Kauai Lagoons Golf Club.

Cost is $18. ✉ *5-273 Kuhio Hwy, Kilauea* ☎ 808/828–2118 ⊕ *www. kauaiminigolf.com.*

Kiahuna Plantation Golf Course. A meandering creek, lava outcrops, and thickets of trees give Kiahuna its character. Robert Trent Jones Jr. was given a smallish piece of land just inland at Poipu, and defends par with smaller targets, awkward stances, and optical illusions. In 2003 a group of homeowners bought the club and brought Jones back to renovate the course (it was originally built in 1983), adding tees and revamping bunkers. The pro here boasts his course has the best putting greens on the island. This is the only course on Kauai with a complete set of junior's tee boxes. ✉ *2545 Kiahuna Plantation Dr., Koloa* ☎ 808/742–9595 ⊕ *www.kiahunagolf.com* ⛳ *18 holes. 6214 yds. Par 70. Greens fee: $103* ☞ *Facilities: Driving range, putting green, rental clubs, lessons, pro shop, restaurant, bar.*

Kukuiolono Golf Course. Local legend Toyo Shirai designed this fun, funky 9-holer where holes play across rolling, forested hills that afford views of the distant Pacific. Though Shirai has an eye for a good golf hole, Kukuiolono is out of the way and a bit rough, and so probably not for everyone. But at $9 for the day, it's a deal—bring cash, though, as they don't accept credit cards. No tee times. ✉ *854 Puu Rd., Kalaheo* ☎ 808/332–9151 ⛳ *9 holes. 3173 yds. Par 36. Greens fee: $9* ☞ *Facilities: Driving range, putting green, golf carts, pull carts, rental clubs.*

Poipu Bay Golf Course. Poipu Bay has been called the Pebble Beach of Hawaii, and the comparison is apt. Like Pebble Beach, Poipu is a links course built on headlands, not true links land. And as at Monterey Bay, there's wildlife galore—except that the animals are not quite as intrusive to play. It's not unusual for golfers to see monk seals sunning on the beach below, sea turtles bobbing outside the shore break, and humpback whales leaping offshore. From 1994 to 2006, the course (designed by Robert Trent Jones Jr.) hosted the annual PGA Grand Slam of Golf. That means Tiger was a frequent visitor—and winner—here. Call ahead to take advantage of varying prices for tee times. ⊠ *2250 Ainako St., Koloa* ☎ *808/742-8711* ⊕ *www.poipubaygolf.com* ⚐ *18 holes. 6612 yds. Par 72. Greens fee: $240* ☞ *Facilities: Driving range, putting green, rental clubs, golf carts, golf academy/lessons, restaurant, bar.*

Fodor's Choice ★ **Princeville Resort.** Robert Trent Jones Jr. built two memorable courses overlooking Hanalei Bay, the 27-hole Princeville Makai Course (1971) and the 18-hole Prince Course (1990). The combination earned Princeville Resort the 20th spot in *Golf Digest's* list of the "Best 75 Golf Resorts in North America." The Makai Course underwent extensive renovations in 2009, including new turf throughout, reshaped greens and bunkers, refurbished cart paths and comfort stations, and the creation of an extensive practice facility. They also offer free rounds for junior golfers (15 and under) when accompanied by one paying adult. Rated Hawaii's second toughest course (behind Oahu's Koolau), this is jungle golf, with holes running through dense forest and over tangled ravines, out onto headlands for breathtaking ocean views, then back into the jungle.

Makai Golf Course ⊠ *4080 Lei O Papa Rd., Princeville* ☎ *808/826-3580* ⊕ *www.makaigolf.com* ⚐ *27 holes. 6886 yds. Par 72. Greens fee: $220* ☞ *Facilities: Driving range, putting green, rental clubs, golf carts, pro shop, golf academy/lessons, snack bar.*

Prince Golf Course ⊠ *5-3900 Kuhio Hwy., Princeville* ☎ *808/826-5001* ⊕ *www.princeville.com* ⚐ *18 holes. 6960 yds. Par 72. Greens fee: $170* ☞ *Facilities: Driving range, putting green, rental clubs, golf carts, pro shop, golf academy/lessons, restaurant, bar.*

Wailua Municipal Golf Course. Voted by *Golf Digest* as one of Hawaii's 15 best golf courses, this seaside course was first built as a 9-hole golf course in the 1930s. The second 9 holes were added in 1961. Course designer Toyo Shirai created a course that is fun but not punishing. Not only is this an affordable game with minimal water hazards, but it is challenging enough to have been chosen to host three USGA Amateur Public Links Championships. The trade winds blow steadily on the East Side of the island and make the game all the more challenging. An ocean view and affordability make this one of the most popular courses on the island. Tee times are accepted up to seven days in advance. ⊠ *3-5350 Kuhio Hwy., five mins north of airport* ☎ *808/241-6666* ⚐ *18 holes. 6585 yds. Par 72. Greens fee: $48 weekdays, $60 weekends. Half price after 2 pm. Cart rental: $18. Cash or traveler's checks only* ☞ *Facilities: Driving range, rental clubs, golf carts, pro shop, lessons, snack bar.*

HIKING

The best way to experience the *aina*—the land—on Kauai is to step off the beach and hike into the remote interior. You'll find waterfalls so tall you'll strain your neck looking, pools of crystal clear water for swimming, tropical forests teeming with plant life, and ocean vistas that will make you wish you could stay forever.

■ TIP→ For your safety wear sturdy shoes—preferably water-resistant ones.

All hiking trails on Kauai are free, so far. There's a development plan in the works that will turn the Waimea Canyon and Kokee state parks into admission-charging destinations. Whatever it may be, it will be worth it.

★ **Hanalei-Okolehao Trail.** *Okolehao* basically translates to "moonshine" in Hawaiian. This trail follows the Hihimanu Ridge, which was established in the days of Prohibition, when this backyard liquor was distilled from the roots of ti plants. The 2-mile hike climbs 1,200 feet and offers a 360-degree view of Hanalei Bay and Waioli Valley. Thanks to Kauai Sierra Club volunteers, this trail survived Hurricane Iniki. It took eight years of hauling chain saws and weed whackers up the ridge to clear the trail. Your ascent begins at the China Ditch off the Hanalei River. Follow the trail through a lightly forested grove, at the Y take the first right, and then take the next left up a steep embankment. From here the trail is well marked. Most of the climb is lined with hala, ti, wild orchid, and eucalyptus. You'll get your first of many ocean views at mile marker 1. ⊠ *Hanalei, Follow Ohiki Rd. (north of the Hanalei Bridge) 7 miles to the U.S. Fish and Wildlife Service parking area. Directly across the street is a small bridge that marks the trailhead.*

Ho opii Falls. Tucked among the winding roads and grassy pastures of Kapahi, 3 miles inland from Kapaa town, is an easy hike to two waterfalls. A 10-minute walk will deliver you to the creek. Follow it around to see the first set of falls. The more impressive second falls are a mere 25 minutes away. The swimming hole alone is worth the journey. Just climb the rooted path next to the first falls and turn left on the trail above. Turn left on the very next trail to descend back into the canyon and follow the leafy path that zigzags along the creek. The falls and the swimming hole will lie below. ⊠ *Kapaa ♦ On the north end of Kapaa, ¼ mile past the last lookout, is a small side road called Kawaihau. Follow the road up 3 miles, then turn right on Kapahi Rd. into a residential neighborhood. Kapahi Rd. dead-ends near the trailhead. Look for the yellow gate on your left.*

Fodor's Choice **Kalalau Trail.** Of all the hikes on the island, Kalalau Trail is by far the
★ most famous and in many regards the most strenuous. A moderate hiker can handle the 2-mile trek to Hanakapiai Beach, and for the seasoned outdoorsman, the additional 2 miles up to the falls is manageable. But be prepared to rock-hop along a creek and ford waters that can get waist high during the rain. Round-trip to Hanakapiai Falls is 8 miles. This steep and often muddy trail is best approached with a walking stick. If there has been any steady rain, waiting for drier days would provide a more enjoyable trek. The narrow trail will deliver one startling ocean view after another along a path that is alternately shady

Continued on page 150

BIRTH OF THE ISLANDS

How did the volcanoes of the Hawaiian Islands evolve here, in the middle of the Pacific Ocean? The ancient Hawaiians believed that the volcano goddess Pele's hot temper was the key to the mystery; modern scientists contend that it's all about plate tectonics and one very hot spot.

Plate Tectonics & the Hawaiian Question: The theory of plate tectonics says that the Earth's surface is comprised of plates that float around slowly over the planet's molten interior. The vast majority of earthquakes and volcanic eruptions occur near plate boundaries—the San Francisco earthquakes in 1906 and 1989, for example, were the result of activity along the nearby San Andreas Fault, where the Pacific and North American plates meet. Hawaii, more than 1,988 miles from the nearest plate boundary, is a giant exception. For years scientists struggled to explain the island chain's existence—if not a fault line, what caused the earthquakes and volcanic eruptions that formed these islands?

What's a hotspot? In 1963, J. Tuzo Wilson, a Canadian geophysicist, argued that the Hawaiian volcanoes must have been created by small concentrated areas of extreme heat beneath the plates. Wilson hypothesized that there is a hotspot beneath the present-day position of the Big Island. Its heat produced a persistent source of magma by partly melting the Pacific Plate above it. The magma, lighter than the surrounding solid rock, rose through the mantle and crust to erupt onto the sea floor, forming an active seamount. Each flow caused the seamount to grow until it finally emerged above sea level as an island volcano. Plausible so far, but why then, is there not one giant Hawaiian island?

Holo Mai Pele, often played out in hula, is the Hawaiian creation myth. Pele sends her sister Hiiaka on an epic quest to fetch her lover Lohiau. Overcoming many obstacles, Hiiaka reaches full goddess status and falls in love with Lohiau herself. When Pele finds out, she destroys everything dear to her sister, killing Lohiau and burning Hiiaka's ohia groves. Each time lava flows from a volcano, ohia trees sprout shortly after, in a constant cycle of destruction and renewal.

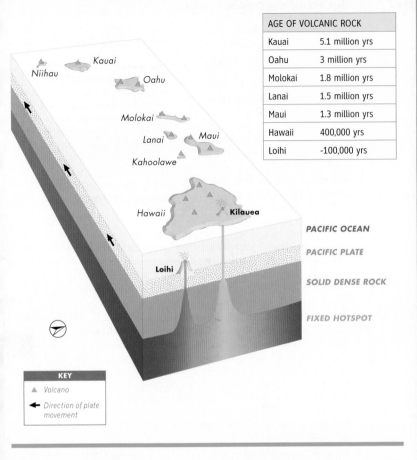

AGE OF VOLCANIC ROCK	
Kauai	5.1 million yrs
Oahu	3 million yrs
Molokai	1.8 million yrs
Lanai	1.5 million yrs
Maui	1.3 million yrs
Hawaii	400,000 yrs
Loihi	-100,000 yrs

PACIFIC OCEAN

PACIFIC PLATE

SOLID DENSE ROCK

FIXED HOTSPOT

KEY

▲ Volcano

← Direction of plate movement

Volcanoes on the Move: Wilson further suggested that the movement of the Pacific Plate itself eventually carries the island volcano beyond the hotspot. Cut off from its magma source, the island volcano becomes dormant. As the plate slowly moved, one island volcano would become extinct just as another would develop over the hotspot. After several million years, there is a long volcanic trail of islands and seamounts across the ocean floor. The oldest islands are those farthest from the hotspot. The exposed rocks of Kauai, for example, are about 5.1 million years old, but those on the Big Island are less than .5 million years old, with new volcanic rock still being formed.

An Island on the Way: Off the coast of the Big Island, the volcano known as Loihi is still submerged but erupting. Scientists long believed it to be a retired seamount volcano, but in the 1970s they discovered both old and new lava on its flanks, and in 1996 it erupted with a vengeance. It is believed that several thousand years from now, Loihi will be the newest addition to the Hawaiian Islands.

and sunny. Wear hiking shoes or sandals, and bring drinking water since the creeks on the trail are not potable. Plenty of food is always encouraged on a strenuous hike such as this one. If your plan is to venture the full 11 miles into Kalalau, you need to acquire a camping permit. ⊠ *Drive north past Hanalei to end of road. Trailhead is directly across from Kee Beach.*

Mahaulepu Heritage Trail. This trail offers the novice hiker an accessible way to appreciate the rugged southern coast of Kauai. A cross-country course wends its way along the water, high above the ocean, through a lava field and past a sacred *heiau* (stone structure). Walk all the way to Mahaulepu, 2 miles north for a two-hour round-trip. ⊠ *Drive north on Poipu Rd., turn right at Poipu Bay Golf Course sign. The street name is Ainako, but the sign is hard to see. Drive down to beach and park in lot ⊕ www.hikemahaulepu.org.*

Sleeping Giant Trail. An easy and easily accessible trail practically in the heart of Kapaa, the Sleeping Giant Trail—or simply Sleeping Giant—gains 1,000 feet over 2 miles. We prefer an early-morning—say, sunrise—hike, with sparkling blue-water vistas, up the East Side trailhead. At the top you can see a grassy grove with a picnic table. Experienced hikers may want to go a step farther, all the way to the giant's nose and chin. From here there are 360-degree views of the island. It is a local favorite with many East-Siders meeting here to exercise. ⊠ *Haleilio Rd., Wailua, turn mauka off Rte. 56 onto Haleilio Rd.; proceed 1 mile to small parking area on right.*

Waimea Canyon and Kokee State Parks. This park contains a 50-mile network of hiking trails of varying difficulty that take you through acres of native forests, across the highest-elevation swamp in the world, to the river at the base of the canyon, and onto pinnacles of land sticking their necks out over Napali Coast. All hikers should register at Kokee Natural History Museum, where you can find trail maps, current trail information, and specific directions.

All mileage mentioned below is one-way.

The **Kukui Trail** descends 2½ miles and 2,200 feet into Waimea Canyon to the edge of the Waimea River—it's a steep climb. The **Awaawapuhi Trail,** with 1,600 feet of elevation gains and losses over 3¼ miles, feels more gentle than the Kukui Trail, but it offers its own huffing-and-puffing sections in its descent along a spiny ridge to a perch overlooking the ocean.

The 3½-mile **Alakai Swamp Trail** is accessed via the **Pihea Trail**, or a four-wheel-drive road. There's one strenuous valley section, but otherwise it's a pretty level trail—once you access it. This trail is a bird-watcher's delight and includes a painterly view of Wainiha and Hanalei

---

WORD OF MOUTH

"Our all time favorite anywhere hike was the Nualolo/Cliffs/Awaawapuhi Loop Trail. We started the hike at about 11 am after parking at Kokee Lodge. Check trail conditions when you stop at the lodge. You don't want to do this trail when it is muddy or slippery, particularly the Cliff section. That part of the trail can wash out." —LindainOhio

DID YOU KNOW?

Kauai is called the "Garden Isle," and it's easy to see why as you hike through the lush, green Hanakapiai Valley.

LEPTOSPIROSIS

Leptospirosis is a bacterial disease that is transmitted from animals to humans. It can survive for long periods of time in freshwater and mud contaminated by the urine of infected animals, such as mice, rats, and goats.

The bacteria enter the body through the eyes, ears, nose, mouth, and broken skin. To avoid infection, don't drink untreated water from the island's streams; don't wade in waters above the chest or submerge skin with cuts and abrasions in island streams or rivers.

Symptoms are often mild and resemble the flu—fever, diarrhea, chills, nausea, headache, vomiting, and body pains—and may occur 2 to 20 days after exposure. If you think you have these symptoms, see a doctor right away.

valleys at the trail's end. The trail traverses the purported highest-elevation swamp in the world on a boardwalk so as not to disturb the fragile plant- and wildlife. It is typically the coolest of the hikes due to the tree canopies, elevation, and cloud coverage.

The **Canyon Trail** offers much in its short trek: spectacular vistas of the canyon and the only dependable waterfall in Waimea Canyon. The easy 2-mile hike can be cut in half if you have a four-wheel-drive vehicle. If you were outfitted with a headlamp, this would be a great hike at sunset as the sun's light sets the canyon walls ablaze in color. ⊠ *Kokee Natural History Museum, Rte. 550, 3600 Kokee Rd., Kekaha* ☎ *808/335–9975 for trail conditions.*

EQUIPMENT AND TOURS

Fodor's Choice ★ **Kauai Nature Tours.** Father and son scientists started this hiking tour business. As such, their emphasis is on education and the environment. If you're interested in flora, fauna, volcanology, geology, oceanography, and the like, this is the company for you. They offer daylong hikes along coastal areas, beaches, and in the mountains. ■ TIP→ If you have a desire to see a specific location, just ask. They will do custom hikes to spots they don't normally hit if there is interest. Hikes range from easy to strenuous and rates range from $125 to $150. Transportation is often provided from hotel. ⊠ *Meets at designated spots around island* ☎ *808/742–8305, 888/233–8365* ⊕ *www.kauainaturetours.com.*

Princeville Ranch Adventures. This 4-mile hike traverses Princeville Ranch, crossing through a rain forest and to a five-tier waterfall for lunch and swimming. Moderately strenuous hiking is required. Fee is $129. ⊠ *West of Princeville Airport on Rte. 56, between mile markers 27 and 28, Princeville* ☎ *808/826–7669, 888/955–7669* ⊕ *www. adventureskauai.com.*

HORSEBACK RIDING

Most of the horseback-riding tours on Kauai are primarily walking tours with little trotting and no cantering or galloping, so no experience is required. Zip. Zilch. Nada. If you're interested, most of the stables offer private lessons. The most popular tours are the ones including a picnic lunch by the water. Your only dilemma may be deciding what kind of water you want—waterfalls or ocean. You may want to make your decision based on where you're staying. The "waterfall picnic" tours are on the wetter North Shore, and the "beach picnic" tours take place on the South Side.

> **LILIKO'I ALERT**
>
> If you're hiking in May and June, you'll see *lilikoi*—often referred to as passion fruit—scattered like yellow eggs among the ferns. It tastes as sweet and floral as it smells—bite the tip of the rind off and you'll see speckled jelly with tiny black seeds; then slurp it right out of the skin. If you miss lilikoi season, scout out delicious lilikoi mustards and jams sold by local grocers. Lilikoi pie is also served at a few Hawaiian eateries.

CJM Country Stables. Just past the Hyatt in Poipu, CJM Stables offers a three-hour picnic ride with noshing on the beach, as well as their more popular two-hour trail ride. The landscape here is rugged and beautiful, featuring sand dunes and limestone bluffs. They can get you as close as anyone to the secluded Mahaulepu bay. CJM sponsors seasonal rodeo events that are free and open to the public. Prices range from $103 to $135. ⊠ *Poipu Rd., 1½ miles from Grand Hyatt Kauai, Koloa* ☎ *808/742–6096* ⊕ *www.cjmstables.com.*

Esprit de Corps. If you ride, this is the company for you. Esprit de Corps has three- to eight-hour rides for experienced riders who know how to trot and canter. They also have a two-hour beginner ride that requires no experience. What's also nice is the maximum group size: six. Weddings on horseback can be arranged (in fact, Dale, the owner, is a wedding officiant, specializing in Jewish and interfaith marriages), and custom rides for less experienced and younger riders (as young as two) are available, as well as private lessons (starting at age six). Make sure to call ahead because they are by appointment only. Rates range from $130 to $390. ⊠ *End of Kualapa Pl., 1491 Kualapa Place, Kapaa* ☎ *808/822–4688* ⊕ *www.kauaihorses.com.*

Fodor's Choice ★ **Princeville Ranch Stables.** A longtime *kamaaina* (resident) family operates Princeville Ranch. They originated the waterfall picnic tours, which run three or four hours and include a short but steep hike down to Kalihiwai Falls, a dramatic three-tier waterfall, for swimming and picnicking. Princeville also has shorter, straight riding tours and private rides, and if they're moving cattle while you're visiting, you can sign up for a cattle drive. Prices range from $135 up to $245 for some private tours. ⊠ *Kuhio Hwy. West of Princeville Airport, mauka between mile markers 27 and 28, Princeville* ☎ *808/826–7669* ⊕ *www.princevilleranch.com.*

5

It's said to be the wettest place on Earth—Mt. Waialeale gets about 450 inches of rain per year.

MOUNTAIN TUBING

For the past 40 years, Hawaii's sugarcane plantations have closed one by one. In the fall of 2009, Gay and Robinson announced the closure of Kauai's last plantation, leaving only one in Maui, the last in the state. The sugarcane irrigation ditches remain, striating these islands like spokes in a wheel. Inspired by the Hawaiian *auwai*, which diverted water from streams to taro fields, these engineering feats harnessed the rain. One ingenious tour company on Kauai has figured out a way to make exploring them an adventure: float inflatable tubes down the route.

☼ **Kauai Backcountry Adventures.** Popular with all ages, this laid-back adventure can book up two weeks in advance in busy summer months. Here's how it works: you recline in an inner tube and float down fern-lined irrigation ditches that were built more than a century ago—the engineering is impressive—to divert water from Mt. Waialeale to sugar and pineapple fields around the island. They'll even give you a headlamp so you can see as you float through five covered tunnels. The scenery from the island's interior at the base of Mt. Waialeale on Lihue Plantation land is superb. Ages five and up are welcome. The tour takes about three hours and includes a picnic lunch and a swim in a swimming hole. ■TIP→ You'll definitely want to pack water-friendly shoes (or rent some from the outfitter), sunscreen, a hat, bug repellent, and a beach towel. Tours cost $102 per person and are offered morning and afternoon, daily. ✉ *3-4131 Kuhio Hwy., across from gas station, Hanamaulu* ☎ *808/245–2506, 888/270–0555* ⊕ *www.kauaibackcountry.com.*

SKYDIVING

If you're a full-throttle adrenaline junkie, it doesn't get any better than jumping out of an airplane over an island—oh, the views—and floating peacefully back down to earth tethered to a parachute. There aren't many options, though, on Kauai; in fact, there's just one.

Skydive Kauai. Ten thousand feet over Kauai and falling at a rate of 120 mph is probably as thrilling as it gets while airborne. First, there's the 25-minute plane ride to altitude in a Cessna 182, then the exhilaration of the first step into sky, the sensation of sailing weightless in the air over Kauai, and finally the peaceful buoyancy beneath the canopy of your parachute. A tandem free-fall rates among the most unforgettable experiences of a lifetime. Wed that to the aerial view over Kauai and you've got a winning marriage that you can relive with an HD video memory. Tandem dive: $229. ⊠ *Salt Pond Beach Park, Port Allen Airport* ☎ *808/335–5859* ⊕ *skydivekauai.com.*

5

TENNIS

If you're interested in booking some court time on Kauai, there are public tennis courts in Waimea, Kekaha, Hanapepe, Koloa, Kalaheo, Puhi, Lihue, Wailua Homesteads, Wailua Houselots, and Kapaa New Park.

Many hotels and resorts have tennis courts on property; even if you're not staying there, you can still rent court time. Rates range from $10 to $15 per person per hour. On the South Shore, try the **Grand Hyatt Kauai** (☎ *808/742–1234*) and **Kiahuna Swim and Tennis Club** (☎ *808/742–9533*). On the North Shore try the **Hanalei Bay Resort** (☎ *808/826–6522 Ext. 8225*).

For specific directions or more information, call the **County of Kauai Parks and Recreation Office** (☎ *808/241–4463*). Many hotels and resorts have tennis courts on property; even if you're not staying there, you can still rent court time. Rates range from $10 to $15 per person per hour. On the South Side, try the **Grand Hyatt Kauai** (☎ *808/742–1234*) and **Kiahuna Swim and Tennis Club** (☎ *808/742–9533*). On the North Shore, try the **Princeville Racquet Club** (☎ *808/826–1230*).

ZIPLINE TOURS

The latest adventure on Kauai is "zipping," or "ziplining." Regardless of what you call it, chances are you'll scream like a rock star while trying it. Strap on a harness, clip onto a cable running from one side of a river or valley to the other, and zip across. The step off is the scariest part. ■ TIP➡ Pack knee-length shorts or pants, athletic shoes, and courage for this adventure.

Fodor'sChoice ★ **Just Live.** When Nichol Baier and Julie Lester started Just Live in 2003, their market was exclusively school-age children, but soon they added visitor tours. Experiential education through adventure is how they describe it. Whatever you call it, sailing 70 feet above the ground for 3½ hours will take your vacation to another level. This is the only

DID YOU KNOW

Most of Kauai's land is not accessible by road. You can explore the island's lush interior on a zipline tour.

treetop zipline in the state where your feet never touch ground once you're in the air: Seven zips and four canopy bridges make the Tree Top Tour ($120) their most popular one. For the heroic at heart, there's the Zipline Eco Adventure ($125), which includes three ziplines, two canopy bridges, a climbing wall, a 100-foot rappelling tower, and a "Monster Swing." If you're short on time—or courage—you can opt for the Wikiwiki Zipline Tour ($79), which includes three ziplines and two canopy bridges in under two hours. They still incorporate team building in the visitor tours, although their primary focus remains community programming. Enjoy knowing that money spent here serves Kauai's children. ⊠ *4 miles west of Lihue on Hwy. 50* ☎ *808/482–1295* ⊕ *www.zipkauai.com.*

★ **Outfitters Kauai.** This company added new zipline offerings in the summer of 2009. They still have a half-day, multisport adventure of ziplining, suspension bridge crossings, and aerial walkways with hiking in between. Their most popular tour (Zipline Trek Nui Loa) features a 1,800-foot tandem zip—that's right, you don't have to go it alone. Plus, a unique WaterZip cools things off if you work up a sweat. The price is $152. A shorter version of this adventure—the Zipline Trek Iki Mua—is available and runs $112. Outfitters Kauai also includes ziplining as part of its Kipu Safari tour *(⇨ see Kayaking in chapter 4).* ⊠ *2827-A Poipu Rd., Poipu* ☎ *808/742–9667, 888/742–9887* ⊕ *www. outfitterskauai.com.*

Princeville Ranch Adventures. The North Shore's answer to ziplining is a nine-zipline course with a bit of hiking, and suspension bridge crossing thrown in for a half-day adventure. The 4½-hour Zip N' Dip tour includes lunch and swimming at a waterfall pool, while the Zip Express whizzes you through the entire course in three hours. Both excursions conclude with a 1,200-foot tandem zip across a valley. Guides are energetic and fun and can offer good dining and nightlife recommendations. This is as close as it gets to flying; just watch out for the albatross. Prices start at $125 for the Zip Express and $145 for the Zip N' Dip. ⊠ *West of Princeville Airport on Rte. 56, between mile markers 27 and 28, Princeville* ☎ *808/826–7669, 888/955–7669* ⊕ *www.adventureskauai.com.*

6

Shops and Spas

WORD OF MOUTH

"Find out where you can get a lomilomi massage. OMG—I thought I'd died and gone to heaven."

—PamSF

Join, Ask, Share. www.fodors.com/community/

Updated by
Lois Ann Ell

There aren't a lot of shops and spas on Kauai, but what you will find here are a handful of places very much worth checking out for the quality of their selection of items sold and services rendered. Many shops now make an effort to sell as many locally made products as possible. When buying an item, ask where it was made or even who made it.

Often you will find that a product handcrafted on the island may not be that much more expensive than a similar product made overseas. You can also look for the purple "Kauai Made" sticker many merchants display.

Along with one major shopping mall, a few shopping centers, and a growing number of big-box retailers, Kauai has some delightful mom-and-pop shops and specialty boutiques with lots of character. The Garden Isle also has a large and talented community of artisans and fine artists, with galleries all around the island showcasing their creations. You can find many island-made arts and crafts in the small shops, and it's worthwhile to stop in at crafts fairs and outdoor markets to look for bargains and mingle with island residents.

If you're looking for a special memento of your trip that is unique to Kauai County, check out the distinctive Niihau shell lei. The tiny shells are collected from beaches on Kauai and Niihau, pierced, and strung into beautiful necklaces, chokers, and earrings. It's a time-consuming and exacting craft, and these items are much in demand, so don't be taken aback by the high price tags. Those made by Niihau residents will have certificates of authenticity and are worth collecting. You often can find cheaper versions made by non-Hawaiians at crafts fairs.

Kauai is often touted as the healing island, and local spas try hard to fill that role. With the exception of the Hyatt's ANARA Spa, the facilities aren't as posh as some might want, but it's in the human element that Kauai excels. Island residents are known for their warmth, kindness, and humility, and you can find all these attributes in the massage therapists and technicians who work long hours at the resort spas. These professionals take their therapeutic mission seriously; they genuinely want you to experience the island's relaxing, restorative qualities. Private massage services abound on the island, and your spa therapist may offer the same services at a much lower price outside the resort, but if you're looking for a variety of health-and-beauty treatments, an exercise workout, or a full day of pampering, a spa will prove most convenient.

SHOPS

Stores are typically open daily from 9 or 10 am to 5 pm, although some stay open until 9 pm, especially those near resorts. Don't be surprised if the posted hours don't match the actual hours of operation at the smaller shops, where owners may be fairly casual about keeping to a regular schedule.

THE NORTH SHORE

The North Shore has three main shopping areas, all in towns off the highway. Hanalei has two shopping centers directly across from each other, which offer more than you would expect in a remote, relaxed town. Princeville Shopping Center is a bustling little mix of businesses, necessities, and some unique shops, often pricey. Kilauea is a bit more sprawled out and offers a charming, laid-back shopping scene with a neighborhood feel.

SHOPPING CENTERS

Ching Young Village. This popular shopping center looks a bit worn, but that doesn't deter business. Hanalei's only grocery store is here along with a number of other shops useful to locals and visitors, such as a Hawaiian music outlet, jewelry stores, art galleries, a surf shop and several restaurants. ⊠ *5-5190 Kuhio Hwy., makai after mile marker 2, Hanalei* ☎ *808/826-7222* ⊕ *www.chingyoungvillage.com.*

Hanalei Center. Once an old Hanalei schoolhouse, the Hanalei Center is now a bevy of boutiques and restaurants. You can dig through '40s and '50s vintage memorabilia, find Polynesian artifacts or search for that unusual gift. Buy beach gear as well as island wear and women's clothing. Find a range of fine jewelry and paper art jewelry. There is a full service salon and a yoga studio in the two-story modern addition to the center, which also houses a well-stocked health food store. ⊠ *5-5161 Kuhio Hwy., mauka after mile marker 2, Hanalei* ☎ *808/826-7677.*

Princeville Shopping Center. The big draws at this small center are a full-service grocery store and a hardware store, but there's also a wine market, a yoga studio, a sandal boutique, a comic-book store, and an ice-cream shop. This is also the last stop for gas and banking on the North Shore. ⊠ *5-4280 Kuhio Hwy., makai after mile marker 28, Princeville* ☎ *808/826-9497.*

GIFTS

Kong Lung Co. Sometimes called the Gump's of Kauai, this gift store sells elegant clothing, exotic glassware, ethnic books, gifts, and artwork—all very lovely and expensive. The shop is housed in a beautiful 1892 stone building right in the heart of Kilauea. It's the showpiece of the pretty little Kong Lung Center, where everything from handmade soaps to hammocks to excellent pizza can be found. Next door is the Kilauea Town Market & Deli, a good place to buy natural and gourmet foods, wines, and sandwiches. ⊠ *2484 Keneke St., Kilauea* ☎ *808/828–1822.*

Village Variety Store. How about a fun beach towel for the folks back home? That's just one of the gifts you can find here, along with shell lei, Kauai shirts, macadamia nuts, and other souvenirs at low prices. The store also has many small, useful items such as envelopes, housewares, and toiletries. ⊠ *Ching Young Village, Kuhio Hwy., Hanalei* ☎ *808/826–6077.*

JEWELRY

Crystal & Gems Gallery. Sparkling crystals of every shape, size, type, and color are sold in this small, amply stocked boutique. The knowledgeable staff can help you choose crystals for specific healing purposes. ⊠ *4489 Aku Rd., Hanalei* ☎ *808/826–9304* ⊕ *www.crystals-gems.com.*

THE EAST SIDE

KAPAA AND WAILUA

Kapaa is the most heavily populated area on Kauai, so it's not surprising that it has the most diverse shopping opportunities on the island. Unlike the North Shore's retail scene, shops here are not neatly situated in centers; they are spread out along a long stretch of road, with many local retail gems tucked away that you may not find if you're in a rush.

SHOPPING CENTERS

Kauai Village Shopping Center. The buildings of this Kapaa shopping village are in the style of a 19th-century plantation town. **ABC Discount Store** sells sundries; **Safeway** carries groceries and alcoholic beverages; **Longs Drugs** has a pharmacy, health and beauty products, and a good selection of Hawaiian merchandise; **Papaya's** has health foods and an excellent cafe. There's also a **Vitamin World** and a **UPS store**. Other shops sell jewelry, art, and home decor. Check out the **Children of the Land Cultural Center,** which holds workshops, classes, and other events. Restaurants include Chinese, vegetarian, and Vietnamese options, and there's also a **Starbucks.** ⊠ *4-831 Kuhio Hwy., Kapaa* ☎ *808/822–3777.*

Kinipopo Shopping Village. Kinipopo is a tiny little center on Kuhio Highway. **Korean Barbeque** fronts the highway, as does **Goldsmith's Kauai Gallery,** which sells handcrafted Hawaiian-style gold jewelry. **Monaco's** has authentic Mexican food, and **Cakes by Kristin** is a new pastry shop specializing in cakes. There's also a clothing shop, an art gallery, and a café open for breakfast and lunch called **Tutu's Soup Hale.** ⊠ *4-356 Kuhio Hwy., Kapaa.*

Waipouli Town Center. Foodland is the focus of this small retail plaza, one of three shopping centers anchored by grocery stores in Kapaa. You can also find a **McDonald's, Fun Factory** video arcade, a clothing shop called **Kauai Kraze,** and **The Coffee Bean,** along with a local-style restaurant. ⊠ *4-901 Kuhio Hwy., Kapaa.*

CLOTHING

★ **Bambulei.** Two 1930s-style plantation homes have been transformed into a boutique featuring vintage and contemporary clothing, antiques, jewelry, and accessories. You'll also find rare Hawaiian collectibles and furniture here. ⊠ *4-369 Kuhio Hwy., Wailua* ☎ *808/823–8641* ⊕ *www. bambulei.com.*

Deja Vu Surf Outlet. This mom-and-pop operation has a great assortment of surfwear and clothes for outdoor fanatics, including tank tops, visors, swimwear, and Kauai-style T-shirts. They also carry body boards and water sports accessories. Good deals can be found at sidewalk sales. ⊠ *4-1419 Kuhio Hwy., Kapaa* ☎ *808/822–4401.*

Divine Planet. This friendly, hip boutique sells unusual merchandise from India and other exotic Asian locales. Dangly earrings, loose, natural clothing, beads, campy home furnishings, and other eclectic offerings make this fun shop worth a stop. If you miss it here, you can check out the Hanalei location. ⊠ *4-1351 Kuhio Hwy., Kapaa* ☎ *808/821–1835* ⊠ *Ching Young Village, 5–1590 Kuhio Hwy., Hanalei* ☎ *808/826–8970.*

Marta's Boat. This charming boutique sells handmade, one-of-a-kind clothing by husband-and-wife team Ambrose and Marta Curry. He creates silk-screen art with nontoxic paint on fabric in his studio next door; then she cuts and sews the fabric into bags and clothing for men, women, and children. ⊠ *4-770 Kuhio Hwy., Kapaa* ☎ *808/822–3926* ⊕ *www.martasboat.com.*

GALLERIES

ALOHA Images. ALOHA in this gallery's title stands for "Affordable Location of Original Hawaiian Art." A self-proclaimed "candy store for art lovers," it has a large selection of Hawaiian-theme art, ranging from $75 up to the rare $15,000, and owner Ray offers layaway plans to those who request one. ⊠ *4–1383 Kuhio Hwy., Kapaa* ☎ *808/ 821–1382.*

Kela's Glass Gallery. The colorful vases, bowls, and other fragile items sold in this distinctive gallery are definitely worth viewing at Kela's Glass Gallery if you appreciate quality handmade glass art. It's expensive, but if something catches your eye, they'll happily pack it for safe transport home. They also ship worldwide. ⊠ *4-1354 Kuhio Hwy., Kapaa* ☎ *808/822–4527* ⊕ *www.glass-art.com.*

GIFTS

Pagoda. The new sister store of the iconic Bambulei, Pagoda is a tiny shop big on exceptional antiques, Hawaiiana, and gifts. The owner, Liane, has been collecting rare finds most of her life and now has a place to showcase them. ⊠ *4-369 Kuhio Hwy, Kapaa* ☎ *808/821–2172* ⊕ *www.pagodastore.com.*

Vicky's Fabric Shop. This small store is packed full of tropical and Hawaiian prints, silks, slinky rayons, soft cottons, and other fine fabrics. A variety of sewing patterns and notions are featured as well at Vicky's Fabric Shop, making it a must-stop for any seamstress. If you're seeking something that's truly one-of-a-kind, check out the selection of purses,

6

aloha wear, and other quality hand-sewn items. ⊠ *4-1326 Kuhio Hwy., Kapaa* ☎ *808/822–1746.*

HOME DECOR

Otsuka's Furniture & Appliances. Family-owned Otsuka's Furniture and Appliances has a large clientele of visitors, who appreciate the wide selection of unique furniture, artwork, candles, tropical-print pillows, accessories, and knickknacks that can be found here. ⊠ *4-1624 Kuhio Hwy., Kapaa* ☎ *808/822–7766* ⊕ *www.otsukas.com.*

JEWELRY

Jim Saylor Jewelers. Jim Saylor has been designing beautiful keepsakes for over 30 years on Kauai. Gems from around the world, including black pearls, diamonds and more, appear in his unusual settings. ⊠ *1318 Kuhio Hwy., Kapaa* ☎ *808/822–3591.*

Kauai Gold & Kauai Pearl. A wonderful selection of rare Niihau shell lei at Kauai Gold & Kauai Pearl ranges in price from $20 to $200. To appreciate the craftsmanship, understand the sometimes-high prices, and learn to care for and preserve these remarkable necklaces, ask how they are made. The store, which has been in business since 1985, also sells a selection of 14-karat gold jewelry and Tahitian black pearls. ⊠ *Coconut Marketplace, 4-484 Kuhio Hwy., Kapaa* ☎ *808/822–9361.*

MARKET

Kauai Products Fair. Open daily, the Kauai Products Fair outdoor market features fresh produce, tropical plants and flowers, a red dirt shirt shop, a coffee shop, aloha wear, jewelry and gifts. ⊠ *Outside on north side of Kapaa, across from Otsuka's Furniture* ☎ *808/246–0988.*

LIHUE

Lihue is the business area on Kauai, as well as home to all the big-box stores and the only real mall. Do not mistake this town as lacking in rare finds, however. Lihue is steeped in history and diversity while simultaneously welcoming new trends and establishments.

SHOPPING CENTERS

Kilohana Plantation. This 16,000-square-foot Tudor mansion contains art galleries, a jewelry store, and the farm-to-table restaurant 22 North. Kilohana Plantation is filled with antiques from its original owner and the restored outbuildings house a craft shop and a Hawaiian-style clothing shop. Train rides on a restored railroad are available, with knowledgeable guides reciting the history of sugar on Kauai. The site is also now the home of Luau Kalamaku and Koloa Rum Company. ⊠ *3-2087 Kaumualii Hwy., 1 mile west of Lihue* ☎ *808/245–5608* ⊕ *www.kilohanakauai.com.*

Kukui Grove Center. This is Kauai's only true mall. Besides **Sears Roebuck** and **Kmart,** anchor tenants are **Longs Drugs, Macy's,** and **Times Supermarket.** The mall's stores offer women's clothing, surf wear, art, toys, athletic shoes, jewelry, a hair salon, and locally made crafts. Restaurants range from fast food and sandwiches to Mexican and Korean. The center stage often has entertainment, and there is a farmers' market on Mondays and "Toddler Thursdays" offers entertainment for young children. ✉ *3-2600 Kaumualii Hwy., west of Lihue* ☎ *808/245–7784* ⊕ *www.kukuigrovecenter.com.*

CLOTHING

Hilo Hattie, The Store of Hawaii, Fashion Factory. This is the big name in aloha wear for tourists throughout the Islands, and Hilo Hattie, The Store of Hawaii, Fashion Factory only has a store on Kauai, located a mile from Lihue Airport. Come here for cool, comfortable aloha shirts and muumuu in bright floral prints, as well as other souvenirs. Also, be sure to check out the line of Hawaii-inspired home furnishings. ✉ *3252 Kuhio Hwy.* ☎ *808/245–3404* ⊕ *www.hilohattie.com.*

GIFTS

Fodor's Choice ★ **Kapaia Stitchery.** Hawaiian quilts made by hand and machine, a beautiful selection of fabrics, quilting kits, and fabric arts fill Kapaia Stitchery, a cute little red plantation-style building. There are also many locally made gifts for sale. The staff is friendly and helpful, even though a steady stream of customers keeps them busy. ✉ *3-3551 Kuhio Hwy., ½ mile north of Lihue* ☎ *808/245–2281.*

★ **Kauai Museum.** The gift shop at the museum sells some fascinating books, maps, and prints, as well as lovely feather lei hatbands, Niihau shell jewelry, handwoven *lau hala* hats, and koa wood bowls. Also featured at the Kauai Museum are tapa cloth, authentic *tikis* (hand-carved wooden figurines), as well as other good-quality local crafts at reasonable prices. ✉ *4428 Rice St.* ☎ *808/246–2470.*

HOME DECOR

Two Frogs Hugging. At Two Frogs Hugging, you'll find lots of interesting housewares, accessories, knickknacks, and hand-carved collectibles, as well as baskets and furniture from Indonesia, the Philippines, and China. ✉ *3215 Kuhio Hwy.* ☎ *808/246–8777* ⊕ *www.twofrogshugging.com.*

FOOD SPECIALTIES

Kauai Fruit and Flower Company. At this shop near Lihue and five minutes away from the airport, you can buy fresh Hawaii-grown sugarloaf pineapple, sugarcane, ginger, tropical flowers, coconuts, local jams, jellies, and honey, plus papayas, bananas, and mangoes from Kauai. All the fruit at Kauai Fruit and Flower Company has been inspected and approved to ship out of state. ✉ *3-4684 Kuhio Hwy., Kapaa* ☎ *808/245–1814.*

MARKETS

Kauai Community Market. This is no regular farmers' market. Join the locals at the Community College in Lihue on Saturdays, and you'll find fresh produce and flowers, as well as packaged products like breads, goat cheese, pasta, honey, coffee, soaps, lotions and more, all made locally. Seating areas are available to grab a snack or lunch from the food booths and lunch wagons set up there. ✉ *3-1901 Kaumualii Hwy.* ☎ *808/337–9944* ⊙ *Saturday 9:30–1.*

6

THE SOUTH SHORE

The South Shore, like the North Shore, has convenient shopping clusters, including Poipu Shopping Village and the new Kukuiula Shopping Village. There are many high-priced shops but some unique clothing and gift selections.

SHOPPING CENTERS

The Shops at Kukuiula. This is the South Shore's newest shopping center, with chic, high-end shops, exclusive galleries, restaurants, and cafés. Check out the Kauai Culinary Market on Wednesday from 4 to 6, to see cooking demonstrations, listen to live Hawaiian music, visit the beer and wine garden, and browse wares from local vendors. This attractive open-air, plantation-style center is just beyond the roundabout as you enter Poipu. ⊠ *2829 Kalanikaumaka, Poipu* ☎ *808/742–0234* ⊕ *www. shops@kukuiula.com* ⌚ *Daily 10–9.*

Poipu Shopping Village. Convenient to nearby hotels and condos on the South Shore, the two-dozen shops at Poipu Shopping Village sell resort wear, gifts, souvenirs, and art. This complex also has great food choices, from hot dog stands to excellent restaurants. There are a few upscale and appealing jewelry stores and fun clothing stores. A Tahitian dance troupe performs in the open-air courtyard Tuesday and Thursday at 5 pm. ⊠ *2360 Kiahuna Plantation Dr., Poipu Beach* ☎ *808/742–2831.*

GALLERIES

Fodor's Choice ★   **Galerie 103.** This gallery sells art, but the owners want you to experience it as well. Sparse and dramatic, the main room at Galerie 103 consists of concrete floors and walls of featured pieces, from internationally acclaimed artists and local Kauai ones. Most of the artwork is contemporary or modern with a focus on environmental issues. ⊠ *2829 Ala Kalanikaumaka, Kohala* ☎ *808/742–0103* ⊕ *www.galerie103.com* ⌚ *Tuesday through Saturday 12–8.*

Halele'a Gallery. In addition to offering original Hawaiian artwork, this stylish gallery doubles as a boutique that sells a unique sampling of clothing, jewelry, and gifts made by local designers. ⊠ *2829 Kalanikaumaka Rd, Suite K, Poipu, Koloa* ☎ *808/742–9525* ⊕ *www. haleleagallery.com.*

WEST SIDE

The West Side is years behind the South Shore in development, offering charming, simple shops with authentic local flavor.

SHOPPING CENTERS

Eleele Shopping Center. Kauai's West Side has a scattering of stores, including those at this no-frills strip-mall, Eleele Shopping Center. It's a good place to rub elbows with local folk at **Big Save** grocery store or to grab a quick bite to eat at the casual **Grinds Cafe** or **Tois Thai Kitchen.** ⊠ *Rte. 50 near Hanapepe, Eleele.*

Waimea Canyon Plaza. As Kekaha's retail hub and the last stop for supplies before heading up to Waimea Canyon, Waimea Canyon Plaza is a tiny, tidy complex of shops that is surprisingly busy. Look for local

Continued on page 170

ALL ABOUT LEI

Lei brighten every occasion in Hawaii, from birthdays to bar mitzvahs to baptisms. Creative artisans weave nature's bounty—flowers, ferns, vines, and seeds—into gorgeous creations that convey an array of heartfelt messages: "Welcome," "Congratulations," "Good luck," "Farewell," "Thank you," "I love you." When it's difficult to find the right words, a lei expresses exactly the right sentiment.

WHERE TO BUY THE BEST LEI

Some nice lei on Kauai can be found—believe it or not—in the major chain stores, including **Foodland** (✉ 5-4290 Kuhiu Hwy., Princeville ☎ 808/862–7513), in the Princeville Shopping Center, and **Safeway** (✉ 4-831 Kuhiu Hwy., Poipu Beach), in the Kauai Village Shopping Center. Also fabulous lei can be found at the various roadside vendors you'll see as you drive around the island.

LEI ETIQUETTE

■ To wear a closed lei, drape it over your shoulders, half in front and half in back. Open lei are worn around the neck, with the ends draped over the front in equal lengths.

■ Pikake, ginger, and other sweet, delicate blossoms are "feminine" lei. Men opt for cigar, crown flower, and ti leaf, which are sturdier and don't emit as much fragrance.

■ Lei are always presented with a kiss, a custom that supposedly dates back to World War II when a hula dancer fancied an officer at a U.S.O. show. Taking a dare from members of her troupe, she took off her lei, placed it around his neck, and kissed him on the cheek.

■ You shouldn't wear a lei before you give it to someone else. Hawaiians believe the lei absorbs your *mana* (spirit); if you give your lei away, you'll be giving away part of your essence.

ORCHID

Growing wild on every continent except Antarctica, orchids—which range in color from yellow to green to purple—comprise the largest family of plants in the world. There are more than 20,000 species of orchids, but only three are native to Hawaii—and they are very rare. The pretty lavender vanda you see hanging by the dozens at local lei stands has probably been imported from Thailand.

MAILE

Maile, an endemic twining vine with a heady aroma, is sacred to Laka, goddess of the hula. In ancient times, dancers wore maile and decorated hula altars with it to honor Laka. Today, "open" maile lei usually are given to men. Instead of ribbon, interwoven lengths of maile are used at dedications of new businesses. The maile is untied, never snipped, for doing so would symbolically "cut" the company's success.

ILIMA

Designated by Hawaii's Territorial Legislature in 1923 as the official flower of the island of Oahu, the golden ilima is so delicate it lasts for just a day. Five to seven hundred blossoms are needed to make one garland. Queen Emma, wife of King Kamehameha IV, preferred ilima over all other lei, which may have led to the incorrect belief that they were reserved only for royalty.

PLUMERIA

This ubiquitous flower is named after Charles Plumier, the noted French botanist who discovered it in Central America in the late 1600s. Plumeria ranks among the most popular lei in Hawaii because it's fragrant, hardy, plentiful, inexpensive, and requires very little care. Although yellow is the most common color, you'll also find plumeria lei in shades of pink, red, orange, and "rainbow" blends.

PIKAKE

Favored for its fragile beauty and sweet scent, pikake was introduced from India. In lieu of pearls, many brides in Hawaii adorn themselves with long, multiple strands of white pikake. Princess Kaiulani enjoyed showing guests her beloved pikake and peacocks at Ainahau, her Waikiki home. Interestingly, pikake is the Hawaiian word for both the bird and the blossom.

KUKUI

The kukui (candlenut) is Hawaii's state tree. Early Hawaiians strung kukui nuts (which are quite oily) together and burned them for light; mixed burned nuts with oil to make an indelible dye; and mashed roasted nuts to consume as a laxative. Kukui nut lei may not have been made until after Western contact, when the Hawaiians saw black beads from Europe and wanted to imitate them.

foods, souvenirs, and island-made gifts for all ages. ⊠ *Kokee Rd. at Rte. 50, Kekaha.*

BOOKS

Talk Story Bookstore. Located in a historic building in quiet Hanapepe town, this cozy bookstore becomes the gathering place on busy Friday evenings during the weekly art nights. Local authors sign their books inside while outside there's live music and food trucks for treats. Mostly used books are sold here, and at this writing after the closing of Borders Books in Lihue, it is the only official bookstore on Kauai. ⊠ *3785 Hanapepe Rd., Hanapepe* ☏ *808/335–6469* ⊕ *www. talkstorybookstore.com.*

CLOTHING

Paradise Sportswear. This is the retail outlet of the folks who invented Kauai's popular "red dirt" shirts, which are dyed and printed with the characteristic local soil. Ask the salesperson at Paradise Sportswear to tell you the charming story behind these shirts. Sizes from infants up to 5X are available. ⊠ *4350 Waialo Rd., Port Allen* ☏ *808/335–5670.*

FLOWERS

Kauai Tropicals. You can have Kauai Tropicals ship heliconia, anthuriums, ginger, and other tropicals in 5-foot-long boxes directly from its flower farm in Kalaheo. ⊠ *Kalaheo* ☏ *800/303–4385.*

FOOD SPECIALTIES

Kauai Coffee Visitor Center and Museum. Kauai produces more coffee than any other island in the state. The local product can be purchased from grocery stores or here at the Kauai Coffee Visitor Center and Museum, where a sampling of the nearly one-dozen coffees is available. Be sure to try some of the estate-roasted varieties. ⊠ *870 Halawili Rd., Kalaheo* ✛ *Off Rte. 50, west of Kalaheo* ☏ *808/335–0813, 800/545–8605* ⊕ *www.kauaicoffee.com.*

SPAS

Though most spas on Kauai are associated with resorts, none are restricted to guests only. And there's much by way of healing and wellness to be found on Kauai beyond the traditional spa—or even the day spa. More and more retreat facilities are offering what some would call alternative healing therapies. Others would say there's nothing alternative about them; you can decide for yourself.

Alexander Day Spa & Salon at the Kauai Marriott. This sister spa of Alexander Simson's Beverly Hills spa focuses on body care rather than exercise, so don't expect any fitness equipment or exercise classes. The Alexander Day Spa & Salon at the Kauai Marriott has the same ambience of stilted formality as the rest of the resort, but it is otherwise a sunny, pleasant facility. Massages are available in treatment rooms and on the beach, although the beach locale isn't as private as you might imagine. Wedding-day and custom spa packages can be arranged. ⊠ *Kauai Marriott Resort & Beach Club, 3610 Rice St., Suite 9A, Lihue* ☏ *808/246–4918* ⊕ *www.alexanderspa.com* ☞ *$65–$190*

massage. Facilities: Hair salon, steam room. Services: Body treat-
ments—including masks, scrubs, and wraps—facials, hair styling,
makeup, manicures, massages, pedicures, waxing.

Fodor's Choice
★

ANARA Spa. The luxurious ANARA Spa has all the equipment and services you expect from a top resort spa, along with a pleasant, professional staff. Best of all, it has indoor and outdoor areas that capitalize
on the tropical locale and balmy weather, further distinguishing it from
the Marriott and St. Regis spas. Its 46,500 square feet of space includes
the new Garden Treatment Village, an open-air courtyard with private
thatched-roof huts, each featuring a relaxation area, misters, and open-
air shower in a tropical setting. Ancient Hawaiian remedies and local
ingredients are featured in many of the treatments, such as a Lokahi
Garden facial, and a Hawaiian Herbal Aromatherapy body wrap. The
open-air lava-rock showers are wonderful, introducing many guests to
the delightful island practice of showering outdoors. The spa, which
includes a full-service salon, adjoins the Hyatt's legendary swimming
pool. ⊠ *Hyatt Regency Kauai Resort and Spa, 1571 Poipu Rd., Poipu*
☎ *808/240–6440* ⊕ *www.anaraspa.com* ☞ *Massages start at $160.*
Facilities: Hair salon, outdoor hot tubs, sauna, steam room. Gym with:
Cardiovascular machines, free weights, weight-training equipment. Ser-
vices: Body scrubs and wraps, facials, manicures, massage, pedicures.
Classes and programs: Aerobics, aquaerobics, body sculpting, fitness
analysis, flexibility training, personal training, Pilates, step aerobics,
weight training, yoga.

Angeline's Muolaulani Wellness Center. It doesn't get more authentic than
this. In the mid-1980s Aunty Angeline Locey opened her Anahola home
to offer traditional Hawaiian healing practices. Now her son and grand-
daughter carry on the tradition. At Angeline's Muolaulani Wellness
Center, there's a two-hour treatment ($150) that starts with a steam,
followed by a sea-salt-and-clay body scrub and a two-person massage.
The real treat, however, is relaxing on Aunty's open-air garden deck.
Hot-stone lomilomi is also available. Aunty's mission is to promote a
healthy body image; as such, au naturel is the accepted way here, so if
you're nudity-shy, this may not be the place for you. On second thought,
Aunty would say it most definitely is; *Muolaulani* translates to "a place
for young buds to bloom." ⊠ *Anahola, directions provided upon reser-*
vation ☎ *808/822–3235* ⊕ *www.angelineslomikauai.com* ☞ *Facilities:*
Steam room. Services: Body scrubs and massage.

Golden Lotus Studio. This small studio, tucked off the main road in
Kapaa, offers a variety of yoga and dance classes daily, including Kauai
Power Yoga with Jessica Krull. Various types of massage are available
by appointment, including lomilomi, Ayurveda, deep tissue, and Thai
style. Check their website for special events and workshops, offered
frequently. ⊠ *4-941a Kuhio Hwy., Kapaa* ☎ *808/823–9810* ⊕ *www.*
goldenlotuskauai.org.

Fodor's Choice
★

Halelea Spa. This superb spa at The St. Regis Princeville Resort is indeed
a House of Joy, as its Hawaiian name translates. Opened in 2009, the
11,000-square-foot Halelea Spa transports users to a place of utter
tranquillity. The spa's 12 luxurious treatment rooms afford a subdued

ANARA Spa

Halelea Spa

KAUAI: THE HEALING ISLAND

If you look at a globe, you'll notice that, yes, Hawaii is in the middle of the ocean, and then you'll realize that it's also a connecting point between East and West. Over the centuries, as people have migrated, the islands have become a melting pot not only of cultures but of healing practices as well. You'll find healing modalities from around the world on Kauai. Some practitioners have offices; many work out of their homes. ■TIP→ Virtually all will require a reservation—no walk-ins—except in yoga studios. Here is a sampling of the healing arts offered on Kauai. You can also visit ⊕ www.kauaihealing.org and ⊕ www.kauaihwa.org.

Pilates Kauai. A full studio offering private and semiprivate lessons in a secluded setting is what you can expect at Pilates Kauai. ⊠ Kilauea ☎ 808/639–3074 ⊕ www.pilateskauai.com.

Yoga Hanalei. There are a wide variety of daily classes at Yoga Hanalei, given at the Hanalei Center. ⊠ 5-5161 Kuhio Hwy, Hanalei ☎ 808/826–9642 ⊕ www.yogahanalei.com.

6

indoor setting only outmatched by the professional service. Take advantage of the dedicated couples' room and enjoy a taro butter *pohaku* (hot-stone) massage. Follow that with a few hours sipping tea in the relaxation lounge, sweating in the sauna, and rinsing in an overhead rain shower. There is a qualified wellness consultant and spa programs are inspired by native Hawaiian healing rituals. You can find health, beauty, and inner peace at this spa, but expect to pay for it. ⊠ *The St. Regis Princeville Resort, 5520 Ka Haku Rd., Princeville* ☎ *877/787–3447, 808/826–9644* ⊕ *www.stregisprinceville.com* ☞ *Massage $170–$245. Services: Body scrubs and wraps, facials, massage, waxing.*

Hanalei Day Spa. As you travel beyond tony Princeville, life slows down. The single-lane bridges may be one reason. Another is the Hanalei Day Spa, an open-air, thatched-roof, Hawaiian-style hut nestled just off the beach on the grounds of Hanalei Colony Resort in Haena. Though this no-frills day spa offers facials, waxing, wraps, scrubs, and the like, its specialty is massage: Ayurveda, Zen Shiatsu, Swedish, and even a baby massage (and lesson for Mom, to boot). Owner Darci Frankel teaches yoga, a discipline she started as a young child. That practice led her to start the Ayurveda Center of Hawaii, which operates out of the spa and offers an ancient Indian cleansing and rejuvenation program known as Pancha Karma. Think multiday wellness retreat. ⊠ *Hanalei Colony Resort, Rte. 560, 6 miles past Hanalei, Haena* ☎ *808/826–6621* ⊕ *www.hanaleidayspa.com* ☞ *Massage $95–$210. Services: Body scrubs and wraps, facials, massage, waxing. Classes and programs: Yoga.*

★ **A Hideaway Spa.** This is the only full-service day spa on the laid-back West Side. A Hideaway Spa is in one of the restored plantation cottages that make up the guest quarters at Waimea Plantation Cottages, creating a cozy and comfortable setting you won't find elsewhere. The overall feel is relaxed, casual, and friendly, as you'd expect in this quiet country town. The staff is informal, yet thoroughly professional. Beach yoga and massages are available, as well as a full-service salon with hair, nails, and makeup services. Try the kava kava ginger wrap followed by the lomi *iliili*—hot-stone massage. ⊠ *Waimea Plantation Cottages, 9400 Kaumualii Hwy., Cottage No. 30, Waimea* ☎ *808/338–0005* ⊕ *www.ahideawayspa.com* ☞ *Massage $50–$170. Facilities: Outdoor hot tub, steam room. Services: Acupuncture, body scrubs and wraps, facials, hydrotherapy, massage. Classes and programs: Yoga.*

Tri Health Ayurveda Spa. The goal at the Tri Health Ayurveda Spa isn't a one-time massage for momentary bliss, although relaxation is a key ingredient. Rather, this spa's focus is a multiweek, multitreatment, intensive program designed to eliminate toxins stored in the body and increase the flow and energy of all systems. Treatments are designed around the ancient Ayurvedic tradition of heat to open the pores, oil to deliver nutrients to tissues and nerve endings, and massage (by two therapists working in synchronized movement) to accelerate circulation. Note: Because the massage strokes are long and can run the length of the body, there is no draping involved. Ayurvedic doctors, food, and treatments are available, as is lodging in the 10-bedroom retreat facility, on 25 acres hidden by design for privacy—hence, no glaring signs. Single sessions are available. ⊠ *Kilauea* ☎ *808/828–2104* ⊕ *www.trihealthayurvedaspa.com* ☞ *Massage $130–$275. Facilities: Steam room. Services: Herbal body scrubs, massage.*

The Yoga House. If you want authentic Bikram yoga, this is the place to find it. It's owned by sisters Aimee and McKell, who teach classes in this bright, clean studio twice daily. Other yoga classes are offered here too, as well as massage and a weekly acupuncture clinic. ⊠ *4-885 Kuhio Hwy., Kapaa* ☎ *808/823–9642* ⊕ *www.bikramyogakapaa.com.*

TRY A LOMI MASSAGE

Living in ancient Hawaii wasn't all sunbathing and lounging at the beach. Growing taro was hard work, you know. So, too, were building canoes, fishing for dinner, and pounding tapa for clothing, sails, and blankets. Enter *lomilomi*—Hawaiian-style massage. It's often described as being more vigorous, more rhythmical, and faster than Swedish massage, and it incorporates more elbow and forearm work. It might even involve chanting, music, and four hands (in other words, two people).

Entertainment and Nightlife

WORD OF MOUTH

"Nice place to go for drinks and see a hula show is the Terrace at the Grand Hyatt. Liked to do that with early dinner afterward at Tidepools (never been to Dondero's but it looked nice) and after-dinner drink at Stevenson Library there."

—Jamie99

Updated by
David Simon

Kauai has never been known for its nightlife. It's a rural island, where folks tend to retire early, and the streets are dark and deserted well before midnight. The island does have its nightspots, though, and the after-dark entertainment scene may not be expanding, but it is consistently present in areas frequented by tourists.

Most of the island's dinner and luau shows are held at hotels and resorts. Hotel lounges are a good source of live music, often with no cover charge, as are a few bars and restaurants around the island.

Check the local newspaper, the *Garden Island,* as well as its own Kauai Times entertainment guide, for listings of weekly happenings, or tune in to community radio station KKCR—found at 90.9, 91.9, or 92.7 on the FM dial, depending on where on the island you are at that moment— at 5:30 pm for the arts and entertainment calendar. Free publications such as *Kauai Gold, This Week on Kauai,* and *Essential Kauai* also list entertainment events. You can pick them up at Lihue Airport near the baggage claim area, as well as at numerous retail areas on the island.

ENTERTAINMENT

Although luau remain a primary source of evening fun for families on vacation, there are a handful of other possibilities. There are no traditional dinner cruises, but some boat tours do offer an evening buffet with music along Napali Coast. A few times a year, Women in Theater (WIT), a local women's theater group, performs dinner shows at the Hukilau Lanai in Wailua. You can always count on a performance of *South Pacific* at the Kauai Beach Resort, and the Kauai Community College Performing Arts Center draws well-known artists.

Kauai Community College Performing Arts Center. This is a main venue for island entertainment, hosting a concert music series, visiting musicians, dramatic productions, and special events such as the International Film Festival. ⊠ *3-1901 Kaumualii Hwy., Lihue* ☎ *808/245–8352* ⊕ *kauai. hawaii.edu/pac.*

DINNER SHOW

South Pacific Dinner Show. It seems a fitting tribute to see the play that put Kauai on the map. Rodgers and Hammerstein's original *South Pacific* has been playing at the Kauai Beach Resort to rave reviews since 2002. The full musical production, accompanied by a buffet dinner, features local talent. ⊠ *Jasmine Ballroom, Kauai Beach Resort, 4331 Kauai Beach Dr., Lihue* ☎ *808/346–6500* ⊕ *www.southpacifickauai.com* ✉ *$85* ⊙ *Wed., doors open at 5:30 pm, show at 6:45.*

FESTIVAL

☾ **Bon Festival.** Traditional Japanese celebrations in honor of loved ones who have died are held from late June through August at various Buddhist temples all over the island. It sounds somber, but it's really a community festival of dance. To top it off, you're welcome to participate. Dance, eat, play carnival games, and hear Japanese *taiko* drumming by Kauai youth at one of the Bon folk dances, which take place on temple lawns every Friday and Saturday night from dusk to midnight. Some dancers wear the traditional kimono; others wear board shorts and a tank top. The moves are easy to follow, the event is lively and wholesome, and it's free. A different temple hosts a dance each weekend. Watch the local paper for that week's locale.

LUAU

Although the commercial luau experience is a far cry from the backyard luau thrown by local residents to celebrate a wedding, graduation, or baby's first birthday, they're nonetheless entertaining and a good introduction to the Hawaiian food that isn't widely sold in restaurants. Besides the feast, there's often an exciting dinner show with Polynesian-style music and dancing. It all makes for a fun evening that's suitable for couples, families, and groups, and the informal setting is conducive to meeting other people. Every luau is different, reflecting the cuisine and tenor of the host facility, so compare prices, menus, and entertainment before making your reservation. Most luau on Kauai are offered only on a limited number of nights each week, so plan ahead to get the luau you want. We tend to prefer those *not* held on resort properties, because they feel a bit more authentic. *The luau shows listed below are our favorites.*

Grand Hyatt Kauai Luau. What used to be called Drums of Paradise has a new name and a new dance troupe but still offers a traditional luau buffet and an exceptional performance. This oceanfront luau comes with a view of the majestic Keoneloa Bay. ⊠ *Grand Hyatt Kauai Resort and Spa, 1571 Poipu Rd., Poipu* ☎ *808/240–6456* ⊕ *www.hyatt.com/ gallery/kauailuau* ✉ *$94* ⊙ *Thurs. and Sun., doors open at 5 pm, show begins at 6.*

★ **Luau Kalamaku.** Set on historic sugar-plantation land, this new luau bills itself as the only "theatrical" luau on Kauai. The luau feast is served buffet-style, there's an open bar, and the performers aim to both entertain and educate about Hawaiian culture. Guests sit at tables around a circular stage; tables farther from the stage are elevated, providing unobstructed views. Additional packages offer visitors the opportunity to tour the 35-acre plantation via train or special romantic perks

7

Hula is hot in Hawaii, and on Kauai the top places to see it include Smith's Tropical Paradise, Luau Kalamaku, and Poipu Shopping Village.

like a lei greeting and champagne. ✉ *3-2087 Kaumualii St., Lihue* ☎ *877/622–1780* ⊕ *www.luaukalamaku.com* 🖵 *$99* ⏱ *Tues. and Fri. check-in begins at 5, dinner at 6:30, show at 7:30.*

Fodor'sChoice
★ **Smith's Tropical Paradise Luau.** A 30-acre tropical garden provides the lovely setting for this popular luau, which begins with the traditional blowing of the conch shell and *imu* (pig roast) ceremony, followed by cocktails, an island feast, and an international show in the amphitheater overlooking a torch-lighted lagoon. It's fairly authentic and a better deal than the pricier resort events. ✉ *174 Wailua Rd., Kapaa* ☎ *808/821–6895* 🖵 *$88* ⏱ *Sept.–May, Mon., Wed., and Fri. 5–9:15; June–Aug., weekdays 5–9:15.*

MUSIC

Check the local paper for outdoor reggae and Hawaiian-music shows.

Hanalei Slack Key Concerts. Relax to the instrumental music form created by Hawaiian *paniolo* (cowboys) in the early 1800s. Shows are at Hale Halawai Ohana O Hanalei, which is *mauka* down a dirt access road across from St. William's Catholic Church (Malolo Road) and then left down another dirt road. Look for a thatched-roof *hale* (house), several little green plantation-style buildings, and the brown double-yurt community center around the gravel parking lot. There is also a weekly Saturday show in Kapaa town.

Kapaa Slack Key Concerts ✉ *The Children of the Land (in the Safeway shopping center), 4-831 Kuhio Hwy, #332, Kapaa* ☎ *808/821–1234* ⏱ *Sat. at 5 pm.* ✉ *Hanalei Family Community Center, 5-5299 Kuhio*

Hwy., Hanalei ☎*808/826–1469* ⊕ *www.hawaiianslackkeyguitar. com* ⊒ *$20* ⊘ *Fri. at 4, Sun. at 3.*

Kauai Concert Association. This group offers a seasonal program at the Kauai Community College Performing Arts Center. A range of big-name artists, from Ricky Lee Jones to Taj Mahal, have been known to show up on Kauai for planned or impromptu performances. ⊠ *3-1901 Kaumualii Hwy., Lihue* ☎ *808/245–7464* ⊕ *www.kauai-concert.org.*

THEATER

Kauai Community Players. This talented local group presents plays throughout the year. ⊠ *4411 Kikowaena Street, behind Harley Davidson shop, across from Kauai Community College, Lihue* ☎ *808/245–7700* ⊕ *www.kauaicommunityplayers.org.*

WORD OF MOUTH

"We enjoyed Smith's family on Kauai. This was on our first visit to Hawaii. Not sure I would go again, but I wouldn't miss it once. It's family-run; you are greeted by multiple generations of family. There is a little golf-cart-type tour of their grounds, very pretty. The imu ceremony is really interesting. I was pleasantly surprised by the food, and enjoyed the dancing/performances, too. I think kids would like it: fire, knife dancing, etc." —rncheryl

NIGHTLIFE

For every new venue that opens on Kauai, another one closes. Perhaps it's simply the result of the island's ubiquitous but little-known epidemic: paradise paralysis. Symptoms include a slight fragrance of coconut wafting from the pores, pink cheeks and nose, a relaxed gait, and a slight smile curving on the lips. Let's face it: Kauai lulls people into a stupor that puts them to bed before 10 pm. But if you are one of those immune to the disease, Kauai may have a place or two for you to while away your spare hours.

BARS AND CLUBS

Nightclubs that stay open until the wee hours are rare on Kauai, and the bar scene is limited. The major resorts generally host their own live entertainment and happy hours. All bars and clubs that serve alcohol must close at 2 am, except those with a cabaret license, which allows them to close at 4 am. For information on events or specials, check out the nightlife section of the *Kauai Times* (⊕ *kauaitimes.net*).

THE NORTH SHORE

Hanalei Gourmet. The sleepy North Shore stays awake—until 10:30, that is—each evening in this small, convivial setting inside Hanalei's restored old school building. The emphasis here is on local live Hawaiian, jazz, rock, and folk music. ⊠ *5-5161 Kuhio Hwy., Hanalei Center, Hanalei* ☎ *808/826–2524* ⊕ *www.hanaleigourmet.com.*

★ **St. Regis Bar.** This spacious lounge overlooking Hanalei Bay offers drinks daily from 3:30 to 11. Stop by between 5:30 and 10 for *pupu*

Continued on page 184

7

HULA: MORE THAN A FOLK DANCE

Hula has been called "the heartbeat of the Hawaiian people" and also "the world's best-known, most misunderstood dance." Both are true. Hula isn't just dance. It is storytelling.

Chanter Edith McKinzie calls it "an extension of a piece of poetry." In its adornments, implements, and customs, hula integrates every important Hawaiian cultural practice: poetry, history, genealogy, craft, plant cultivation, martial arts, religion, protocol. So when 19th century Christian missionaries sought to eradicate a practice they considered depraved, they threatened more than just a folk dance.

With public performance outlawed and private hula practice discouraged, hula went underground for a generation, to rural villages. The fragile verbal link by which culture was transmitted from teacher to student hung by a thread. Even increasing literacy did not help because hula's practitioners were a secretive and protected circle.

As if that weren't bad enough, vaudeville, Broadway, and Hollywood got hold of the hula, giving it the glitz treatment in an unbroken line from "Oh, How She Could Wicky Wacky Woo" to "Rock-A-Hula Baby." Hula became shorthand for paradise: fragrant flowers, lazy hours. Ironically, this development assured that hundreds of Hawaiians could make a living performing and teaching hula. Many danced *auana* (modern form) in performance; but taught *kahiko* (traditional), quietly, at home or in hula schools.

Today, 30 years after the cultural revival known as the Hawaiian Renaissance, language immersion programs have assured a new generation of proficient—and even eloquent—chanters, songwriters, and translators. Visitors can see more, and more authentic, traditional hula than at any other time in the last 200 years.

Like the culture of which it is the beating heart, hula has survived.

Lei *poo*. Head lei. In kahiko, greenery only. In auana, flowers.

Face emotes appropriate expression. Dancer should not be a smiling automaton.

Shoulders remain relaxed and still, never hunched, even with arms raised. No bouncing.

Eyes always follow leading hand.

Lei. Hula is rarely performed without a shoulder lei.

Arms and hands remain loose, relaxed, below shoulder level—except as required by interpretive movements.

Traditional hula skirt is loose fabric, smocked and gathered at the waist.

Hip is canted over weight-bearing foot.

Knees are always slightly bent, accentuating hip sway.

Kupee. Ankle bracelet of flowers, shells, or—traditionally—noise-making dog teeth.

In kahiko, feet are flat. In auana, they may be more arched, but not tiptoes or bouncing.

BASIC MOTIONS

Speak or Sing

Moon or Sun

Grass Shack or House

Mountains or Heights

Love or Caress

At backyard parties, hula is performed in bare feet and street clothes, but in performance, adornments play a key role, as do rhythm-keeping implements.

In hula *kahiko* (traditional style), the usual dress is multiple layers of stiff fabric (often with a pellom lining, which most closely resembles *kapa*, the paperlike bark cloth of the Hawaiians). These wrap tightly around the bosom but flare below the waist to form a skirt. In pre-contact times, dancers wore only kapa skirts. Men traditionally wear loincloths.

Monarchy-period hula is performed in voluminous muumuu or high-necked muslin blouses and gathered skirts. Men wear white or gingham shirts and black pants.

In hula *auana* (modern), dress for women can range from grass skirts and strapless tops to contemporary tea-length dresses. Men generally wear aloha shirts, but sometimes grass skirts over pants or even everyday gear.

SURPRISING HULA FACTS

■ Grass skirts are not traditional; workers from Kiribati (the Gilbert Islands) brought this custom to Hawaii.

■ In olden-day Hawaii, *mele* (songs) for hula were composed for every occasion—name songs for babies, dirges for funerals, welcome songs for visitors, celebrations of favorite pursuits.

■ Hula *mai* is a traditional hula form in praise of a noble's genitals; the power of the *alii* (royalty) to procreate gave *mana* (spiritual power) to the entire culture.

■ Hula students in old Hawaii adhered to high standards: scrupulous cleanliness, no sex, daily cleansing rituals, certain food prohibitions, and no contact with the dead. They were fined if they broke the rules.

WHERE TO WATCH

■ Coconut Marketplace, ⊠ 4-484 Kuhio Hwy., Kapaa, ⏱ Sat. 1 PM.

■ Poipu Shopping Village, ⊠ 2360 Kiahuna Plantation Dr., Poipu Beach, ☎ 808/742–7444 ⏱ Tues. and Thurs. 5 pm.

■ Smith's Tropical Paradise, ⊠ 174 Wailua Rd., Kapaa, ☎ 808/821–6895, ⏱ Mon., Wed., and Fri. 5–9:15. Dinner included.

■ Festivals: There are many festivals on the island year-round where you can see hula performed. For more information visit *www.kauaifestivals.com*.

Kauai: Undercover Movie Star

Though Kauai has played itself in the movies, most recently starring in *The Descendants* (2011), most of its screen time has been as a stunt double for a number of tropical paradises. The island's remote valleys portrayed Venezuelan jungle in Kevin Costner's *Dragonfly* (2002) and a Costa Rican dinosaur preserve in Steven Spielberg's *Jurassic Park* (1993). Spielberg was no stranger to Kauai, having filmed Harrison Ford's escape via seaplane from Menehune Fishpond in *Raiders of the Lost Ark* (1981).

The fluted cliffs and gorges of Kauai's rugged Napali Coast play the misunderstood beast's island home in *King Kong* (1976), and a jungle dweller of another sort, in *George of the Jungle* (1997), frolicked on Kauai. Harrison Ford returned to the island for 10 weeks during the filming of *Six Days, Seven Nights* (1998), a romantic adventure set in French Polynesia. Part-time Kauai resident Ben Stiller used the island as a stand-in for the jungles of Vietnam in *Tropic Thunder* (2008) and Johnny Depp came here to film some of *Pirates of the Caribbean: On Stranger Tides* (2011). But these are all relatively contemporary movies. What's truly remarkable is that Hollywood discovered Kauai in 1933 with the making of *White Heat*, which was set on a sugar plantation and—like another more memorable movie filmed on Kauai—dealt with interracial love stories.

Then, it was off to the races, as Kauai saw no fewer than a dozen movies filmed on island in the 1950s, not all of them Oscar contenders. Rita Hayworth starred in *Miss Sadie Thompson* (1953) and no one you'd recognize starred in the tantalizing *She Gods of Shark Reef* (1956).

The movie that is still immortalized on the island in the names of restaurants, real estate offices, a hotel, and even a sushi item is *South Pacific* (1957). (You guessed it, right?) That mythical place called Bali Hai is never far away on Kauai.

In the 1960s Elvis Presley filmed *Blue Hawaii* (1961) and *Girls! Girls! Girls!* (1962) on the island. A local movie tour likes to point out the stain on a hotel carpet where Elvis's jelly doughnut fell.

Kauai has welcomed a long list of Hollywood's A-List: John Wayne in *Donovan's Reef* (1963); Jack Lemmon in *The Wackiest Ship in the Army* (1961); Richard Chamberlain in *The Thorn Birds* (1983); Gene Hackman in *Uncommon Valor* (1983); Danny DeVito and Billy Crystal in *Throw Momma from the Train* (1987); and Dustin Hoffman, Morgan Freeman, Renee Russo, and Cuba Gooding Jr. in *Outbreak* (1995).

Yet the movie scene isn't the only screen on which Kauai has starred. A long list of TV shows, TV pilots, and made-for-TV movies make the list as well, including *Gilligan's Island, Fantasy Island, Starsky & Hutch, Baywatch Hawaii*—even reality TV shows *The Bachelor* and *The Amazing Race 3*.

For the record, just because a movie did some filming here doesn't mean the entire movie was filmed on Kauai. *Honeymoon in Vegas* filmed just one scene here, while the murder mystery *A Perfect Getaway* (2009) was set on the famous Kalalau Trail and featured beautiful Kauaian backdrops but was shot mostly in Puerto Rico.

(hors d'oeuvres), acoustic guitar or piano music, and an ocean view. ⊠ *Princeville Resort, 5520 Ka Haku Rd., Princeville* ☎ *808/826–9644.*

Tahiti Nui. This venerable and decidedly funky institution in sleepy Hanalei no longer offers its famous luau, ever since owner and founder Auntie Louise Marston died. But spirits are always high at this popular hangout for locals and visitors alike, which houses live nightly entertainment, including Hawaiian music earlier in the evening and rock and roll starting around 9. Patrons can show off their own pipes during Monday karaoke festivities. For a more intimate setting, don't miss the new wine bar, Tahiti Iti, located right next door. ⊠ *5-5134 Kuhio Hwy., Hanalei* ☎ *808/826–6277* ⊕ *www.thenui.com.*

THE EAST SIDE

Duke's Barefoot Bar. This is one of the liveliest bars in Nawiliwili. Contemporary Hawaiian music is usually performed at this beachside bar every day during "Aloha Hours" from 4 to 6 pm. Thursday, Friday and Saturday nights also feature more music from 8:30 to 10:30. ⊠ *3610 Rice St., Kalapaki Beach, Lihue* ☎ *808/246–9599* ⊕ *www.dukeskauai.com.*

Hukilau Lanai. This open-air bar and restaurant is on the property of the Kauai Coast Resort but operates independently. Trade winds trickle through the modest little bar, which looks out into a coconut grove. If the mood takes you, go on a short walk to the sea, or recline in big, comfortable chairs while listening to mellow jazz or Hawaiian slack-key guitar. Live music plays every night, though the bar is closed on Mondays. Poolside happy hour runs from 3 to 5. Freshly infused tropical martinis—perhaps locally grown lychee and pineapple or a Big Island vanilla bean infusion—are house favorites. ⊠ *520 Aleka Loop Kuhio Hwy., Wailua* ☎ *808/822–0600* ⊕ *www.hukilaukauai.com.*

Rob's Good Times Grill. Let loose at this popular sports bar, which features DJs spinning Friday and Saturday from 10 pm to 2 am with the occasional live band. Tuesday offers swing dancing, while Wednesday you can kick up your heels with country line dancing from 8 to 10 pm. Karaoke follows both, while Sunday and Monday are full-on karaoke all night. ⊠ *4303 Rice St., Lihue* ☎ *808/246–0311* ⊕ *www.kauaisportsbarandgrill.com.*

Trees Lounge. Behind the hokey Coconut Marketplace and next to the Kauai Coast Resort in Kapaa, you'll find Trees Lounge. For a while, this chic wood-filled bar and restaurant hosted good live music but didn't allow any dancing, to the chagrin of its patrons. Now with the proper liquor licenses in hand, Trees will let you move much more than just some solo toe tapping as live bands, singer-songwriters and open-mikers all take the stage. Closed Sundays. ⊠ *440 Aleka Pl., Kapaa* ☎ *808/823–0600* ⊕ *www.treesloungekauai.com.*

THE SOUTH SHORE

Keoki's Paradise. A young, energetic crowd makes this a lively spot on Friday and Saturday nights. There's live music every night, usually for two hours between 6 pm and 9 pm. When the dining room clears out, there's a bit of a bar scene for singles. The bar closes at 10:30 pm. ⊠ *Poipu Shopping Village, 2360 Kiahuna Plantation Dr., Poipu* ☎ *808/742–7534* ⊕ *www.keokisparadise.com.*

7

Lavas at Sheraton Kauai. This is *the* place to be on the South Shore to celebrate sunset with a drink; the ocean view is unsurpassed. There is live music every night from 9 until closing at 11. The lineup isn't set in stone, so call before you arrive to see who's playing that night. ⊠ *Sheraton Kauai Resort, 2440 Hoonani Rd., Poipu* ☎ *808/742–1661* ⊕ *www. sheraton-kauai.com/dining.*

THE WEST SIDE

The Grove Cafe. Formerly the Waimea Brewing Company, this location allows you to sip on some locally brewed beers in an airy plantation-style house on the grounds of Waimea Plantation Cottages. Outdoor seating and a wraparound lanai make this eatery a worthwhile West Side experience. Expect slow service and mediocre fare. There is usually live music Wednesday through Friday, or grab a growler to go, take a stroll out back to the beach, and enjoy views of Niihau while the sun sets. ⊠ *9400 Kaumualii Hwy., Waimea* ☎ *808/338–1625.*

COFFEEHOUSES

The island has a few coffeehouses where you can keep the night's entertainment going by taking in some live music in a quiet setting.

Fodor's Choice
★
Caffé Coco. Nestled in a bamboo forest draped in bougainvillea and flowering vines and hidden from view off the Kuhio Highway is a charming little venue where local musicians perform nightly. Caffé Coco offers pupu (appetizers), entrées, and desserts. It may not have a liquor license, but don't let that stop you from enjoying the local talent; just bring your own wine or beer. The outdoor setting—twinkle lights and tiki torches beneath a thatched hut—is what the Kauai of old must have been like. There's hula every Friday, and Hawaiian music on Thursdays. It's open until 9 Tuesday through Sunday. ⊠ *4-369 Kuhio Hwy., Wailua* ☎ *808/822–7990.*

Where to Eat

WORD OF MOUTH

"On our first night with family, we always like to have a casual dinner in the tropical open-air setting at Keoki's. We really feel we've arrived in paradise . . . When just the two of us arrive, my husband and I enjoy pupus and drinks or dinner surrounded by orchids in the quieter Plantation Gardens in Kiahuna complex."

—jojo46

Updated by
Charles E.
Roessler

On Kauai, if you're lucky enough to win an invitation to a potluck, baby luau, or beach party, don't think twice—just accept. The best grinds (food) are homemade, and so you'll eat until you're full, then rest, eat some more, and make a plate to take home, too.

But even if you can't score a spot at one of these parties, don't despair. Great local-style food is easy to come by at countless low-key places around the island. As an extra bonus, these eats are often inexpensive, and portions are generous. Expect plenty of meat—usually deep-fried or marinated in a teriyaki sauce and grilled *pulehu*-style (over an open fire)—and starches. Rice is standard, even for breakfast, and often served alongside potato-macaroni salad, another island specialty. Another local favorite is *poke*, made from chunks of raw tuna or octopus seasoned with sesame oil, soy sauce, onions, and pickled seaweed. It's a great *pupu* (appetizer) when paired with a cold beer.

Kauai's cultural diversity is apparent in its restaurants, which offer authentic Chinese, Korean, Japanese, Thai, Mexican, Italian, Vietnamese, and Hawaiian specialties. Less specialized restaurants cater to the tourist crowd, serving standard American fare—burgers, pizza, sandwiches, surf-and-turf combos, and so on. Kapaa offers the best selection of restaurants, with options for a variety of tastes and budgets; most fast-food joints are in Lihue.

KAUAI DINING PLANNER

EATING-OUT STRATEGY

Where should we eat? With dozens of island eateries competing for your attention, it may seem like a daunting question. But our expert writers and editors have done most of the legwork—the dozens of selections here represent the best eating experience this island has to offer. Search "Best Bets" for top recommendations by price, cuisine, and experience. Or find a restaurant quickly—reviews are ordered alphabetically within their geographic area.

WITH KIDS

Hawaii is a kid-friendly destination in many regards, and that includes taking the little ones out to eat with you. Because of the overall relaxed vibe and casual dress here, you won't have to worry too much about your tot's table manners or togs—within reason, of course. Take advantage of treats and eating experiences unique to Hawaii, such as shave ice, sunshine markets (perfect for picnic lunches or beach provisions), and luau.

RESERVATIONS

It's always a good idea to make reservations when you can, and if you plan to dine at one of Kauai's top eateries, reservations are essential. However, you'll find that many places on the island don't take reservations at all, and service is first-come, first-served.

WHAT TO WEAR

Just about anything goes on Kauai. At lunch you can dine in your bathing suit, a sarong, or T-shirt and shorts, and flip-flops at most places. Dinner is only a slight step up. That said, if you're out for a special occasion and want to don your fanciest duds, no one will look twice.

SMOKING

Smoking is prohibited in all Hawaii restaurants and bars.

HOURS AND PRICES

Restaurants on Kauai significantly quiet down by 9 pm; the limited bar scene continues past midnight—but not much past. It seems as if the entire island is in bed before 10 pm to get up early the next day and play. In general, peak dining hours here tend to be on the earlier side, during sunset hours from 6 to 8 pm.

A tip of 18% to 20% is standard for good service.

WHAT IT COSTS			
$	$$	$$$	$$$$
under $17	$17–$26	$27–$35	over $35

AT DINNER

Restaurant prices are for a main course at dinner.

THE NORTH SHORE

Because of the North Shore's isolation, restaurants have enjoyed a captive audience of visitors who don't want to make the long, dark trek into Kapaa town for dinner. As a result, dining in this region has been characterized by expensive fare that isn't especially tasty, either. Fortunately, the situation is slowly improving as new restaurants open and others change hands or menus.

Still, dining on the North Shore can be pricier than other parts of the island, and not especially family-friendly. Most of the restaurants are found either in Hanalei town or the Princeville resorts. Consequently, you'll encounter delightful mountain and ocean views, but just one restaurant with oceanfront dining.

BEST BETS FOR KAUAI DINING

Where can I find the best food the island has to offer? Fodor's writers and editors have selected their favorite restaurants by price, cuisine, and experience in the lists below. In the first column, the Fodor's Choice properties represent the "best of the best" across price categories. You can also search by area for excellent eats—just peruse our complete reviews on the following pages.

Fodor'sChoice★

Bar Acuda, $$$$,
p. 191
Beach House, $$$,
p. 203
Dondero's, $$, p. 204
Hukilau Lanai, $$,
p. 196
Restaurant Kintaro,
$$, p. 197

By Price

$

Dani's Restaurant,
p. 200
Eggbert's, p. 196
Hamura Saimin,
p. 201
Hanamaulu Restaurant, p. 202
Joe's on the Green,
p. 209
Kilauea Fish Market,
p. 191
Lihue Barbecue Inn,
p. 203

Mema Thai Chinese
Cuisine, p. 197
Mermaid's Café,
p. 197
Papaya's, p. 197
Toi's Thai Kitchen,
p. 214
Verde, p. 198

$$

Dondero's, p. 204
Hukilau Lanai, p. 196
Kalaheo Café & Coffee Co., p. 209
Kauai Pasta, p. 196
Plantation Gardens,
p. 211
Poipu Tropical Burgers, p. 211
Scotty's Beachside
BBQ, p. 197
Wrangler's Steakhouse, p. 214

$$$

Beach House, p. 203
Pomodoro Ristorante
Italiano, p. 212

Roy's Poipu Bar &
Grill, p. 212
Tidepools, p. 212

$$$$

Bar Acuda, p. 191

By Cuisine

HAWAIIAN

Dani's Restaurant, $,
p. 200
Hamura Saimin, $,
p. 201
Hanamaulu Restaurant, $, p. 202

PLATE LUNCH

Dani's Restaurant, $,
p. 200
Kilauea Fish Market,
$, p. 191
Hanamaulu Restaurant $, p. 202
Keoki's Paradise, $$,
p. 211
Restaurant Kintaro,
$$, p. 197

By Experience

BEST VIEW

Beach House, $$$,
p. 203
Brennecke's Beach
Broiler, $$$, p. 204
Bull Shed, $$, p. 195
Café Portofino, $$,
p. 200

MOST KID-FRIENDLY

Eggbert's, $, p. 196
Keoki's Paradise, $$,
p. 211
Kilauea Bakery and
Pau Hana Pizza, $,
p. 191
Pizzetta, $, p. 211
Poipu Tropical Burgers, $$, p. 211

MOST ROMANTIC

Beach House, $$$,
p. 203
Café Portofino, $$,
p. 200
Dondero's, $$, p. 204

$$$$ MEDITERRANEAN Fodor's Choice ★ **Bar Acuda.** This tapas bar is a very welcome addition to the Hanalei dining scene, rocketing right near top place in the categories of tastiness, creativity, and pizzazz. Owner-chef Jim Moffat's brief menu changes regularly: You might find *banderillas* (grilled flank steak skewers with honey and chipotle chili oil), Gorgonzola endive salad, or Spanish chorizo with grilled apples. The food is consistently remarkable, but it's the subtly intense sauces that elevate the cuisine to outstanding. It's super casual, but chic, with a nice porch for outdoor dining. ✉ *Hanalei Center, 5-5161 Kuhio Hwy., Hanalei* ☎ *808/826–7081* 🌐 *www.restaurantbaracuda.com* ⏲ *Closed Mon.*

$$ AMERICAN **Hanalei Gourmet.** This spot in Hanalei's restored old schoolhouse offers dolphin-safe tuna, low-sodium meats, fresh-baked breads, and homemade desserts as well as a casual atmosphere where both families and the sports-watching crowds can feel equally comfortable. Early birds can order coffee and toast or a hearty breakfast. Lunch and dinner menus feature sandwiches, burgers, filling salads, and nightly specials of fresh local fish. They also will prepare a picnic and give it to you in an insulated backpack. A full bar and frequent live entertainment keep things hopping even after the kitchen closes. Thursday evenings fill up for fish taco night, which begins at 6. ✉ *5-5161 Kuhio Hwy., Hanalei* ☎ *808/826–2524* 🌐 *www.hanaleigourmet.com.*

$$$$ ECLECTIC **Kauai Grill.** Savor an artful meal created by world-renowned chef Jean-Gorges Vongerichten, surrounded by a dramatic Hanalei Bay scene. Located at the recently renovated St. Regis Princeville Resort, Kauai Grill has dark wood decor and an ornate red chandelier, the centerpiece of the room. The attention here is on the flavors of robust meat and local, fresh seafood. Most dishes are plainly grilled, accompanied by exotic sauces and condiments. The specials change frequently and use as many Hawaiian-grown ingredients as possible. Expect attentive service with the somewhat stiff feel of an exclusive hotel, and an expertly created meal. ✉ *St. Regis Princeville, 5520 Ka Haku Rd., Princeville* ☎ *808/826–9644* ⚠ *Reservations essential* ⏲ *No lunch. Closed Sun.–Mon.*

$ AMERICAN **Kilauea Bakery and Pau Hana Pizza.** This bakery has garnered tons of well-deserved good press for its starter of Hawaiian sourdough made with guava as well as its specialty pizzas topped with such yummy ingredients as smoked *ono* (a Hawaiian fish), Gorgonzola-rosemary sauce, barbecued chicken, goat cheese, and roasted onions. Open from 6:30 am, the bakery serves coffee drinks, delicious fresh pastries, bagels, and breads in the morning. Late risers beware: breads and pastries sell out quickly on weekends. Pizza, soup, and salads can be ordered for lunch or dinner. If you want to hang out or do the Wi-Fi coffee shop bit in Kilauea, this is the place. A cute courtyard with covered tables is a pleasant place to linger. ✉ *Kong Lung Center, 2484 Keneke St., Kilauea* ☎ *808/828–2020.*

$ SEAFOOD **Kilauea Fish Market.** If you're not in a hurry, this tiny restaurant serves up fresh fish in quality preparations, including tucked into hearty wraps and salads, stir-fried, and grilled with tasty sauces made from scratch. All fish and vegetables are locally purchased. The ahi wrap is the most popular selection, while the chicken plate lunch, with a choice of brown

8

Dining is a scenic affair at the St. Regis Princeville Resort, whose restaurants overlook Hanalei Bay and Mt. Makana.

or white rice, is the best deal for the budget conscious. After placing your order inside, you can eat outside at covered tables (bug alert) or take out. ⊠ *Kilauea Lighthouse Rd., Kilauea* ☎ *808/828–6244* ☾ *Closed Sun.*

$$$$ ✗ **Makana Terrace.** Enjoy dining while gazing at one of the most exqui-
MODERN   site snapshots of Hanalei Bay. There's no doubt it's pricey, but you're
HAWAIIAN paying for the view—sit on the terrace if you can—and for an attentive
staff. There is a focus on local, Hawaiian-grown foods here, including
the fish plate of a fresh Pacific catch, which is your best bet for lunch.
Feast at the extensive breakfast buffet for $34 per person from 6:30
to 11:00 am, but note that it's traditional fare: nothing spectacular or
exotic. For a special evening, splurge on the surf and turf (around $45)
and time your dinner around sunset for an unforgettable Hawaiian
vista. ⊠ *5520 Ka Haku Rd., Princeville* ☎ *808/826–9644.*

$$$ ✗ **Mediterranean Gourmet.** A trip to this romantic Middle Eastern oasis
MEDITERRANEAN pays off after a narrow, beach-hugging ride along the exquisite North
Shore coastline. Owner-chef Imad Beydoun, a native of Beirut, serves
multiple hummus appetizers, stuffed grape leaves, baba ghanoush,
crispy spinach and lamb *fatayers* alongside traditional favorites like
rib eyes and rosemary rack of lamb. The seafood tower is an impres-
sive presentation of shrimp, scallops and fresh fish resting on grilled
pineapple and mashed potatoes. Local fish including ahi, ono and
seasonal catches add Pacific Rim touches when combined with fresh
local produce. Belly-dancing performances and live music along with
Tuesday's luau (reservations suggested), add to the relaxed ambiance.
■ TIP→ Arrive early (around 6 pm) for prime seats and to enjoy the lovely

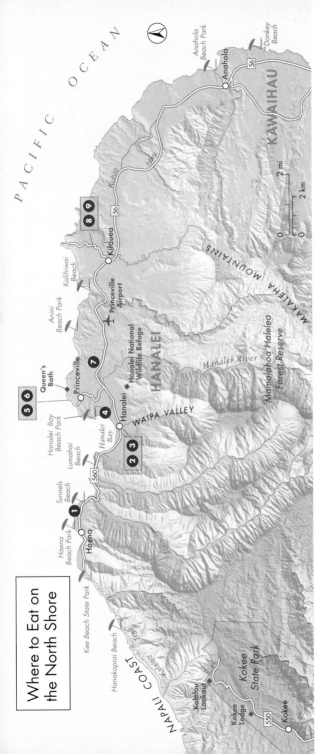

Where to Eat on the North Shore

Bar Acuda **3**
Hanalei Gourmet **2**
Kauai Grille **5**
Kilauea Bakery
and Pau Hana Pizza **9**
Kilauea Fish Market **8**

Makana Terrace **6**
Mediterranean Gourmet....**1**
Postcards Café **4**
The Tavern at Princeville ...**7**

8

BUDGET-FRIENDLY EATS: NORTH SHORE

It's not easy to find cheap food on the North Shore, but these little eateries serve up dinner for two for under $20.

Foodland. In a pinch, you can pick up pretty good sushi, ready-to-eat hot entrées, and panini sandwiches at the Foodland grocery store. ✉ *Princeville Shopping Center, 5–4280 Kuhio Hwy., Princeville* ☎ *808/826–9880.*

Hanalei Pizza. Excellent pizza (the pesto with whole-wheat crust is a winner), salads, and a few pasta dishes can be taken out or enjoyed at inside and outside tables at Ching Young Village. Strange as it may seem, pizza is pricey on Kauai. ✉ *5-5190 Kuhio Hwy., Hanalei* ☎ *808/826–9494.*

Neide's Salsa & Samba. This is one of the best low-cost eateries, with unusual and tasty Brazilian and Mexican food to take out or eat in a casual garden setting at the Hanalei Center. ✉ *5-5161 Kuhio Hwy., Hanalei* ☎ *808/826–1851.*

Harvest Market. Health foods, such as rice dishes, soups, and salads, are served in the back of this natural-foods store at the Hanalei Center; takeout only. ✉ *5-5161 Kuhio Hwy., Hanalei* ☎ *808/826–0089.*

Tropical Taco. This is a safe choice for a quick take-out meal of basic Mexican food. ✉ *5-5088 Kuhio Hwy., Hanalei* ☎ *808/827–8226* ⊕ *www.tropicaltaco.com.*

ocean views at day's end. ✉ *Hanalei Colony Resort, 5-7130 Kuhio Hwy., Haena* ☎ *808/826–9875* ⊕ *www.kauaimedgourmet.com* ☾ *Closed Sun.*

$$
AMERICAN
✕ **Postcards Café.** With its vintage photos of the North Shore, beamed ceilings, and light interiors, this plantation-cottage restaurant has a menu stressing seafood but also offering additive-free vegetarian and vegan options. But don't get the wrong idea—this isn't simple cooking: specials might include carrot-ginger soup, taro fritters, or fresh fish served with peppered pineapple-sage sauce, or blackened ahi. Desserts are made without refined sugar. Try the chocolate silk pie made with barley malt chocolate, pure vanilla, and creamy tofu with a gingery crust. This is probably your best bet for dinner in Hanalei town. ✉ *5-5075A Kuhio Hwy., Hanalei* ☎ *808/826–1191* ⊕ *www.postcardscafe.com* ☾ *No lunch.*

AMERICAN
✕ **The Tavern at Princeville.** Roy Yamaguchi's tasteful restaurant overlooking the beautiful Prince Golf Course offers a convivial, lively atmosphere to dine in. Though it lacks charm after the sun goes down, the food is high-quality, with specialties like parmesan-crusted ono, ahi poke spiked with a kukui nut base, an excellent onion soup gratin, plus steak, burger, and chicken choices. Kid- and small-group friendly, the Tavern lends itself to a casual come-and-go vibe. ✉ *5-3900 Kuhio Hwy, Princeville* ☎ *808/826-8700.*

THE EAST SIDE

Since the East Side is the island's largest population center, it makes sense that it should boast the widest selection of restaurants. It's also a good place to get both cheaper meals and the local-style cuisine that residents favor.

Most of the eateries are found along Kuhio Highway between Kapaa and Wailua; a few are tucked into shopping centers and resorts. In Lihue, it's easier to find lunch than dinner because many restaurants cater to the business crowd.

You'll find all the usual fast-food joints in both Kapaa and Lihue, as well as virtually every ethnic cuisine available on Kauai. Although fancy gourmet restaurants are less abundant in this part of the island, there's plenty of good, solid food, and a few stellar attractions. But unless you're staying on the East Side, or passing through, it's probably not worth the long drive from the North Shore or Poipu resorts to eat here.

WORD OF MOUTH

"Postcards Café in Hanalei. When you're on the North Shore, absolutely be sure to go here for dinner. They are open 6 to 9 pm and serve outstanding, mostly organic food. The preparations are unique and so, so delicious. If you get there around 6 you'll even see them cutting the herbs and lettuce from the garden. It's in a small, intimate house."
—MelissaMorgan

KAPAA AND WAILUA

In recent years, the most affordable, hip new eateries on the island have opened in Kapaa. Unlike the resort-dominated South and North shores, Kapaa is local, fun, and eclectic, with hamburger stands on the side of the road, vegetarian venues, and swanky bars serving up artful appetizers. Diversity is the key to this area; there is something for everyone, especially those on a budget.

$$ ✕ **Bull Shed.** The A-frame structure makes this popular restaurant look
STEAKHOUSE distinctly rustic from the outside. Inside, light-color walls and a full wall of glass highlight an ocean view that is one of the best on Kauai. Come early for a window seat and watch the surf crashing on the rocks while you study the menu. The food is simple and basic—think white bread and iceberg lettuce—but they know how to do surf and turf. You can try both in one of several combo dinner platters or order fresh island fish and thick steaks individually. The restaurant is best known for its prime rib and Australian rack of lamb. Longtime visitors and locals love this place, which hasn't changed much in 30 years. Arrive early for the best seats. ✉ *796 Kuhio Hwy., Kapaa* ☎ *808/822–3791, 808/822–1655* ⊕ *www.bullshedrestaurant.com* ⊗ *No lunch*.

$ ✕ **Caffé Coco.** A restored plantation cottage set back off the highway and
CAFÉ surrounded by tropical foliage is the setting for this island café. You'll know it by its bright blue storefront. An attached black-light art gallery and an apparel shop called Bambulei make this a fun stop for any meal. Outdoor seating in the vine-covered garden is pleasant during nice weather, although on calm nights, it can get buggy. Acoustic music is

8

offered regularly, attracting a laid-back local crowd. Pot stickers filled with tofu and chutney, ahi wraps, Greek and organic salads, fresh fish and soups, and a daily list of specials are complemented by wonderful desserts. Allow plenty of time, because the tiny kitchen can't turn out meals quickly. ⊠ *4-369 Kuhio Hwy., Wailua* ☎ *808/822–7990* ⊗ *Closed Mon.*

$
AMERICAN
☉

✕**Eggbert's.** If you're big on breakfasts, try Eggbert's, which serves breakfast items until 2 pm daily. This traditional favorite has moved to the north end of the Coconut Marketplace but still welcomes families. It's a great spot for omelets, banana pancakes, and eggs Benedict in two sizes. Lunch selections include sandwiches, burgers, a pork and cabbage plate, and fresh fish. Take-out orders are also available. And if you'd like a bloody mary with those pancakes, Eggbert's bar can oblige. ⊠ *Coconut Marketplace, 4-484 Kuhio Hwy., Kapaa* ☎ *808/822–4422.*

$$
AMERICAN
Fodor's Choice
★

✕**Hukilau Lanai.** Relying heavily on superfresh island fish and locally grown vegetables, this restaurant offers quality food that is competently and creatively prepared. The fish—grilled, steamed, or sautéed and served with succulent sauces—shines here. Other sound choices are the savory meat loaf and prime rib. Mac-nut-crusted chicken and a few pasta dishes round out the menu. The ahi nachos appetizer is not to be missed, nor is the warm chocolate dessert soufflé. The spacious dining room looks out to the ocean, and it's lovely to eat at the outdoor tables when the weather is nice. Overall, it's a solid choice on the East Side. ⊠ *Kauai Coast Resort, Coconut Marketplace, 520 Aleka Loop, Kapaa* ☎ *808/822–0600* ⊕ *www.hukilaukauai.com* ⊗ *No lunch. Closed Mon.*

$
ITALIAN

✕**Kauai Pasta.** If you don't mind a no-frills atmosphere for affordable food, this is the place. The husband of the husband-and-wife team that runs the restaurant left his executive-chef position at Roy's to open a catering business. He leased a kitchen that happened to have a small dining area and gradually upgraded and expanded it. Rather than let it go to waste, they open for dinner every evening. Their specials are satisfying and delicious, and their 10-inch pizzettas make a fine meal for one. The locals have this place figured out; they show up in droves. The chic KP Lounge stays open late, offering a handsome hideout for tasty nighttime grinds and cocktails. There's a branch in Lihue that also serves lunch. ⊠ *4-939B Kuhio Hwy., Kapaa* ☎ *808/822–7447* ⊕ *www.kauaipasta.com.*

$
AMERICAN
☉

✕**Kountry Kitchen.** If you're big on breakfast, try Kountry Kitchen, which serves breakfast and lunch items until 1:30 pm daily. Across the street from the library in Kapaa, this family-friendly restaurant has a sunny interior, and a cozy, greasy-spoon atmosphere with friendly service. It is a great spot for omelets, banana pancakes, and eggs Benedict in two sizes. Lunch selections include sandwiches, burgers, and *loco mocos* (a popular local rice, beef, gravy, and eggs concoction). Take-out orders are also available. ⊠ *1485 Kuhio Hwy., Kapaa* ☎ *808/822–3511* ⊗ *No dinner.*

$$ ✕ **Lemongrass Grill.** The inside of Kapaa's Lemongrass Grill may remind
ECLECTIC you of a Pacific Rim–theme rustic tavern, with its stained wood interior,
numerous paintings and carvings, and food that is as fresh as it can get.
There's something for everybody here: salads, poultry, steaks and ribs,
vegetarian fare, and, of course, a wide selection of seafood, all with an
island flair. Specials include a heaping seafood platter featuring lobster
tails, scallops, shrimp scampi, the fish of the day, and an assortment
of vegetables—they say it's "for two," but it could easily feed three
or four. Service is laid-back but friendly. ⊠ *4-885 Kuhio Hwy., Kapaa*
☎ *808/821–2888* ⊗ *No lunch.*

$ ✕ **Mema Thai Chinese Cuisine.** Refined and intimate, Mema Thai serves its
THAI dishes on crisp white linens accented by tabletop orchid sprays. Menu
items such as broccoli with oyster sauce and cashew chicken reveal
Chinese origins, but the emphasis is on Thai dishes. A host of curries—
red, green, yellow, and house—made with coconut milk and kaffir-lime
leaves—run from mild to mouth searing. The traditional green-papaya
salad adds a cool touch for the palate. ⊠ *Wailua Shopping Plaza, 369
Kuhio Hwy., Kapaa* ☎ *808/823–0899* ⊗ *No lunch weekends.*

$ ✕ **Mermaid's Café.** Sit and watch as your meal is prepared at this café
ECLECTIC in Kapaa. The small yet diverse menu of sophisticated dishes features
homemade sauces and local ingredients. Try the ahi nori wrap with
fresh seared tuna, rice, cucumber, and wasabi cream sauce with pickled
ginger and soy sauce—their most popular pick. Other dishes include
rice, fresh vegetables, and either tofu or chicken served with a peanut
sauce or coconut curry sauce. Everything can be made either vegetarian
or vegan. Fish is caught daily by local fisherman, and produce is grown
on the island. ⊠ *1384 Kuhio Hwy., Kapaa* ☎ *808/821–2026.*

$ ✕ **Papaya's.** Kauai's largest natural-foods market contains a buffet-style
VEGETARIAN café with good food at low prices. Food items change daily, but there's
always a hot and cold salad bar, and favorites like taro burgers for lunch
and dinner. Meals are made with fresh organic lettuce and vegetables,
most grown nearby. You can order takeout or eat at a covered table in
the courtyard. ⊠ *Kauai Village Shopping Center, 4-831 Kuhio Hwy.,
Kapaa* ☎ *808/823–0190* ⊕ *www.papayasnaturalfoods.com.*

$$ ✕ **Restaurant Kintaro.** If you want to eat someplace that's a favorite with
JAPANESE locals, visit Kintaro's. But be prepared to wait on weekends, because
Fodor's Choice the dining room and sushi bar are always busy. Try the unbeatable Bali
★ Hi Bomb, a roll of crab and smoked salmon, baked and topped with
wasabi mayonnaise. For an "all-in-one-dish" meal, consider the *Yosen-
abe,* a single pot filled with a healthful variety of seafood and vegetables.
Teppanyaki dinners are meat, seafood, and vegetables flash-cooked on
tabletop grills in an entertaining display. Tatami-mat seating is available behind shoji screens that provide privacy for groups. Like many
longtime restaurants, it's an enduring favorite. ⊠ *4-370 Kuhio Hwy.,
Wailua* ☎ *808/822–3341* ⊗ *No lunch. Closed Sun.*

$$ ✕ **Scotty's Beachside BBQ.** Ribs and other succulent smoked meats are the
AMERICAN stars at this casual upstairs restaurant that has a large, often noisy din-
ing room and lovely ocean view. While the BBQ is best here, the menu
also has shrimp, chicken, and burgers. You can choose your BBQ sauce
and two side dishes; the coleslaw and baked beans are noteworthy.

8

Some of the best eats on Kauai come from the sea. Ask what the local catch of the day is for the freshest option.

If you still have room for dessert, try the make-your-own s'mores. ✉ *4-1546 Kuhio Hwy., Kapaa* 🕿 *808/823–8480* ⊕ *www.scottysbbq. com* ⊗ *Closed Sun.*

$$
INDIAN
✕ **Shivalik Indian Cuisine.** This recently opened eatery provides a refreshing alternative to the typical fish and seafood offerings at most of Kauai's upscale restaurants. Boasting no particular Indian regional style, this small-plaza hideaway with a tandoor oven has delicious curried vegetables, chicken dishes, and naan. Their samosas are especially noteworthy. ▪TIP➜ The lunch buffet is a bargain at $14. ✉ *4-771 Kuhio Hwy, Kapaa* 🕿 *808/821-2333* ⊕ *www.shivalikindiancuisne.com.*

$
MEXICAN
✕ **Verde.** Combining classic Mexican food with chili-based sauces and creations from the chef's home state of New Mexico, Verde's menu includes tostadas, enchiladas, and tacos served with fresh fish or slow-cooked beef or chicken. The seared tuna tacos with red chili aioli and the stacked enchilada, with chicken or beef short ribs smothered in red or green chili sauce, are favorites. Beers and margaritas served with premium tequila complement the spicy sauces perfectly. Don't be misled by the location of this spot—a small space in a shopping complex. ✉ *4-1101 Kuhio Hwy., Kapaa* 🕿 *808/821–1400* ⊕ *www.verdehawaii.com.*

$$
SEAFOOD
✕ **Wailua Marina Restaurant.** Offering the island's only river view, this marina restaurant—an island fixture for almost 40 years—is a good spot to stop for lunch after a boat ride up the Wailua River to the Fern Grotto, and worth a visit on its own merit. With more than 40 selections, the menu is a mix of comfort food and more sophisticated dishes; portions are gigantic. The chef is fond of stuffing: You'll find stuffed baked pork chops, stuffed chicken baked in plum sauce, and ahi

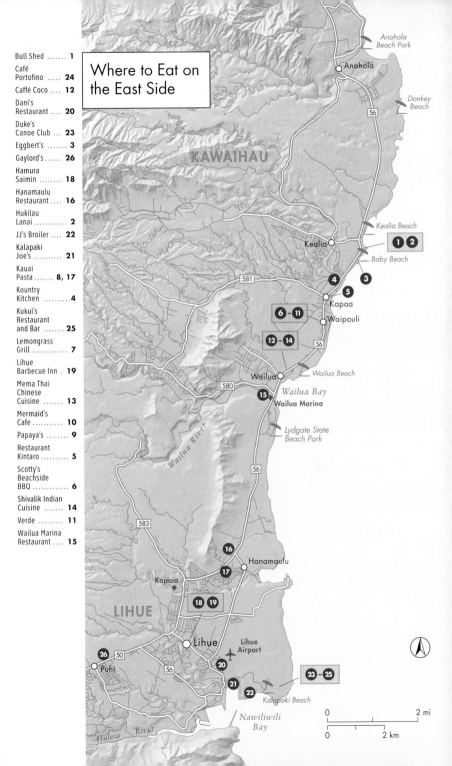

Where to Eat on the East Side

Bull Shed 1

Café
Portofino 24

Caffé Coco 12

Dani's
Restaurant 20

Duke's
Canoe Club ... 23

Eggbert's 3

Gaylord's 26

Hamura
Saimin 18

Hanamaulu
Restaurant 16

Hukilau
Lanai 2

JJ's Broiler 22

Kalapaki
Joe's 21

Kauai
Pasta 8, 17

Kountry
Kitchen 4

Kukui's
Restaurant
and Bar 25

Lemongrass
Grill 7

Lihue
Barbecue Inn . 19

Mema Thai
Chinese
Cuisine 13

Mermaid's
Cafe 10

Papaya's 9

Restaurant
Kintaro 5

Scotty's
Beachside
BBQ 6

Shivalik Indian
Cuisine 14

Verde 11

Wailua Marina
Restaurant 15

KAWAIHAU

Anahola
Beach Park

Anahola

Donkey
Beach

56

Kealia Beach

Kealia

Baby Beach

581

Kapaa

Waipouli

56

Wailua

Wailua Beach

580

Wailua Bay

Wailua Marina

Lydgate State
Beach Park

56

Wailua River

583

Hanamaulu

Kapaia

LIHUE

Lihue

Lihue
Airport

26

50

Puhi

56

Kalapaki Beach

Nawiliwili
Bay

Huleia River

0   2 mi

0   2 km

stuffed with crab. The steamed mullet is a classic island dish. ⊠ *Wailua River State Park, Wailua Rd., Wailua* ☏ *808/822–4311* ⊙ *Closed Mon.*

LIHUE

You will probably find yourself in Lihue at least a few times during your stay. When it comes to restaurants, Lihue is somewhat extreme. There are some remarkable (and expensive) restaurants and some great low-cost eateries that feed the business lunch crowd—but not much in between. If you are in town for lunch, don't pass up some of the authentic, local spots.

$$ ✕ **Café Portofino.** The menu at this
ITALIAN mostly authentic northern Italian restaurant is as impressive as the views of Kalapaki Bay and the Haupu range. Owner Giuseppe Avocadi's better-sounding-than-tasting dishes have managed to garner a host of culinary awards and raves from dining critics. The fresh ahi carpaccio is a signature dish, and pasta, scampi, and veal are enhanced by sauces. Linger over coffee and ice cream-filled profiteroles or traditional tiramisu while enjoying romantic harp music. Solid service and a soothing, dignified atmosphere complete the dining experience, making this a great place for a date if only the food was better and wine less overpriced. ⊠ *Kauai Marriott Resort & Beach Club, 3610 Rice St.* ☏ *808/245–2121* ⊕ *cafeportofino.com* ⊙ *No lunch.*

$ ✕ **Dani's Restaurant.** Kauai residents frequent this big, sparsely furnished
HAWAIIAN eatery near the Lihue Fire Station for a hearty, local-style breakfast and lunch. Dani's is a good place to try traditional luau cuisine without commercial luau prices. You can order Hawaiian-style *laulau* (pork and taro leaves wrapped in ti leaves and steamed) or kalua pig, slow roasted in an underground oven. Other island-style dishes include Japanese-prepared *tonkatsu* (pork cutlet) and teriyaki beef, and there's always the all-American New York steak. Omelets are whipped up with fish cake, kalua pig, or seafood; everything is served with rice. ⊠ *4201 Rice St.* ☏ *808/245–4991* ⊙ *Closed Sun. No dinner.*

$$ ✕ **Duke's Canoe Club.** Surfing legend Duke Kahanamoku is immortal-
SEAFOOD ized at this casual bi-level restaurant set on Kalapaki Bay. Guests can admire surfboards, photos, and other memorabilia marking the Duke's long tenure as a waterman. It's an interesting collection, and an indoor garden and waterfall add to the pleasing sights. You'll find simple fare ranging from fish tacos and stir-fried cashew chicken to hamburgers, served 11 am to 11 pm. At dinner, fresh fish prepared in a variety of styles is the best choice. Duke's claims to have the biggest salad bar on

BUDGET-FRIENDLY EATS: EAST SIDE

At these small, local-style eateries, two people can generally eat dinner for less than $20.

Garden Island BBQ and Chinese Restaurant ⊠ *4252-A Rice St., Lihue* ☏ *808/245-8868.*

Hamura Saimin ⊠ *2956 Kress St., Lihue* ☏ *808/245-3271.*

Korean BBQ ⊠ *4-356 Kuhio Hwy., Wailua* ☏ *808/823-6744.*

Waipouli Restaurant ⊠ *Waipouli Town Center, 4-771 Kuhio Hwy., Kapaa* ☏ *808/822-9311.*

SHAVE ICE

Nothing goes down quite as nicely as shave ice on a hot day. This favorite island treat has been likened to a sno-cone, but that description doesn't do a good shave ice justice. Yes, it is ice served up in a cone-shape cup and drenched with sweet syrup, but the similarities end there. As its name implies, the ice should be feathery, light—the texture of snowflakes, not frozen slush. And alongside the standard cherry and grape, you'll find all sorts of exotic island flavorings, such as passion fruit, pineapple, coconut, mango, and, of course, a rainbow mix.

Not all shave ice meets these high standards, and when you're hot, even the average ones taste great. But a few places are worth seeking out. On the East Side, the best is **Hawaiian Blizzard** (⊠ *Kapaa Shopping Center, 4-1105 Kuhio Hwy.*), a true shave ice stand that opens up midday in front of the Big Save grocery store in Kapaa. In Lihue, try **Halo Halo Shave Ice** (⊠ *2956 Kress St.*). And on the hot, dry West Side, make a beeline for **Jo-Jo's Clubhouse** (⊠ *Mile marker 23, Kaumualii, Hwy. 50*), on the main drag in Waimea. All three places have benches where you can sit and slurp.

the island, though given the lack of competition, that isn't saying much. A happy-hour drink and appetizer is a less expensive way to enjoy the moonrises and ocean views here—though it can get pretty crowded. The Barefoot Bar is a hot spot for after-dinner drinks, too. ⊠ *Kauai Marriott Resort & Beach Club, 3610 Rice St.* ☎ *808/246–9599* ⊕ *www.dukeskauai.com.*

$$$

ECLECTIC

✕**Gaylord's.** This restaurant recently received a welcome overhaul. Located in what was at one time Kauai's most expensive plantation estate, Gaylord's pays tribute to the elegant dining rooms of 1930s high society. Tables with candlelight sit on a cobblestone patio surrounding a fountain and overlooking a wide lawn. The sustainability-minded menu features classic American cooking with a focus on locally produced ingredients. Try the quiche or ceviche with avocado and citrus, followed with a Wailua lamb chop, stuffed eggplant or Aakukui Ranch beef tenderloin with gorgonzola-stuffed potato cake. Lunches feature the tasty (grilled eggplant and peppers with pickled vegetables, rouille, and smoked provolone) and the daily burger, the chef's "whimsical preparation" of ground local meat. The lavish Sunday brunch includes a variety of eggs Benedict offerings in addition to standard omelets with farm-fresh eggs and a pancake station. Before or after dining you can wander around the estate grounds. ⊠ *Kilohana Plantation, 3-2087 Kaumualii Hwy.* ☎ *808/245–9593* ⊕ *22northkauai.com.*

$

HAWAIIAN

✕**Hamura Saimin.** Folks just love this funky old plantation-style diner. Locals and tourists stream in and out all day long, and neighbor islanders stop in on their way to the airport to pick up take-out orders for friends and family back home. *Saimin* is the big draw, and each day the Hiraoka family dishes up about 1,000 bowls of steaming broth and homemade noodles, topped with a variety of garnishes. The barbecued chicken and meat sticks adopt a smoky flavor during grilling. The landmark eatery is also famous for its *lilikoi* (passion fruit) chiffon

Nothing beats shave ice (no, not "shaved" ice) on a hot Hawaiian day.

pie. ■ TIP→ As one of the few island restaurants open late, until 8:30 pm on weeknights and midnight on Friday and Saturday, it's favored by night owls. ⊠ 2956 Kress St. ☎ 808/245–3271 ▭ No credit cards.

$ ✕ **Hanamaulu Restaurant, Tea House, Sushi Bar, and Robatayaki.** Business is
JAPANESE brisk at this landmark Kauai eatery. The food is a mix of Japanese, Chinese, and local-style cooking, served up in hearty portions. The ginger chicken and fried shrimp are wildly popular, as are the fresh sashimi and sushi. Other choices include tempura, chicken *katsu* (Japanese-style fried chicken), beef broccoli, and *robatayaki* (grilled seafood and meat). The main dining room is rather unattractive, but the private rooms in back look out on the Japanese garden and fishponds and feature traditional seating on tatami mats at low tables. These tearooms can be reserved and are favored for family events and celebrations. ⊠ 3-4291 Kuhio Hwy., Rte. 56, Hanamaulu ☎ 808/245–2511 ☉ Closed Mon.

$$ ✕ **JJ's Broiler.** This spacious, low-key restaurant serves hearty fare, with
AMERICAN dinner specials such as lobster and Slavonic steak, a broiled sliced tenderloin dipped in buttery wine sauce. On sunny afternoons, ask for a table on the lanai overlooking Kalapaki Bay and try one of the generous salads. The upstairs section is currently only available for private events, but you can still eat at the restaurant's lower level, which is open-air and casual. JJ's is a relaxed place to enjoy lunch, dinner, or just sit at the bar for a drink, with one of the best ocean views in Lihue. ⊠ Anchor Cove, 3416 Rice St., Nawiliwili ☎ 808/246–4422 ⊕ www.jjsbroiler.com.

$ ✕ **Kalapaki Joe's.** Hit the original Kalapaki Joe's down in Nawiliwili
AMERICAN for happy hour and enjoy 25-cent wings and $3 fish tacos at this well-situated sports bar. Whoop it up with the crowd of locals and tourists watching everything from football to rugby on strategically placed

TVs. Stay for dinner to have generous portions of sports-bar fare, plus local fish dishes including an excellent seared ahi sashimi plate, and take in the postcard-perfect view of Kalapaki Bay. ⊠ *3501 Rice St, #208, Nawiliwili* ☎ *808/245–6266.*

$$
ECLECTIC
✕ **Kukui's Restaurant and Bar.** The healthful choices and cross-cultural flavors on Kukui's menu are well matched with its casual, open-air setting. The meals have hints of Hawaiian, Asian, and contemporary American cuisines. Slow-roasted prime rib, fresh catch, penne pasta with salmon, and a surf-and-turf option are representative of the well-rounded fare. A prime rib and king crab buffet ($45) is served on Friday night in addition to the regular menu. An extensive breakfast buffet ($25) is offered every morning, or choose from the à la carte menu. Renovated with a modern theme in 2009, there is also now a hip sushi bar called Toro Tei—try "da spida roll," a crispy fried shrimp roll with crab, cucumber, sprouts, and avocado. You can also order from the bar menu. ⊠ *Kauai Marriott Resort & Beach Club, 3610 Rice St.* ☎ *808/ 245–5050* ⊕ *kukuiskauaimarriott.com.*

WORD OF MOUTH

"I also wouldn't want to miss a meal at Hamura's on Rice St. at Kress. Try not to go right at lunchtime, because it can be really crowded. Even if you're stuffed, order some lilikoi pie for dessert."
—glimmer2

$
AMERICAN
✕ **Lihue Barbecue Inn.** Few Kauai restaurants are more beloved than this family-owned eatery, a mainstay of island dining since 1940. The menu runs from traditional American to Asian. The dishes are decent but nothing to send a postcard home about. Try the baby back ribs, or fried loco moco, or choose a full Japanese dinner from the other side of the menu. If you can't make up your mind, strike a compromise with the inn's tri-sampler. Opt for the fruit cup—fresh, not canned—instead of soup or salad, and save room for a hefty slice of homemade cream pie, available in all sorts of flavors. ⊠ *2982 Kress St.* ☎ *808/245–2921* ⊗ *Closed Sun.*

THE SOUTH SHORE

Most South Shore restaurants are more upscale and located within the Poipu resorts. If you're looking for a gourmet meal in a classy setting, the South Shore is where you'll find it. Poipu has a number of excellent restaurants in dreamy settings and decidedly fewer family-style, lower-price eateries.

$$$
AMERICAN
Fodor's Choice
★
✕ **Beach House.** This restaurant partners a dreamy ocean view with impressive cuisine. Few Kauai experiences are more delightful than sitting at one of the outside tables and savoring a delectable meal while the sun sinks into the glassy blue Pacific. It's the epitome of tropical dining, and no other restaurant on Kauai can offer anything quite like it. Chef Robin Moe's menu changes often, but the food is consistently creative and delicious. A few trademark dishes appear regularly, such as mint-coriander lamb rack, fire-roasted ahi, and lemongrass and kaffir-lime sea scallops. Seared macadamia-nut-crusted mahimahi, a dish ubiquitous on island menus, gets a refreshing new twist when served

8

with a *lilikoi* (passion fruit)–lemongrass beurre blanc. Save room for the signature molten chocolate desire, a decadent finale at this pleasing and deservedly popular restaurant. ✉ *5022 Lawai Rd., Koloa* ☎ *808/742–1424* ⊕ *www.the-beach-house.com* ✍ *Reservations essential* ☾ *No lunch.*

$$$ ✕ **Brennecke's Beach Broiler.** Brennecke's is decidedly casual and fun, with a busy bar, windows overlooking the beach, and a cheery blue-and-white interior. It specializes in big portions in a wide range of offerings including rib-eye steak, prime rib, crab legs, shrimp, and the fresh catch of the day. Can't decide? Then, create your own combination meal. This place is especially good for happy hours (3 pm to 5 pm and 8 to 9:30), as the drink and pupu menus bring the prices closer to reality. The fare is fair, but the ocean view and convenient location compensate for the food's shortcomings. There's a take-out deli downstairs. ✉ *2100 Hoone Rd., Poipu* ☎ *808/742–7588* ⊕ *www.brenneckes.com.*

STEAKHOUSE

$$ ✕ **Casablanca at Kiahuna.** Outdoor dining in a pleasant garden setting and consistently good food make this restaurant at the Kiahuna Swim and Tennis Club worth a visit. The fresh fish of the day and the beef filet with porcini truffle sauce are noteworthy, or try the fresh mozzarella wrapped in prosciutto and served with poached figs in a distinctive pork-fig sauce. A tapas menu rounds out the offerings. ✉ *2290 Poipu Rd., Poipu* ☎ *808/742–2929* ⊕ *www.casablancakauai.com* ☾ *No dinner Mon.*

MEDITERRANEAN

$$ ✕ **Casa di Amici.** Tucked away in a quiet neighborhood above Poipu Beach, this "House of Friends" has live classical piano music on Saturday nights and an outside deck open to sweeping ocean views. Entrées from the internationally eclectic menu include a saffron-vanilla paella risotto made with black tiger prawns, fresh fish, chicken breast, and homemade Italian sausage. For dessert, take the plunge with a baked Hawaii: a chocolate-macadamia-nut brownie topped with coconut and passion-fruit sorbet and flambéed Italian meringue. ✉ *2301 Nalo Rd., Poipu* ☎ *808/742–1555* ⊕ *www.casadiamici.com* ☾ *No lunch.*

ITALIAN

$$ ✕ **Dondero's.** The inlaid marble floors, ornate tile work, and Italianate murals that compose the elegant interior at this restaurant compete with a stunning ocean view. In addition to the beautiful setting, Dondero's offers outstanding food, a remarkable wine list, and impeccable service, making this one of Kauai's best restaurants. Chef Patrick Shimada's elegant tasting menu features Italian dishes, including homemade pastas, risotto, and flatbread pizza. Try the four-cheese risotto with Kauai cherry tomatoes, or the grilled Pacific swordfish filet, served with oregano, lemon, olive oil, and baby bell pepper relish. The waitstaff deserves

ITALIAN

Fodor's Choice
★

BUDGET-FRIENDLY: SOUTH SHORE & WEST SIDE

Grind's Cafe and Espresso
✉ *Rte. 50, 4469 Waialo Rd.*
⌂ *Box 809, Eleele* ☎ *808/335–6027* ⊕ *www.grindscafe.net.*

Puka Dog ✉ *2650 Kiahuna Plantation Dr., Koloa* ☎ *808/742–6044* ⊕ *www.pukadog.com.*

Wong's Chinese Restaurant ✉ *Kaumuali Hwy.,* ⌂ *Box 129, Hanapepe* ☎ *808/335–5066.*

Continued on page 209

LUAU: A TASTE OF HAWAII

The best place to sample Hawaiian food is at a backyard luau. Aunts and uncles are cooking, the pig is from a cousin's farm, and the fish is from a brother's boat.

But even locals have to angle for invitations to those rare occasions. So your choice is most likely between a commercial luau and a Hawaiian restaurant.

Some commercial luau are less authentic; they offer little of the traditional diet and are more about umbrella drinks, spectacle, and fun.

For greater authenticity, folksy experiences, and rock-bottom prices, visit a Hawaiian restaurant (most are in anonymous storefronts in residential neighborhoods). Expect rough edges and some effort negotiating the menu.

In either case, much of what is known today as Hawaiian food would be as foreign to a 16th-century Hawaiian as risotto or chow mien. The pre-contact diet was simple and healthy—mainly raw and steamed seafood and vegetables. Early Hawaiians used earth ovens and heated stones to cook seafood, taro, sweet potatoes, and breadfruit and seasoned their food with sea salt and ground kukui nuts. Seaweed, fern shoots, sweet potato vines, coconut, banana, sugarcane, and select greens and roots rounded out the diet.

Successive waves of immigrants added their favorites to the ti leaf–lined table. So it is that foods as disparate as salt salmon and chicken long rice are now Hawaiian—even though there is no salmon in Hawaiian waters and long rice (cellophane noodles) is Chinese.

AT THE LUAU: KALUA PORK

The heart of any luau is the *imu*, the earth oven in which a whole pig is roasted. The preparation of an imu is an arduous affair for most families, who tackle it only once a year or so, for a baby's first birthday or at Thanksgiving, when many Islanders prefer to imu their turkeys. Commercial luau operations have it down to a science, however.

THE ART OF THE STONE
The key to a proper imu is the *pohaku*, the stones. Imu cook by means of long, slow, moist heat released by special stones that can withstand a hot fire without exploding. Many Hawaiian families treasure their imu stones, keeping them in a pile in the backyard and passing them on through generations.

PIT COOKING
The imu makers first dig a pit about the size of a refrigerator, then lay down *kiawe* (mesquite) wood and stones, and build a white-hot fire that is allowed to burn itself out. The ashes are raked away, and the hot stones covered with banana and ti leaves. Well-wrapped in ti or banana leaves and a net of chicken wire, the pig is lowered onto the leaf-covered stones. *Laulau* (leaf-wrapped bundles of meats, fish, and taro leaves) may also be placed inside. Leaves—ti, banana, even ginger—cover the pig followed by wet burlap sacks (to create steam). The whole is topped with a canvas tarp and left to steam for the better part of a day.

OPENING THE IMU
This is the moment everyone waits for: The imu is unwrapped like a giant present and the imu keepers gingerly wrestle out the steaming pig. When it's unwrapped, the meat falls moist and smoky-flavored from the bone, looking just like Southern-style pulled pork, but without the barbecue sauce.

WHICH LUAU?
Grand Hyatt Kauai Luau. Choose this oceanfront luau if it's a romantic evening you're after.

Luau Kalamaku. This luau is on a former sugar plantation and has a more theatrical style than the resort type.

Paina o Hanalei. Lavish, with upscale Pacific Rim cuisine.

Smith's Tropical Paradise. Our top pick, set on a lovely 30-acre tropical garden.

MEA AI ONO.
GOOD THINGS TO EAT.

LAULAU
Steamed meats, fish, and taro leaf in ti-leaf bundles: fork-tender, a medley of flavors; the taro resembles spinach.

LOMI LOMI SALMON
Salt salmon in a piquant salad or relish with onions, tomatoes.

POI
Poi, a paste made of pounded taro root, may be an acquired taste, but it's a must-try during your visit.

Consider: The Hawaiian Adam is descended from *kalo* (taro). Young taro plants are called "keiki"—children. Poi is the first food after mother's milk for many Islanders. Ai, the word for food, is synonymous with poi in many contexts.

Not only that, we love it. "There is no meat that doesn't taste good with poi," the old Hawaiians said.

But you have to know how to eat it: with something rich or powerfully flavored. "It is salt that makes the poi go in," is another adage. When you're served poi, try it with a mouthful of smoky kalua pork or salty lomi lomi salmon. Its slightly sour blandness cleanses the palate. And if you don't like it, smile and say something polite. (And slide that bowl over to a local.)

Laulau

Lomi Lomi Salmon

Poi

E HELE MAI AI! COME AND EAT!

Hawaiian restaurants tend to be inconveniently located in well-worn storefronts with little or no parking, outfitted with battered tables and clattering Melmac dishes, but they personify aloha, invariably run by local families who welcome tourists who take the trouble to find them.

Many are cash-only operations and combination plates are a standard feature: one or two entrées, a side such as chicken long rice, choice of poi or steamed rice and—if the place is really old-style—a tiny portion of coarse Hawaiian salt and some raw onions for relish.

Most serve some foods that aren't, strictly speaking, Hawaiian, but are beloved of ka-maaina, such as salt meat with watercress (preserved meat in a tasty broth), or *akubone*

(skipjack tuna fried in a tangy vinegar sauce).

Our favorite: **Dani's Restaurant** (✉ 4201 Rice St., Lihue, ☎ 808/245–4991).

MENU GUIDE

Much of the Hawaiian language encountered during a stay in the Islands will appear on restaurant menus and lists of luau fare. Here's a quick primer.

ahi: *yellowfin tuna.*

aku: *skipjack, bonito tuna.*

amaama: *mullet; it's hard to get but tasty.*

bento: *a box lunch.*

chicken luau: *a stew made from chicken, taro leaves, and coconut milk.*

haupia: *a light, pudding-like sweet made from coconut.*

imu: *the underground oven in which pigs are roasted for luau.*

kalua: *to bake underground.*

kau kau: *food. The word comes from Chinese but is used in the Islands.*

kimchee: *Korean dish of pickled cabbage made with garlic and hot peppers.*

Kona coffee: *coffee grown in the Kona district of the Big Island.*

laulau: *literally, a bundle. Laulau are morsels of pork, chicken, butterfish, or other ingredients wrapped with young taro leaves and then bundled in ti leaves for steaming.*

lilikoi: *passion fruit, a tart, seedy yellow fruit that makes delicious desserts, juice, and jellies.*

lomi lomi: *to rub or massage; also a massage. Lomi lomi salmon is fish that has been rubbed with onions and herbs; commonly served with minced onions and tomatoes.*

luau: *a Hawaiian feast; also the leaf of the taro plant used in preparing such a feast.*

luau leaves: *cooked taro tops with a taste similar to spinach.*

mahimahi: *mild-flavored dolphinfish, not the marine mammal.*

mai tai: *potent rum drink with orange liqueurs and pineapple juice, from the Tahitian word for "good."*

malasada: *a Portuguese deep-fried doughnut without a hole, dipped in sugar.*

manapua: *steamed chinese buns filled with pork, chicken, or other fillings.*

mano: *shark.*

niu: *coconut.*

onaga: *pink or red snapper.*

ono: *a long, slender mackerel-like fish; also called wahoo.*

ono: *delicious; also hungry.*

opihi: *a tiny shellfish, or mollusk, found on rocks; also called limpets.*

papio: *a young ulua or jack fish.*

poha: *Cape gooseberry. Tasting a bit like honey, the poha berry is often used in jams and desserts.*

poi: *a paste made from pounded taro root, a staple of the Hawaiian diet.*

poke: *cubed raw tuna or other fish, tossed with seaweed and seasonings.*

pupu: *appetizers or small plates.*

saimin: *long thin noodles and vegetables in broth, often garnished with small pieces of fish cake, scrambled egg, luncheon meat, and green onion.*

sashimi: *raw fish thinly sliced and usually eaten with soy sauce.*

ti leaves: *a member of the agave family. The leaves are used to wrap food while cooking and removed before eating.*

uku: *deep-sea snapper.*

ulua: *a member of the jack family that also includes pompano and amberjack. Also called crevalle, jack fish, and jack crevalle.*

CLOSE UP

The Plate-Lunch Tradition

To experience island history firsthand, take a seat at one of Hawaii's ubiquitous "plate lunch" eateries, and order a segmented Styrofoam plate piled with rice, macaroni salad, and maybe some fiery pickled vegetable condiment. On the sugar plantations, Native Hawaiians and immigrant workers from many different countries ate together in the fields, sharing food from their "kaukau kits," the utilitarian version of the Japanese *bento* lunchbox. From this "melting pot" came the vibrant language of pidgin and its equivalent in food: the plate lunch.

At beaches and events, you will probably see a few tiny kitchens-on-wheels, another excellent venue for sampling plate lunches. These portable restaurants are descendants of "lunch wagons" that began selling food to plantation workers in the 1930s. Try the deep-fried chicken *katsu* (rolled in Japanese panko bread crumbs and spices). The marinated beef teriyaki is another good choice, as is miso butterfish. The noodle soup, *saimin*, with its Japanese fish stock and Chinese red-tinted barbecue pork, is a distinctly local medley. Koreans have contributed spicy barbecue *kalbi* ribs, often served with chili-laden *kimchi* (pickled cabbage). Portuguese bean soup and tangy Filipino *adobo* stew are also favorites. The most popular Hawaiian contribution to the plate lunch is the *laulau*, a mix of meat and fish and young taro leaves, wrapped in more taro leaves and steamed.

special praise for its thoughtful, discrete service. ⊠ *Grand Hyatt Kauai Resort and Spa, 1571 Poipu Rd., Koloa* ☎ 808/240–6456 ⊗ *No lunch.*

$ ✕ **Joe's on the Green.** Eat an open-air breakfast or lunch with an expansive vista of Poipu. Located on the Kiahuna Golf Course, this restaurant boasts such favorites as eggs Benedict, tofu scramble, and banana-macadamia-nut pancakes. For lunch, try the Reuben sandwich or ribs, or build your own salad. The small plates menu and happy-hour drink specials are available from 3 to 6, including favorites such as herb and garlic chicken skewers, seared ahi tacos, and homemade chili nachos, all accompanied by live Hawaiian music. With a casual atmosphere and generous portions, Joe's is a refreshing alternative to the pricier hotel brunch venues in this area. ⊠ *2545 Kiahuna Plantation Dr., Poipu* ☎ *808/742–9696* ⊗ *No dinner.*

AMERICAN

$$$ ✕ **Josselin's Tapas Bar and Grill.** Chef Jean-Marie Josselin, one of the pioneers of Hawaiian regional cuisine, has a winner with this local favorite. After the roaming sangria cart rolls up with concoctions containing lilikoi and lychee, the feast is on. Daily selections depend on local availability, but there's a wide range of Hawaiian-influenced, Asian and Western choices to satisfy all palates. The ahi poke and sashimi dish is special but the menu also features more traditional steak and lamb options. But the fun is in savoring the variety of complex smaller plates. ⊠ *2829 Ala Kalani Kaumaka, St, Koloa* ☎ *808/742–7117.*

ECLECTIC

$$ ✕ **Kalaheo Café & Coffee Co.** Right off the highway in Kalaheo, locals love this café, especially for breakfast. It's a casual atmosphere, except on weekend mornings when it can get very busy. Order up front and

AMERICAN

8

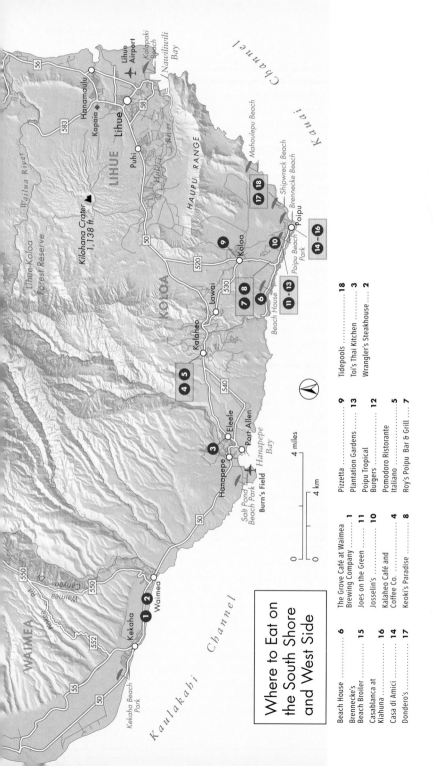

Where to Eat on the South Shore and West Side

Beach House **6**	The Grove Café at Waimea Brewing Company **1**
Brennecke's Beach Broiler **15**	Joes on the Green **11**
Casablanca at Kiahuna **16**	Josselin's **10**
Casa di Amici **14**	Kalaheo Café and Coffee Co. **4**
Dondero's **17**	Keoki's Paradise **8**

Pizzetta **9**	Tidepools **18**
Plantation Gardens **13**	Toi's Thai Kitchen **3**
Poipu Tropical Burgers **12**	Wrangler's Steakhouse **2**
Pomodoro Ristorante Italiano **5**	
Roy's Poipu Bar & Grill **7**	

then find a seat inside or out on the lanai. Favorites include the Kahili Breakfast, scrambled eggs served with Portuguese sausage, ham, and green onions; and the Longboard sandwich, with fried egg, bacon, lettuce, tomato, and melted provolone cheese. Lots of local products are used here, including Anahola Granola, local fish and Kauai coffee, which you can buy by the pound. They are again serving dinner Tuesday through Saturday nights. ✉ *2-2560 Kaumualii Hwy. (Rte. 50), Kalaheo* ☎ *808/332–5858* ⊕ *www.kalaheo.com.*

$$ ✕ **Keoki's Paradise.** Built to resemble a dockside boathouse, this active,
SEAFOOD boisterous place fills up quickly at night thanks to the live music. Seafood appetizers span the tide from sashimi to Thai shrimp sticks, crab cakes, and scallops crusted in *panko* (Japanese-style bread crumbs). The day's fresh catch is available in half a dozen styles and sauces. And there's a sampling of beef, chicken, and pork-rib entrées for the committed carnivore. A lighter menu is available at the bar for lunch and dinner. ✉ *Poipu Shopping Village, 2360 Kiahuna Plantation Dr., Koloa* ☎ *808/742–7534* ⊕ *www.keokisparadise.com.*

$ ✕ **Pizzetta.** Solid food characterizes this family-style Italian restaurant,
ITALIAN which serves up hearty portions of pasta, lasagna, and eggplant Parmesan, along with calzones, pizza with numerous toppings, and salads. The atmosphere is casual and lively and the food is good, especially for the price. Neighborhood delivery is available. ✉ *5408 Koloa Rd., Koloa* ☎ *808/742–8881.*

$$ ✕ **Plantation Gardens.** A historic plantation manager's home has been
ITALIAN converted to a restaurant that serves seafood and kiawe-grilled meats with a Pacific Rim and Italian influence. You'll walk through a tropical setting of torch-lighted orchid gardens and lotus-studded koi ponds to a cozy, European-style dining room with cherrywood floors and a veranda. The menu is based on fresh, local foods: fish right off the boat, herbs and produce picked from the plantation's gardens, fruit delivered by neighborhood farmers. The result is cuisine with island flair—seafood *laulau* (seafood wrapped in ti leaves and steamed)—served alongside traditional classics such as sugarcane-skewered pork tenderloin. Definitely save room for dessert: The lilikoi cheesecake is a dream. In short, the food is excellent and the setting charming. ✉ *Kiahuna Plantation, 2253 Poipu Rd., Koloa* ☎ *808/742–2121* ⊕ *www. pgrestaurant.com* ⊗ *No lunch.*

$$ ✕ **Poipu Tropical Burgers.** Families may find themselves returning for mul-
AMERICAN tiple meals at this all-day casual restaurant, with its children's menu, simple food, and low prices. Veggie, fish, and gourmet half-pound beef burgers are the mainstay, with fresh fish and other specials added at dinner and sandwiches, soups, and hearty salads rounding out the choices. Bottomless soft drinks and milk shakes are a nice touch for the kids; adults can order wine, draft beer, and exotic drinks. Dining rooms at

8

Mahimahi is a popular fish dish on Kauai. The Beach House adds a macadamia nut crust for local flavor.

both locales are airy, cheerful, and casual. ✉ *Poipu Shopping Village, 2360 Kiahuna Plantation Dr., Koloa* ☎ *808/742–1808.*

$$
ITALIAN
✕ **Pomodoro Ristorante Italiano.** Two walls of windows brighten this intimate second-story restaurant in the heart of Kalaheo, where there's good food at reasonable prices. Begin with prosciutto and melon, then proceed directly to the multilayer meat lasagna, a favorite of the chefs—two Italian-born brothers. Other highlights include eggplant or veal parmigiana, chicken saltimbocca, and scampi in a garlic, caper, and white wine sauce. ✉ *Upstairs at Rainbow Plaza, Kaumualii Hwy.(Rte. 50), Kalaheo* ☎ *808/332–5945* ⊗ *Closed Sun. No lunch.*

$$$
MODERN
HAWAIIAN
✕ **Roy's Poipu Bar & Grill.** Hawaii's culinary superstar, Roy Yamaguchi, is fond of sharing his signature Hawaiian fusion cuisine by cloning the successful Honolulu restaurant where he got his start. You'll find one of these copycat eateries on Kauai's South Side in a shopping-center locale that feels too small and ordinary for the exotic food. The menu changes daily, and the hardworking kitchen staff dreams up 5 to 10 (or more) specials each night—an impressive feat. Though the food reflects the imaginative pairings and high-quality ingredients of the original Roy's and the presentation is spectacular, the atmosphere is a little different. As with most restaurant branches, it just doesn't have the heart and soul of the original. ✉ *Poipu Shopping Village, 2360 Kiahuna Plantation Dr., Koloa* ☎ *808/742–5000* ⊕ *www.roysrestaurant.com* ⊗ *No lunch.*

$$$
SEAFOOD
✕ **Tidepools.** The Grand Hyatt Kauai is notable for its excellent restaurants, which differ widely in their settings and cuisine. This one is definitely the most tropical and campy, sure to appeal to folks seeking a bit of island-style romance and adventure. Private grass-thatch huts seem to float on a koi-filled pond beneath starry skies while torches

The Beach House on the South Shore is a prime spot to watch the sun set.

flicker in the lushly landscaped grounds nearby. The equally distinctive food has an island flavor that comes from the chef's advocacy of Hawaii Regional Cuisine and extensive use of Kauai-grown products including fresh herbs from the resort's organic garden. You won't go wrong ordering one of the signature dishes, such as the Hawaiian opah with a tangerine yuzu sauce; macadamia-nut crusted mahimahi; or the Hawaiian-salt and garlic-rubbed prime rib. Start with Tidepools' pupu platter for two—with a crab cake, Kauai shrimp, and ahi sashimi—to wake up your taste buds. If you're still hungry at the end of the meal, the molten chocolate lava cake is sure to satisfy. ⊠ *Grand Hyatt Kauai Resort and Spa, 1571 Poipu Rd., Koloa* ☎ *808/240–6456* ⊗ *No lunch.*

THE WEST SIDE

West Side eateries tend to be more local-style and are generally found along Kaumualii Highway. Pickings start to get slimmer the farther west you travel, and dining choices often are dictated by what's open. Fortunately, West Side restaurants are generally worth patronizing, so you won't go too far wrong if your hunger demands to be satisfied while you're out enjoying the sights.

$$

AMERICAN

✕ **The Grove Café at Waimea Brewing Company.** Housed within the Waimea Plantation Cottages, this old-time restaurant is spacious, with hardwood floors and open-air decks. Dine indoors amid rattan furnishings or at a bar decorated with petroglyphs and colored with Kauai red dirt. Local-style dishes such as Korean garlic chicken, beef short ribs, and fresh fish are highlights. It has live contemporary Hawaiian-style

ROMANTIC DINING

Whether you're already feeling sparks or trying to fan banked embers into flame, a romantic meal can help things along. Fortunately, Kauai has a number of restaurants that are conducive to love.

For divine sunsets, the **Beach House** (☎ *808/742–1424*), in Koloa, is tops, as it puts you right on the water. **Café Portofino** (☎ *808/245–2121*), in Lihue, with its second-story view of Kalapaki Bay and harp music, practically caters to couples. Tops

overall, though, is **Dondero's** (☎ *808/240–6456*), in Koloa, where the food, service, and elegant setting come together to create a special evening. If it's a nice evening, by all means opt for the veranda.

Be sure to make reservations, and don't plan on pinching pennies. If you're on a budget, pick up some take-out food and spread a blanket on the beach for a sunset picnic and dessert beneath brilliant stars.

music on Wednesday, Thursday, and Friday nights. It's a good place to stop while traveling to or from Waimea Canyon, and the island-made microbrews are worth a try. ⊠ *9400 Kaumualii Hwy., Waimea* ☎ *808/338–9733.*

$ ✕ **Toi's Thai Kitchen.** Country-style Thai cuisine, hearty portions, rea-
THAI   sonable prices, and a casual dining room make this family-run eatery a solid choice on the restaurant-sparse West Side. Most dishes can be prepared vegetarian-style or with beef, pork, chicken, or seafood. Try Toi's Temptation, a hearty mix of meats, pineapple, potatoes, and lem-ongrass in a sauce of red-chili-heated coconut milk, or one of the excel-lent curries. Meals include a green papaya or lettuce salad and warm tapioca or black rice pudding. ⊠ *Eleele Shopping Center, 4469 Waialo Rd., Eleele* ☎ *808/335–3111.*

$$ ✕ **Wrangler's Steakhouse.** Denim-covered seating, decorative saddles, and
STEAKHOUSE   a stagecoach in a loft helped to transform the historic Ako General Store in Waimea into a West Side steak house. You can eat under the stars on the deck out back or inside the old-fashioned, wood-panel dining room. The 16-ounce New York steak comes sizzling, and the rib eye is served with capers. A tasty salad is part of each meal. Those with smaller appetites might consider the vegetarian or Japanese-style tempura or the ahi served on penne pasta. Local folks love the special lunch: rice, beef teriyaki, and shrimp tempura with kimchi served in a three-tier *kaukau* tin, or lunch pail, just like the ones sugar-plantation workers once carried. A gift shop has local crafts. ⊠ *9852 Kaumualii Hwy., Waimea* ☎ *808/338–1218* ⊕ *wranglersrestaurant.com* ☼ *Closed Sun.*

Where to Stay

WORD OF MOUTH

"If you are on Kauai for several days, splitting your time between the North and South shores would be nice, in order to allow leisurely visits to Waimea Canyon as well as the sites to the north. If your goal is to relax and stay put at the resort, I would select the South Shore."

—okoshi2002

Updated by
Charles E.
Roessler

The Garden Isle has lodgings for every taste, from swanky resorts to rustic cabins, and from family-friendly condos to romantic bed-and-breakfasts. The savvy traveler can also find inexpensive places that are convenient, safe, and accessible to Kauai's special places and activities.

When you're choosing a place to stay, location is an important consideration. Kauai may seem small on a map, but because it's circular with no through roads, it can take more time than you think to get from place to place. If at all possible, stay close to your desired activities. This way, you'll save time to squeeze in all the things you'll want to do.

Time of year is also a factor. If you're here in winter or spring, consider staying on the South Shore, as the surf on the North Shore and East Side tends to be rough, making many ocean beaches too rough for swimming or water sports.

Before booking accommodations, think hard about what kind of experience you want to have for your island vacation. There are several top-notch resorts to choose from, and Kauai also has a wide variety of condos, vacation rentals, and bed-and-breakfasts. The Kauai Visitors Bureau provides a comprehensive listing of accommodation choices to help you decide.

KAUAI LODGING PLANNER

PROPERTY TYPES

HOTELS AND RESORTS

If you want to golf, play tennis, or hang at a spa, stay at a resort. You'll also be more likely to find activities for children at resorts, including camps that allow parents a little time off. The island's hotels tend to be smaller and older, with fewer on-site amenities. Some of the swankiest places to stay on the island are the St. Regis Princeville Resort on the North Shore, where rooms run more than $1,000 per night in high season, and the Grand Hyatt Kauai on the South Shore for a bit less; of course, those with views of the ocean book faster than those without.

B&BS AND INNS

The island's bed-and-breakfasts allow you to meet local residents and more directly experience the aloha spirit. Many have oceanfront settings and breakfasts with everything from tropical fruits and juices, Kauai coffee, and macadamia waffles to breads made with local bananas and mangoes. Some have pools, hot tubs, services such as *lomilomi* massage, and breakfasts delivered to your lanai. Some properties have stand-alone units on-site.

CONDOS AND VACATION RENTALS

Condos and vacation rentals on Kauai tend to run the gamut from fabulous luxury estates to scruffy little dives. It's buyer-beware in this totally unregulated sector of the visitor industry, though the County of Kauai is in the process of developing new regulations for these types of properties, particularly those in agricultural and rural areas. If you're planning to stay at one of these, be sure to contact the operator prior to traveling to ensure it's still open.

Properties managed by individual owners can be found on online vacation-rental directories such as CyberRentals and Vacation Rentals By Owner, as well as on the Kauai Visitors Bureau's website. There are also several Kauai-based management companies with vacation rentals.

RESERVATIONS

The rule on Kauai—and for Hawaii in general—is book as far in advance as possible. Rooms go most quickly during holidays, but there really isn't any low season to speak of. Some places allow 24 hours' notice to cancel; others require a week or will penalize you the cost of one night. Most hotels allow children under a certain age to stay in their parents' room at no extra charge, but others charge for them as extra adults; find out the cutoff age for discounts.

PRICES

The prices used to establish price categories in this guide are the rack rates given by the hotels at this writing. The tax added to your room rate is 13.42%.

WHAT IT COSTS			
	$	$$	$$$	$$$$
FOR TWO PEOPLE	under $180	$180–$260	$261–$340	over $340

Hotel prices are for two people in a standard double room in high season. Condo price categories reflect studio and one-bedroom rates.

For expanded hotel reviews, visit www.fodors.com.

THE NORTH SHORE

The North Shore is mountainous and wet, which accounts for its rugged, lush landscape. Posh resorts and condominiums await you at Princeville, a community with dreamy views, excellent golf courses, and lovely sunsets. It maintains the lion's share of North Shore accommodations—primarily luxury hotel rooms and condos built on a plateau overlooking the sea. Hanalei, a bayside town in a broad valley, has a

BEST BETS FOR KAUAI LODGING

Where can you find the best lodging experiences this island has to offer? Fodor's writers and editors have selected their favorite hotels, resorts, condos, vacation rentals, and B&Bs by price and experience in the lists below. In the first column, the Fodor's Choice properties represent the "best of the best" across price categories.

Fodor's Choice ★

Grand Hyatt Kauai Resort and Spa, $$$$, p. 228

Hanalei Bay Resort, $$, p. 219

Waimea Plantation Cottages, $, p. 232

Sheraton Kauai Resort, $$$$, p. 230

St. Regis Princeville Resort, $$$$, p. 221

By Price

$

Garden Island Inn, p. 224

Kalaheo Inn, p. 232

Kokee Lodge, p. 232

Mana Yoga Vacation Rentals, p. 221

North Country Farms, p. 221

Plantation Hale Suites, p. 224

Poipu Plantation Resort, p. 230

Rosewood Bed and Breakfast, p. 224

Waimea Plantation Cottages, p. 232

$$

Garden Isle Cottages, p. 226

Hanalei Bay Resort, p. 219

Hanalei Colony Resort, p. 219

Hotel Coral Reef, p. 223

$$$

Aston Aloha Beach Hotel, p. 223

Kauai Beach Resort, p. 224

Makahuena at Poipu, p. 228

Poipu Crater Resort, p. 228

Poipu Shores, p. 230

$$$$

Grand Hyatt Kauai Resort and Spa, p. 228

Kauai Coast Resort, p. 224

St. Regis Princeville Resort, p. 221

Whalers Cove, p. 230

By Experience

BEST BEACH

Aston Aloha Beach Hotel, $$$, p. 223

Aston Islander on the Beach, $$, p. 223

Kauai Marriott Resort on Kalapaki Beach, $$$$, p. 226

Outrigger at Lae Nani, $, p. 224

Waimea Plantation Cottages, $, p. 232

BEST B&BS AND INNS

Aloha Cottages, $$$$, p. 223

Garden Island Inn, $, p. 224

Kalaheo Inn, $, p. 232

Poipu Plantation Resort, $, p. 230

Rosewood Bed and Breakfast, $, p. 224

BEST SPA

Grand Hyatt Kauai Resort and Spa, $$$$, p. 228

Hanalei Colony Resort, $$, p. 219

Kauai Beach Resort, $$$, p. 224

Kauai Marriott Resort on Kalapaki Beach, $$$$, p. 226

St. Regis Princeville Resort, $$$$, p. 221

Waimea Plantation Cottages, $, p. 232

MOST KID-FRIENDLY

Aston Aloha Beach Hotel, $$$, p. 223

Grand Hyatt Kauai Resort and Spa, $$$$, p. 228

Hotel Coral Reef, $$, p. 223

Kauai Marriott Resort on Kalapaki Beach, $$$$, p. 226

North Country Farms, $, p. 221

MOST ROMANTIC

Aloha Cottages, $$$$, p. 223

Grand Hyatt Kauai Resort and Spa, $$$$, p. 228

Hanalei Bay Resort, $$, p. 219

Hanalei Colony Resort, $$, p. 219

St. Regis Princeville Resort, $$$$, p. 221

WHERE TO STAY IN KAUAI

	Local Vibe	Pros	Cons
The North Shore	Properties here have the "wow" factor with ocean and mountain beauty; laid-back Hanalei and Princeville set the high-end pace.	When the weather is good (summer) this side has it all. Epic winter surf, gorgeous waterfalls, and verdant vistas create some of the best scenery in Hawaii.	Lots of rain (being green has a cost) means you may have to travel south to find the sun; expensive restaurants and shopping offer few deals.
The East Side	The most reasonably priced area to stay for the practical traveler; lacks the pizzazz of expensive resorts on North and South shores; more traditional Hawaiian hotels.	The best travel deals show up here; more direct access to the local population; plenty of decent restaurants with good variety, along with delis in food stores.	Beaches aren't the greatest (rocky, reefy) at many of the lodging spots; bad traffic at times; some crime issues in parks.
The South Shore	Resort central; plenty of choices where the consistent sunshine is perfect for those who want to do nothing but play golf or tennis and read a book by the pool.	Beautiful in its own right; many enchanted evenings with stellar sunsets; summer surf easier for beginners to handle.	Some areas are deserty with scrub brush; construction can be brutal on piece of mind.
The West Side	There are few options for lodging in this mostly untouristlike setting with contrasts such as the extreme heat of a July day in Waimea to a frozen winter night up in Kokee.	A gateway area for exploration into the wilds of Kokee or for boating trips on Napali Coast; main hub for boat and helicopter trips; outstanding sunsets.	Least convenient side for most visitors; daytime is languid and dry; river runoff can ruin ocean's clarity.

smattering of hotel rooms and numerous vacation rentals, many within walking distance of the beach. Prices tend to be high in this resort area. If you want to do extensive sightseeing on other parts of the island, be prepared for a long drive—one that's very dark at night.

$$
RESORT
Fodor's Choice
★
Hanalei Bay Resort. This time-share condominium resort has a lovely location overlooking Hanalei Bay and Napali Coast. **Pros:** beautiful views; tennis courts on property; tropical pool. **Cons:** steep walkways; long walk to beach. ☒ *5380 Honoiki Rd., Princeville* ☎ *808/826–6522, 866/507–1428* ⊕ *www.hanaleibayresort.com* ⤳ *134 units* ⌂ *In-room: a/c, safe, kitchen. In-hotel: pool, tennis court, beach, children's programs, laundry facilities.*

$$
HOTEL
Hanalei Colony Resort. This 5-acre property, the only true beachfront resort on Kauai's North Shore, is a laid-back, go-barefoot kind of place sandwiched between towering mountains and the sea. **Pros:** oceanfront setting; private, quiet; seventh night free. **Cons:** remote location; damp in winter. ☒ *5-7130 Kuhio Hwy., Haena* ☎ *808/826–6235, 800/628–3004* ⊕ *www.hcr.com* ⤳ *48 units* ⌂ *In-room: no a/c, kitchen, no TV, Wi-Fi. In-hotel: restaurant, bar, pool, spa, beach, laundry facilities.*

Where to Stay on the North Shore

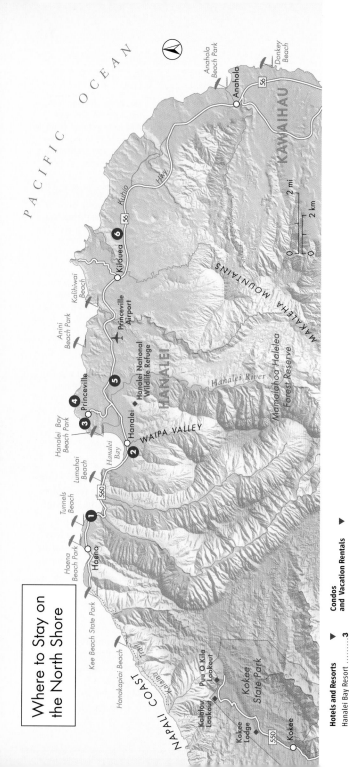

PACIFIC OCEAN

Anahola Beach Park

Donkey Beach

Anahola

56

KAMAIHAU

Kuhio Hwy

Kalihiwai Beach

56

Kilauea ❻

Anini Beach Park

Princeville Airport

Princeville ❹

HANALEI

Hanalei National Wildlife Refuge

Hanalei River

Mamalahoa Halelea Forest Reserve

MAKALEHA MOUNTAINS

Hanalei Bay Beach Park ❸

Hanalei ❷

WAIPA VALLEY

Hanalei Bay

Lumahai Beach

560

Tunnels Beach

Haena Beach Park

Haena ❶

Kee Beach State Park

Honokapiai Beach

NAPALI COAST

Kalalau Trail

Puu O Kila Lookout

Kalahau Lookout

Kokee State Park

Kokee Lodge

550

Kokee

2 mi

2 km

0   0

Hotels and Resorts ▶

Hanalei Bay Resort **3**

Hanalei Colony Resort ...**1**

St. Regis
Princeville Resort **4**

**Condos
and Vacation Rentals** ▶

Hanalei Inn **2**

Mana Yoga Vacation
Rentals **5**

North Country Farms **6**

$
RENTAL

⛫ **Hanalei Inn.** If you're looking for low-priced lodgings a block from gorgeous Hanalei Bay, look no further, as this is the only choice. **Pros:** quick walk to beach. **Cons:** strict cancellation policy; very modest amenities; daytime traffic noise. ⊠ *5-5468 Kuhio Hwy., Hanalei* ☎ *808/826–9333* ⊕ *www.hanaleiinn.com* ⊅ *4 studios* ⚘ *In-room: a/c, kitchen, Wi-Fi.*

$
RENTAL

⛫ **Mana Yoga Vacation Rentals.** If you enjoy yoga, or just a rural environment, these lodgings (a studio and two-bedroom unit) offer peace and quiet, mountain views, and all the amenities of home, as well as the services of yoga instructor and massage therapist Michaelle Edwards, who has a yoga studio on-site. **Pros:** mountain views; yoga and massage on-site; beach accoutrements available. **Cons:** no beach; isolated; 5-minute drive to restaurants and shops. ⊠ *3812 Ahonui Pl., Princeville* ☎ *808/826–9230* ⊕ *www.manayoga.com* ⊅ *2 units* ⚘ *In-room: no a/c, Wi-Fi. In-hotel: laundry facilities.*

$
RENTAL
♻

⛫ **North Country Farms.** These comfortable lodgings are tucked away on a tidy, 4-acre organic fruit, flower, and vegetable farm just east of Kilauea. **Pros:** delightful setting; pick fresh fruit and vegetables; warm and friendly hostess. **Cons:** no beach; no resort-type amenities. ⊠ *Kahili Makai, Box 723, Kilauea* ☎ *808/828–1513* ⊕ *www.northcountryfarms. com* ⊅ *2 cottages* ⚘ *In-room: no a/c, kitchen.*

$$$$
RESORT
Fodor's Choice
★

⛫ **St. Regis Princeville Resort.** Built into the cliffs above Hanalei Bay, this unbeatable Starwood resort offers expansive views of the sea and mountains, including Makana, the landmark peak immortalized as the mysterious Bali Hai island in the film *South Pacific.* **Pros:** great views; excellent restaurants; attractive lobby; professional staff. **Cons:** minimal grounds; reefy beach for swimming. ⊠ *5520 Ka Haku Rd.* ☎ *877/787–3447, 808/826–9644* ⊕ *www.stregisprinceville.com* ⊅ *201 rooms, 51 suites* ⚘ *In-room: a/c, safe, Wi-Fi. In-hotel: restaurant, bar, golf course, pool, tennis court, gym, spa, beach, water sports, children's programs, business center, parking.*

9

THE EAST SIDE

Location, location, location. The East Side, or Coconut Coast, is a good centralized home base if you want to see and do it all. This is one of the few resort areas on Kauai where you can actually walk to the beach, restaurants, and stores from your condo, hotel, or vacation-rental unit. It's not only convenient but comparatively cheap. You pay less for lodging, meals, services, merchandise, and gas here—mainly because the coral-reef coastline isn't as ideal as the sandy-bottom bays that front the fancy resorts. We think the shoreline is just fine. There are pockets in the reef to swim in, and the coast is uncrowded and boasts spectacular views. Warning: Traffic on the main highway can be maddening, and access can be challenging. New traffic and access relief is promised soon. All in all, it's a good choice for families because the prices are right and there's plenty to keep everyone happy and occupied.

The St. Regis Princeville Resort

KAPAA AND WAILUA

Since Kapaa is the island's major population center, this area, including Waipouli and Wailua, has a lived-in, real-world feel. This is where you'll find some of the best deals on accommodations and a wider choice of inexpensive restaurants and shops than in the resort areas. The beaches here are so-so for swimming but nice for sunbathing, walking, and watching the sun and moon rise.

The Wailua area is rather compact and is quite walkable, especially if you avoid the highway, which can be busy and clogged. The resorts here are attractive to middle-class travelers seeking a good bang for their buck. Wailua has rich historic significance among the ancient Hawaiians. Their royalty lived here and ancient sacred grounds, called *heiau*, are clearly marked.

$$$$
RENTAL
Aloha Cottages. Owners Charlie and Susan Hoerner restored a three-bedroom plantation home on Kapaa's Baby Beach to reflect the charm of yesteryear with the conveniences of today. **Pros:** comfortable, home-like atmosphere; good for large groups; safe children's beach. **Cons:** can be windy at times; not great for swimming. ⊠ *1041 Moana Kai Rd., Kapaa* ☎ *808/823–0933, 877/915–1015* ⊕ *www.alohacottages. com* ⇆ *2 cottages* ⅋ *In-room: no a/c, kitchen. In-hotel: beach.*

$$
RESORT
Aston Aloha Beach Hotel. Nestled alongside Wailua Bay and the Wailua River, this low-key, low-rise resort is an easy, convenient place to stay. **Pros:** excellent cultural program; walk to beach and park; convenient locale. **Cons:** exiting hotel parking lot onto highway can be difficult; restaurant meals are average. ⊠ *3-5920 Kuhio Hwy., Kapaa* ☎ *808/823–6000, 888/823–5111* ⊕ *www.astonhotels.com* ⇆ *216 rooms, 10 suites, 24 beach cottages* ⅋ *In-room: a/c, safe, kitchen, Internet. In-hotel: restaurant, pool, tennis court, gym.*

$$
HOTEL
Aston Islander on the Beach. A Hawaii-plantation-style design gives this 6-acre beachfront property a pleasant, low-key feeling. **Pros:** convenient location; kids stay free; online rate deals. **Cons:** smallish pool; no restaurant on the property. ⊠ *440 Aleka Pl., Kapaa* ☎ *808/822–7417, 866/774–2924* ⊕ *www.astonhotels.com* ⇆ *198 rooms, 2 suites* ⅋ *In-room: a/c, safe, Internet. In-hotel: bar, pool, beach, laundry facilities.*

$$
HOTEL
Hotel Coral Reef. Coral Reef has been in business since the 1960s and is something of a beachfront landmark. **Pros:** nice pool; sauna; oceanfront setting; convenient location. **Cons:** located in a busy section of Kapaa; ocean swimming is marginal. ⊠ *4-1516 Kuhio Hwy., Kapaa* ☎ *808/822–4481, 800/843–4659* ⊕ *www.hotelcoralreefresort. com* ⇆ *19 rooms, 2 suites* ⅋ *In-room: a/c, safe. In-hotel: pool, beach, laundry facilities, parking.*

$
RENTAL
Kapaa Sands. An old rock etched with *kanji*, Japanese characters, reminds you that the site of this condominium gem was formerly occupied by a Shinto temple. **Pros:** discounts for extended stays; walking distance to shops, restaurants, and beach; turtle and monk seal sightings common. **Cons:** no-frills lodging; traffic noise in mountain-facing units. ⊠ *380 Papaloa Rd., Kapaa* ☎ *808/822–4901, 800/222–4901* ⊕ *www.kapaasands.com* ⇆ *21 units* ⅋ *In-room: no a/c, kitchen. In-hotel: pool, beach.*

9

$$$$
RENTAL
⌶ **Kauai Coast Resort.** Fronting an uncrowded stretch of beach, this three-story primarily time-share resort is convenient and a bit more upscale than nearby properties. **Pros:** lovely pool; excellent restaurant; convenient. **Cons:** area is a bit touristy. ✉ *520 Aleka Loop, Kapaa* ☎ *808/822–3441, 866/678–3289* ⊕ *www.shellhospitality.com* ↩ *108 units* ⚒ *In-room: a/c, safe, kitchen, Internet. In-hotel: restaurant, pool, tennis court, gym, spa, beach.*

$
RENTAL
⌶ **Outrigger at Lae Nani.** Ruling Hawaiian chiefs once returned from ocean voyages to this spot, now host to condominiums comfortable enough for minor royalty. **Pros:** nice swimming beach; walking distance to playground; attractively furnished. **Cons:** tricky driving in area. ✉ *410 Papaloa Rd., Kapaa* ☎ *808/822–4938, 800/688–7444* ⊕ *www. outrigger.com* ↩ *84 units* ⚒ *In-room: no a/c, safe, kitchen. In-hotel: pool, tennis court, beach, laundry facilities.*

$
RENTAL
⌶ **Plantation Hale Suites.** These attractive plantation-style one-bedroom units have well-equipped kitchenettes and garden lanai. **Pros:** bright, spacious units; three pools; walking distance to shops, restaurant, beach. **Cons:** traffic noise in mountain-view units; coral reef makes ocean swimming challenging. ✉ *484 Kuhio Hwy., Kapaa* ☎ *808/822– 4941, 800/775–4253* ⊕ *www.plantation-hale.com* ↩ *104 units* ⚒ *In-room: a/c, kitchen, Internet. In-hotel: pool, laundry facilities.*

$
B&B/INN
⌶ **Rosewood Bed and Breakfast.** This charming bed-and-breakfast on a macadamia-nut plantation estate offers five separate styles of accommodations, including a two-bedroom Victorian cottage; a three-bedroom, two-bath home; a little one-bedroom grass-thatch cottage; a bunkhouse with three rooms and a shared bath; and the traditional main plantation home with two rooms, each with private bath. **Pros:** varied accommodations; good breakfast; attractive grounds. **Cons:** some traffic noise; no beach. ✉ *872 Kamalu Rd., Kapaa* ☎ *808/822–5216* ⊕ *www. rosewoodkauai.com* ↩ *One 3-bedroom home, one 2-bedroom cottage, one 1-bedroom cottage, 3 rooms in bunkhouse, 2 rooms in main house* ⚒ *In-room: no a/c, kitchen* ▭ *No credit cards.*

LIHUE

Lihue is not the most desirable place to stay on Kauai, in terms of scenic beauty, although it does have its advantages, including easy access to the airport. Restaurants and shops are plentiful, and there's lovely Kalapaki Bay for beachgoers. Aside from the Marriott and the Kauai Beach Resort, most of the limited lodging possibilities are smaller and aimed at the cost-conscious traveler.

$
B&B/INN
⌶ **Garden Island Inn.** Bargain hunters love this three-story inn near Kalapaki Bay and Anchor Cove shopping center. **Pros:** walk to beach, restaurants, and shops; good for families, extended stays, and budget travel. **Cons:** some traffic noise; near a busy harbor; limited grounds; no pool. ✉ *3445 Wilcox Rd., Kalapaki Beach* ☎ *808/245–7227, 800/648–0154* ⊕ *www.gardenislandinn.com* ↩ *22 rooms* ⚒ *In-room: a/c, kitchen, Wi-Fi.*

$$$
RESORT
⌶ **Kauai Beach Resort.** This plantation-style hotel has had a number of different owners and is now under the management of Aqua Hotels

Where to Stay
on the East Side

Hotels and Resorts ▼

Aston Aloha Beach Hotel ... **9**

Aston Islander
on the Beach **5**

Hotel Coral Reef **1**

Kauai
Beach Resort **10**

Kauai Marriott Resort
on Kalapaki Beach **12**

Kauai Palms Hotel **13**

**Condos and
Vacation Rentals** ▼

Aloha Cottages **2**

Kapaa Sands **8**

Kauai Coast Resort **4**

Outrigger at Lae Nani **6**

Plantation Hale Suites **3**

B&Bs and Inns ▼

Garden Island Inn **11**

Rosewood
Bed and Breakfast **7**

and Resorts. **Pros:** nice pool, quiet, resort amenities; shuttle services. **Cons:** not a good swimming beach; windy at times. ⊠ *4331 Kauai Beach Dr.* ☎ *888/805–3843* ⊕ *www.kauaibeachresorthawaii.com* ⤳ *350 rooms, 7 suites* ⌂ *In-room: a/c, safe. In-hotel: restaurant, pool, tennis court, spa, beach.*

$$$$ ⊡ **Kauai Marriott Resort on Kalapaki**
RESORT   **Beach.** An elaborate tropical garden,
  ☺   waterfalls right off the lobby, Greek statues and columns, and an enormous 26,000-square-foot swimming pool characterize the grand—and grandiose—scale of this resort on Kalapaki Bay, which looks out at the dramatic Haupu Mountains. **Pros:** oceanfront setting; good restaurants; convenient location; airport shuttle. **Cons:** distant airport noise; swimming questionable at times. ⊠ *3610 Rice St., Kalapaki Beach* ☎ *808/245–5050, 800/220–2925* ⊕ *www.kauaimarriott.com* ⤳ *356 rooms, 11 suites* ⌂ *In-room: a/c. In-hotel: restaurant, golf course, pool, tennis court, gym, spa, beach, children's programs.*

$ ⊡ **Kauai Palms Hotel.** This low-cost alternative is priced right for the fru-
HOTEL   gal traveler. **Pros:** clean; inexpensive; centrally located. **Cons:** back-street atmosphere; bare-bones amenities; smallish rooms. ⊠ *2931 Kalena St.* ☎ *808/246–0908* ⊕ *www.kauaipalmshotel.com* ⤳ *33 rooms* ⌂ *In-room: a/c, safe, kitchen, Wi-Fi. In-hotel: laundry facilities, parking.*

THE SOUTH SHORE

Sunseekers usually head south to the condo-studded shores of Poipu, where three- and four-story complexes line the coast and the surf is generally ideal for swimming. As the island's primary resort community, Poipu has the bulk of the island's accommodations, and more condos than hotels, with prices in the moderate to expensive range. Although it accommodates many visitors, its extensive, colorful landscaping and low-rise buildings save it from feeling dense and overcrowded, and it has a delightful coastal promenade perfect for sunset strolls. Surprisingly, the South Shore doesn't have as many shops and restaurants as one might expect for such a popular resort region, but the new Kukuiula shopping plaza is doing its best to fill the gaps. ■TIP➔ The area's beaches are among the best on the island for families, with sandy shores, shallow waters, and grassy lawns adjacent to the sand.

$$ ⊡ **Garden Isle Cottages.** Tropical fruit trees and flower gardens surround
RENTAL these spacious ocean-side cottages. **Pros:** gorgeous view; oceanfront setting; comfortable accommodations. **Cons:** no sandy beach; cleaning fee. ⊠ *2658 Puuholo Rd., Koloa* ☎ *808/639–9233, 800/742–6711* ⊕ *www.oceancottages.com* ⤳ *2 cottages* ⌂ *In-room: a/c, kitchen. In-hotel: laundry facilities* ▭ *No credit cards.*

Fodor's Choice ★

Grand Hyatt Kauai Resort and Spa

Grand Hyatt Kauai Resort and Spa

Waimea Plantation Cottages

$$$$ 🖼 **Grand Hyatt Kauai Resort and Spa.** Dramatically handsome, this clas-
RESORT sic Hawaiian low-rise is built into the cliffs overlooking an unspoiled
♨ coastline. **Pros:** fabulous pool; excellent restaurants; Hawaiian charac-
Fodor'sChoice ter. **Cons:** poor swimming beach during summer swells; small balconies.
★ ✉ *1571 Poipu Rd., Koloa* ☎ *808/742–1234, 800/633–7313* ⊕ *www.
grandhyattkauai.com* ↘ *602 rooms, 37 suites* △ *In-room: a/c, safe,
Wi-Fi. In-hotel: restaurant, bar, golf course, pool, tennis court, gym,
spa, beach, children's programs.*

$$ 🖼 **Hideaway Cove.** On a quiet street ending in a cul-de-sac, Hideaway
RENTAL Cove is very quiet, even though it's one block from the ocean's edge
in the heart of Poipu. **Pros:** high-quality furnishings; private lanai;
hot tub or Jacuzzi in each unit. **Cons:** not on the ocean; cleaning fee.
✉ *2307 Nalo Rd., Poipu* ☎ *808/635–8785, 866/849–2426* ⊕ *www.
hideawaycove.com* ↘ *7 units* △ *In-room: a/c, kitchen, Wi-Fi. In-hotel:
laundry facilities.*

$ 🖼 **Kauai Cove Cottages.** Three modern studio cottages sit side by side at
RENTAL the mouth of Waikomo Stream. **Pros:** great snorkeling in the nearby
ocean cove. **Cons:** decor borders on kitsch. ✉ *2672 Puuholo Rd., Poipu*
☎ *808/651–0279, 800/624–9945* ⊕ *www.kauaicove.com* ↘ *3 cottages*
△ *In-room: a/c, kitchen.*

$$$$ 🖼 **Koa Kea Hotel and Resort.** This luxury boutique hotel opened in April
HOTEL 2009 on the grounds of the former Poipu Beach Hotel, a Kauai favor-
ite before its destruction by Hurricane Iniki in 1992. **Pros:** incredibly
comfortable beds; brand-new feeling; good food at Red Salt restaurant.
Cons: not much for children; wind noise in hallways can be distracting.
✉ *2251 Poipu Rd., Poipu* ☎ *808/828–8888, 800/230-4134* ⊕ *www.
koakea.com* ↘ *121 rooms* △ *In-room: a/c, safe, Wi-Fi. In-hotel: res-
taurant, bar, pool, spa, beach, water sports, laundry facilities, parking.*

$$$ 🖼 **Makahuena at Poipu.** Situated close to the center of Poipu, on a rocky
RENTAL point over the ocean, the Makahuena is near Shipwreck and Poipu
beaches. **Pros:** reasonable rates; tennis court; scenic setting. **Cons:** no
swimming beach; small footprint. ✉ *1661 Pee Rd., Poipu* ☎ *808/742–
2482, 800/367–5004* ⊕ *www.castleresorts.com* ↘ *78 units* △ *In-room:
no a/c, kitchen, Internet. In-hotel: pool, tennis court.*

$$$ 🖼 **Outrigger Kiahuna Plantation.** Kauai's largest condo project is lacklus-
RENTAL ter, though the location is excellent. **Pros:** great sunset and ocean views
are bonuses in some units. **Cons:** not the best place to stay if you're
looking for a romantic getaway. ✉ *2253 Poipu Rd., Koloa* ☎ *808/742–
6411, 800/688–7444* ⊕ *www.outrigger.com* ↘ *333 units* △ *In-room:
no a/c, kitchen, Internet. In-hotel: restaurant, golf course, pool, tennis
court, beach.*

$$$ 🖼 **Poipu Crater Resort.** These two-bedroom condominium units are
RENTAL fairly spacious, and the large windows and high ceilings add to the
sense of space and light. **Pros:** attractive and well kept; pretty setting.
Cons: beach isn't good for swimming; few resort amenities. ✉ *2330
Hoohu Rd., Poipu* ☎ *808/742–7400* ⊕ *www.suite-paradise.com* ↘ *30
units* △ *In-room: no a/c, kitchen. In-hotel: pool, tennis court, laundry
facilities.*

$$ 🖼 **Poipu Kapili.** Spacious one- and two-bedroom condo units are minutes
RENTAL from Poipu's restaurants and beaches. **Pros:** units are roomy; good guest

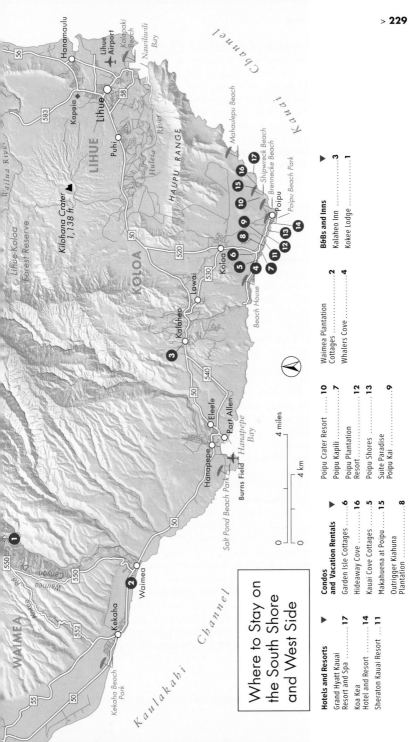

Where to Stay on the South Shore and West Side

Hotels and Resorts ▶
Grand Hyatt Kauai Resort and Spa **17**
Koa Kea Hotel and Resort **14**
Sheraton Kauai Resort ... **11**

Condos and Vacation Rentals ▶
Garden Isle Cottages **6**
Hideaway Cove **16**
Kauai Cove Cottages **5**
Makahuena at Poipu .. **15**
Outrigger Kiahuna Plantation **8**
Poipu Crater Resort **10**
Poipu Kapili **7**
Poipu Plantation Resort **12**
Poipu Shores **13**
Suite Paradise Poipu Kai **9**
Waimea Plantation Cottages **2**
Whalers Cove **4**

B&Bs and Inns ▶
Kalaheo Inn **3**
Kokee Lodge **1**

9

services; property is small. **Cons:** units are ocean-view but not ocean-front. ✉ *2221 Kapili Rd., Koloa* ☎ *808/742–6449, 800/443–7714* ⊕ *www.poipukapili.com* 🛏 *60 units* ☐ *In-room: a/c, kitchen, Internet. In-hotel: pool, tennis court, laundry facilities.*

$
RENTAL
☐ **Poipu Plantation Resort.** Plumeria, ti, and other tropical foliage create a lush landscape for this resort, which has one bed-and-breakfast–style plantation home and nine one- and two-bedroom cottage apartments. **Pros:** attractively furnished; full breakfast at B&B. **Cons:** three-night minimum. ✉ *1792 Pee Rd., Poipu* ☎ *808/742–6757, 800/634–0263* ⊕ *www.poipubeach.com* 🛏 *4 suites, 9 cottages* ☐ *In-room: a/c, kitchen, Wi-Fi. In-hotel: laundry facilities.*

$$$
RENTAL
☐ **Poipu Shores.** Sitting on a rocky point above pounding surf, this is a perfect spot for whale or turtle watching. **Pros:** every unit faces the water; oceanfront pool; wildlife viewing. **Cons:** units vary widely in style; no resort amenities. ✉ *1775 Pee Rd., Koloa* ☎ *808/742–7700, 800/367–5004* ⊕ *www.castleresorts.com* 🛏 *39 units* ☐ *In-room: no a/c, kitchen, Internet. In-hotel: pool, laundry facilities.*

$$$$
RESORT
Fodor's Choice
★
☐ **Sheraton Kauai Resort.** The resort's ocean-wing accommodations here are so close to the water you can practically feel the spray of the surf as it hits the rocks below. **Pros:** ocean-view pool; quiet; nice dining views. **Cons:** no swimming beach; rather staid atmosphere. ✉ *2440 Hoonani Rd., Poipu Beach, Koloa* 📧 *2440 Hoonani Rd. 96756* ☎ *808/742–1661, 888/488–3535* ⊕ *www.sheraton-kauai.com* 🛏 *394 rooms, 8 suites* ☐ *In-room: a/c, safe, Wi-Fi. In-hotel: restaurant, bar, pool, tennis court, gym, beach, children's programs, laundry facilities, business center.*

$$
RENTAL
☐ **Suite Paradise Poipu Kai.** Condominiums, many with cathedral ceilings and all with big windows overlooking the lawns, give this property the feeling of a spacious, quiet retreat inside and out. **Pros:** close to nice beaches; full kitchens; good rates for the location. **Cons:** units aren't especially spacious; beaches not ideal for swimming. ✉ *1941 Poipu Rd., Koloa* ☎ *808/742–6464, 800/367–8020* ⊕ *www.suite-paradise.com* 🛏 *130 units* ☐ *In-room: a/c, safe, kitchen, Internet. In-hotel: restaurant, pool, tennis court.*

$$$$
RENTAL
☐ **Whalers Cove.** Perched about as close to the water's edge as they can get, these two-bedroom condos are the most luxurious on the South Shore. **Pros:** daily service; on-site staff; extremely luxurious; outstanding setting; fully equipped units (1,400–2,000 square feet). **Cons:** rocky beach not ideal for swimming. ✉ *2640 Puuholo Rd., Koloa* ☎ *808/742–7571, 800/225–2683* ⊕ *www.whalerscoveresort.com* 🛏 *39 units* ☐ *In-room: no a/c, kitchen, Internet. In-hotel: pool, beach, laundry facilities.*

Sheraton Kauai Resort

THE WEST SIDE

If you want to do a lot of hiking or immerse yourself in the island's history, find a room in Waimea (though this is not a resort area, so be aware that the pickings are slim). You won't find many restaurants and shops, but you will encounter dark skies, quiet days, miles of largely deserted beach, and a rural environment.

$

B&B/INN

Kalaheo Inn. It isn't easy to find lodgings on the West Side, but this old-fashioned inn does the job in Kalaheo town, where accommodations are otherwise unavailable. **Pros:** some units have kitchens; walking distance to restaurants. **Cons:** no beach; some traffic noise; no-frills lodgings. ⊠ *4444 Papalina Rd., Kalaheo, Kalaheo* ☎ *808/332–6023, 888/332–6023* ⊕ *www.kalaheoinn.com* ⤵ *14 units* ⚬ *In-room: no a/c, kitchen. In-hotel: laundry facilities, parking.*

$

B&B/INN

Kokee Lodge. If you're an outdoors enthusiast, you can appreciate Kauai's mountain wilderness from the 12 rustic cabins that make up this lodge. **Pros:** outstanding setting; more refined than camping; cooking facilities. **Cons:** very austere; no restaurants for dinner; remote. ⊠ *3600 Kokee Rd., at mile marker 15, Waimea* ⌂ *Box 819, Waimea 96796* ☎ *808/335–6061* ⊕ *www.thelodgeatkokee.net* ⤵ *12 cabins* ⚬ *In-room: no a/c, kitchen, no TV. In-hotel: restaurant.*

$

RENTAL

Fodor's Choice

★

Waimea Plantation Cottages. History buffs will adore these reconstructed sugar-plantation cottages, which were originally built in the early 1900s. **Pros:** unique, homey lodging; quiet and low-key. **Cons:** not a white-sand beach; rooms are not luxurious. ⊠ *9400 Kaumualii Hwy., Box 367, Waimea* ☎ *808/338–1625, 800/992–4632* ⊕ *www. waimeaplantation.com* ⤵ *55 cottages* ⚬ *In-room: no a/c, Internet. In-hotel: restaurant, bar, pool, spa, beach, business center.*

UNDERSTANDING KAUAI

HAWAIIAN VOCABULARY

Although an understanding of Hawaiian is by no means required on a trip to the Aloha State, a *malihini,* or newcomer, will find plenty of opportunities to pick up a few of the local words and phrases. Traditional names and expressions are widely used in the Islands. You're likely to read or hear at least a few words each day of your stay.

With a basic understanding and some uninhibited practice, anyone can have enough command of the local tongue to ask for directions and to order from a restaurant menu. One visitor announced she would not leave until she could pronounce the name of the state fish, the *humuhumunukunukuāpua'a.*

Simplifying the learning process is the fact that the Hawaiian language contains only eight consonants—H, K, L, M, N, P, W, and the silent *'okina,* or glottal stop, written '—plus one or more of the five vowels. All syllables, and therefore all words, end in a vowel. Each vowel, with the exception of a few diphthongized double vowels such as *au* (pronounced "ow") or *ai* (pronounced "eye"), is pronounced separately. Thus *'Iolani* is four syllables (ee-oh-la-nee), not three (yo-la-nee). Although some Hawaiian words have only vowels, most also contain some consonants, but consonants are never doubled.

Pronunciation is simple. Pronounce *A* "ah" as in *father; E* "ay" as in *weigh; I* "ee" as in *marine; O* "oh" as in *no; U* "oo" as in *true.*

Consonants mirror their English equivalents, with the exception of W. When the letter begins any syllable other than the first one in a word, it is usually pronounced as a V. *'Awa,* the Polynesian drink, is pronounced "ava," *'ewa* is pronounced "eva."

Almost all long Hawaiian words are combinations of shorter words; they are not difficult to pronounce if you segment them. *Kalaniana'ole,* the highway running east from Honolulu, is easily understood as *Kalani ana 'ole.* Apply the standard pronunciation rules—the stress falls on the next-to-last syllable of most two- or three-syllable Hawaiian words—and Kalaniana'ole Highway is as easy to say as Main Street.

Now about that fish. Try *humu-humu nuku-nuku āpu a'a.*

The other unusual element in Hawaiian language is the *kahakō,* or macron, written as a short line (‾) placed over a vowel. Like the accent (´) in Spanish, the kahakō puts emphasis on a syllable that would normally not be stressed. The most familiar example is probably *Waikīkī.* With no macrons, the stress would fall on the middle syllable; with only one macron, on the last syllable, the stress would fall on the first and last syllables. Some words become plural with the addition of a macron, often on a syllable that would have been stressed anyway. No Hawaiian word becomes plural with the addition of an *S,* since that letter does not exist in the language.

The Hawaiian diacritical marks are not printed in this guide.

Pidgin

You may hear pidgin, the unofficial language of Hawai'i. It is a Creole language, with its own grammar, evolved from the mixture of English, Hawaiian, Japanese, Portuguese, and other languages spoken in 19th-century Hawai'i, and it is heard everywhere.

Glossary

What follows is a glossary of some of the most commonly used Hawaiian words. Hawaiian residents appreciate visitors who at least try to pick up the local language.

'a'ā: rough, crumbling lava, contrasting with *pāhoehoe,* which is smooth.

'ae: yes.

aikane: friend.

āina: land.

akamai: smart, clever, possessing savoir faire.

akua: god.

ala: a road, path, or trail.

ali'i: a Hawaiian chief, a member of the chiefly class.

aloha: love, affection, kindness; also a salutation meaning both greetings and farewell.

'ānuenue: rainbow.

'a'ole: no.

'apōpō: tomorrow.

'auwai: a ditch.

auwē: alas, woe is me!

'ehu: a red-haired Hawaiian.

'ewa: in the direction of 'Ewa plantation, west of Honolulu.

hala: the pandanus tree, whose leaves (*lau hala*) are used to make baskets and plaited mats.

hālau: school.

hale: a house.

hale pule: church, house of worship.

ha mea iki or **ha mea 'ole:** you're welcome.

hana: to work.

haole: ghost. Since the first foreigners were Caucasian, *haole* now means a Caucasian person.

hapa: a part, sometimes a half; often used as a short form of *hapa haole*, to mean a person who is part-Caucasian.

hau'oli: to rejoice. *Hau'oli Makahiki Hou* means Happy New Year. *Hau'oli lā hānau* means Happy Birthday.

heiau: an outdoor stone platform; an ancient Hawaiian place of worship.

holo: to run.

holoholo: to go for a walk, ride, or sail.

holokū: a long Hawaiian dress, somewhat fitted, with a yoke and a train. Influenced by European fashion, it was worn at court, and at least one local translates the word as "expensive mu'umu'u."

holomū: a post–World War II cross between a *holokū* and a mu'umu'u, less fitted than the former but less voluminous than the latter, and having no train.

honi: to kiss; a kiss. A phrase that some tourists may find useful, quoted from a popular hula, is *Honi Ka'ua Wikiwiki:* Kiss me quick!

honu: turtle.

ho'omalimali: flattery, a deceptive "line," bunk, baloney, hooey.

huhū: angry.

hui: a group, club, or assembly. A church may refer to its congregation as a *hui* and a social club may be called a *hui*.

hukilau: a seine; a communal fishing party in which everyone helps to drive the fish into a huge net, pull it in, and divide the catch.

hula: the dance of Hawai'i.

iki: little.

ipo: sweetheart.

ka: the. This is the definite article for most singular words; for plural nouns, the definite article is usually *nā*. Since there is no *S* in Hawaiian, the article may be your only clue that a noun is plural.

kahuna: a priest, doctor, or other trained person of old Hawai'i, endowed with special professional skills that often included prophecy or other supernatural powers; the plural form is *kāhuna*.

kai: the sea, saltwater.

kalo: the taro plant from whose root *poi* (paste) is made.

kamā'aina: literally, a child of the soil; it refers to people who were born in the Islands or have lived there for a long time.

kanaka: originally a man or humanity, it is now used to denote a male Hawaiian or part-Hawaiian, but is occasionally taken as a slur when used by non-Hawaiians. *Kanaka maoli*, originally a full-blooded Hawaiian person, is used by some Native Hawaiian rights activists to embrace part-Hawaiians as well.

kāne: a man, a husband. If you see this word on a door, it's the men's room. If you see *kane* on a door, it's probably a misspelling; that is the Hawaiian name for the skin fungus tinea.

kapa: also called by its Tahitian name, *tapa*, a cloth made of beaten bark and usually dyed and stamped with a repeat design.

kapakahi: crooked, cockeyed, uneven. You've got your hat on *kapakahi*.

kapu: keep out, prohibited. This is the Hawaiian version of the more widely known Tongan word *tabu* (taboo).

kapuna: grandparent; elder.

kēia lā: today.

keiki: a child; *keikikāne* is a boy, *keiki-wahine* a girl.

kona: the leeward side of the Islands, the direction (south) from which the *kona* wind and *kona* rain come.

kula: upland.

kuleana: a homestead or small plot of ground on which a family has been installed for some generations without necessarily owning it. By extension, *kuleana* is used to denote any area or department in which one has a special interest or prerogative. You'll hear it used this way: If you want to hire a surfboard, see Moki; that's his *kuleana*.

lā: sun.

lamalama: to fish with a torch.

lānai: a porch, a balcony, an outdoor living room. Almost every house in Hawai'i has one. Don't confuse this two-syllable word with the three-syllable name of the island, Lāna'i.

lani: heaven, the sky.

lau hala: the leaf of the *hala*, or pandanus tree, widely used in handicrafts.

lei: a garland of flowers.

limu: sun.

lolo: stupid.

luna: a plantation overseer or foreman.

mahalo: thank you.

makai: toward the ocean.

malihini: a newcomer to the Islands.

mana: the spiritual power that the Hawaiians believe inhabit all things and creatures.

manō: shark.

manuwahi: free, gratis.

mauka: toward the mountains.

mauna: mountain.

mele: a Hawaiian song or chant, often of epic proportions.

Mele Kalikimaka: Merry Christmas (a transliteration from the English phrase).

Menehune: a Hawaiian pixie. The *Mene-hune* were a legendary race of little people who accomplished prodigious work, such as building fishponds and temples in the course of a single night.

moana: the ocean.

mu'umu'u: the voluminous dress in which the missionaries enveloped Hawaiian women. Now made in bright printed cottons and silks, it is an indispensable garment. Culturally sensitive locals have embraced the Hawaiian spelling but often shorten the spoken word to "mu'u." Most English dictionaries include the spelling "muumuu."

nani: beautiful.

nui: big.

ohana: family.

'ono: delicious.

pāhoehoe: smooth, unbroken, satiny lava.

Pākē: Chinese. This *Pākē* carver makes beautiful things.

palapala: document, printed matter.

pali: a cliff, precipice.

pānini: prickly pear cactus.

paniolo: a Hawaiian cowboy, a rough transliteration of *español*, the language of the Islands' earliest cowboys.

pau: finished, done.

pilikia: trouble. The Hawaiian word is much more widely used here than its English equivalent.

puka: a hole.

pupule: crazy, like the celebrated Princess Pupule. This word has replaced its English equivalent in local usage.

pu'u: volcanic cinder cone.

waha: mouth.

wahine: a female, a woman, a wife, and a sign on the ladies' room door; the plural form is *wāhine*.

wai: freshwater, as opposed to saltwater, which is *kai*.

wailele: waterfall.

wikiwiki: to hurry, hurry up (since this is a reduplication of *wiki*, quick, neither W is pronounced as a V).

Travel Smart
Kauai

GETTING HERE AND AROUND

▌ AIR TRAVEL

Flying time is about 10 hours from New York, 8 hours from Chicago, and 5 hours from Los Angeles.

Some of the major airline carriers serving Hawaii fly directly from the U.S. mainland to Kauai, allowing you to bypass connecting flights out of Honolulu. Although Lihue Airport is smaller and more casual than Honolulu International, it can also be quite busy during peak times. Allot extra travel time during morning and afternoon rush-hour traffic periods.

Plan to arrive at the airport approximately 60 minutes before departure for interisland flights and slightly longer than that for flights to the mainland.

Plants and plant products are subject to regulation by the Department of Agriculture, both on entering and leaving Hawaii. Upon leaving the Islands, you'll have to have your bags X-rayed and tagged at one of the airport's agricultural inspection stations before you proceed to check-in. Pineapples and coconuts with the packer's agricultural inspection stamp pass freely; papayas must be treated, inspected, and stamped. All other fruits are banned for export to the U.S. mainland. Flowers pass—except for gardenias, rose leaves, jade vine, and mauna loa. Also banned are insects, snails, soil, cotton, cacti, sugarcane, and all berry plants.

You'll have to leave dogs and other pets at home. A 120-day quarantine is imposed to keep out rabies, which is nonexistent in Hawaii. If specific pre- and postarrival requirements are met, animals may qualify for a 30-day or 5-day-or-less quarantine.

Air Travel Resources in Hawaii State of Hawaii Airports Division Offices ☎ *808/836–6417* ⊕ *www.hawaii.gov/dot/ airports.*

AIRPORTS

Honolulu International Airport (HNL) is the main stopover for most domestic and international flights. From Honolulu, there are interisland flights to Kauai departing regularly from early morning until evening. In addition, some carriers now offer nonstop service directly from the U.S. mainland to Lihue Airport (LIH) on a limited basis.

HONOLULU/OAHU AIRPORT

Hawaii's major airport is Honolulu International, on Oahu, 20 minutes (9 mi) west of Waikiki. To travel interisland from Honolulu, you can depart from either the interisland terminal or the commuter-airline terminal, located in two separate structures adjacent to the main overseas terminal building. A free bus service, the Wiki Wiki Shuttle, operates between terminals.

Information Honolulu International Airport (HNL) ☎ *808/836–6413* ⊕ *www.hawaii.gov/ dot/airports.*

KAUAI

On Kauai, visitors fly into Lihue Airport, on the East Side of the island. Visitor Information Booths are outside each baggage-claim area. Visitors will also find news- and lei stands, an HMS Host restaurant, and a Travel Traders gift shop at the airport.

Information Lihue Airport (LIH) ☎ *808/274– 3800* ⊕ *www.hawaii.gov/dot/airports.*

GROUND TRANSPORTATION

Marriott Kauai and Radisson Kauai Beach Resort provide airport shuttles to and from the Lihue Airport. In addition, travelers who've booked a tour with Kauai Island Tours, Roberts Hawaii, or Polynesian Adventure Tours will be picked up at the airport.

SpeediShuttle offers transportation between the airport and hotels, resorts, and time-share complexes on the island. There is an online reservation and fare quote system for information and bookings. Or, you can hire a taxi or limousine. Cabs are available curbside at baggage claim. Cab fares to locations around the island are estimated as follows: Poipu $35–$41, Wailua–Waipouli $17–$20, Lihue–Kukui Grove $10, Princeville–Haena $72–$95. There are two limousine companies that service Lihue Airport: Any Time Shuttle and Kauai North Shore Limo.

Contacts **Any Time Shuttle** ☎ 808/927–1120. **Kauai North Shore Limo** ☎ 808/634–7260. **SpeediShuttle** ☎ 877/242–5777 ⊕ www. speedishuttle.com.

FLIGHTS

Alaska Airlines has a daily Seattle–Lihue flight. America West/US Airways flies into Lihue from San Francisco and Denver and also has flights into Oahu, Maui, and the Big Island. American Airlines offers a daily, nonstop Los Angeles–Kauai flight, in addition to its service into Honolulu, Maui, and the Big Island. Delta has a Los Angeles–Lihue flight and also serves Oahu (Honolulu) and Maui. United Airlines provides direct service to Lihue Airport from Denver, Los Angeles, and San Francisco. The carrier also flies into Honolulu, Maui, and the Big Island.

Airline Contacts **American Airlines** ☎ 800/433–7300 ⊕ www.aa.com. **America West/US Airways** ☎ 800/428–4322 ⊕ www. usairways.com. **Delta Airlines** ☎ 800/221–1212 ⊕ www.delta.com. **Hawaiian Airlines** ☎ 800/367–5320 ⊕ www.hawaiianair.com. **Delta Airlines** ☎ 800/225–2525 ⊕ www. nwa.com. **United Airlines** ☎ 800/864–8331 ⊕ www.united.com.

INTERISLAND FLIGHTS

Interisland flight travel has become expensive in recent years, so be ready to pay should you wish to visit neighboring islands. go! Mokulele Airlines, Hawaiian Airlines, and IslandAir offer regular service between the Islands. In addition to offering a discount for booking online, all have free frequent-flier programs that will entitle you to rewards and upgrades the more you fly. Be sure to compare prices offered by all the interisland carriers. If you are somewhat flexible with your days and times for island hopping, you should have no problem getting a round-trip ticket.

Interisland Carriers **go! Mokulele Airlines** ☎ 888/435–9462, 808/426–7070 ⊕ www. iflygo.com or www.mokuleleairlines.com. **Hawaiian Airlines** ☎ 800/367–5320 ⊕ www. hawaiianair.com. **IslandAir** ☎ 800/652–6541 ⊕ www.islandair.com.

▌ BOAT TRAVEL

CRUISES

For information about cruises, see Chapter 1, "Experience Kauai."

▌ BUS TRAVEL

On Kauai, the County Transportation Agency operates the Kauai Bus, which provides service between Hanalei and Kekaha. It also provides service to the airport and limited service to Koloa and Poipu. The fare is $2 for adults, and frequent-rider passes are available.

Information **Kauai Bus** ☎ 808/241–6410 ⊕ www.kauai.gov/OCA/Transportation.

▌ CAR TRAVEL

The best way to experience all of Kauai's stunning beauty is to get in a car and explore. The 15-mile stretch of Napali Coast, with its breathtaking, verdant-green sheer cliffs, is the only part of the island that's not accessible by car. Otherwise, one main road can get you from Barking Sands Beach on the West Side to Haena on the North Shore.

Asking for directions will almost always produce a helpful explanation from the locals, but you should be prepared for an island term or two. Instead of using compass directions, remember that Hawaii residents refer to places as being either *mauka* (toward the mountains) or *makai* (toward the ocean) from one another. Hawaii has a strict seat-belt law. Those riding in the front seat must wear a seat belt, and children under the age of 17 in the backseats must be belted. The fine for not wearing a seat belt is $92. There is also a law forbidding the use of hand-held devices while driving. Jaywalking is also common in the Islands, so please pay careful attention to the roads. It also is considered rude to honk your horn, so be patient if someone is turning or proceeding through an intersection.

While driving on Kauai, you will come across several one-lane bridges. If you are the first to approach a bridge, the car on the other side will wait while you cross. If a car on the other side is closer to the bridge, then you should wait while the driver crosses. If you're enjoying the island's dramatic views, pull over to the shoulder so you don't block traffic.

GASOLINE
You can count on having to pay more at the pump for gasoline on Kauai than on the U.S. mainland. There are no gas stations past Princeville on the North Shore, and no stations past Waimea on the West Side, so if you're running low, fuel up before heading out to the end of the road.

PARKING
On Kauai there are no parking meters, parking garages, parking tags, or paid parking. If there's room on the side of the road, you can park there. A good rule of thumb is if there are other cars parked in that area, it's safe to do the same.

ROAD CONDITIONS
Kauai has a well-maintained highway running south from Lihue to Barking Sands Beach; a spur at Waimea takes you along Waimea Canyon Drive to Kokee State Park. A northern route also winds its way from Lihue to the end of the road at Haena, the beginning of the rugged and roadless Napali Coast. Opt for a four-wheel-drive vehicle if dirt-road exploration holds any appeal.

ROADSIDE EMERGENCIES
If you find yourself in an emergency or accident while driving on Kauai, pull over if you can. If you have a cell phone with you, call the roadside assistance number on your rental-car contract or AAA Help. If you find that your car has been broken into or stolen, report it immediately to your rental-car company and an agent can assist you. If it's an emergency and someone is hurt, call 911 immediately and stay there until medical personnel arrive.

Emergency Services AAA Help
☎ *800/222-4357.*

CAR RENTAL
Should you plan to do any sightseeing on Kauai, it is best to rent a car. Even if all you want to do is relax at your resort, you may want to hop in the car to check out one of the island's popular restaurants.

While on Kauai, you can rent anything from an econobox to a Ferrari. Rates are usually better if you reserve through a rental agency's website. It's wise to make reservations far in advance and make sure that a confirmed reservation guarantees you a car, especially if you're visiting during peak seasons or for major conventions or sporting events. Rates begin at about $25 to $35 a day for an economy car with air-conditioning, automatic transmission, and unlimited mileage, depending on your pickup location. This does not include the airport concession fee, general excise tax, rental-vehicle surcharge, or vehicle license fee. When you reserve a car, ask about cancellation penalties and drop-off charges should you plan to pick up the car in one location and return it to another. Many rental companies in Hawaii offer coupons for discounts at various attractions that could save you money later on in your trip.

In Hawaii you must be 21 years of age to rent a car, and you must have a valid driver's license and a major credit card. Those under 25 will pay a daily surcharge of $15–$25. Request car seats and extras such as GPS when you book. Hawaii's

CAR RENTAL RESOURCES		
Automobile Associations		
U.S.: American Automobile Association	☎ 315/797–5000	⊕ www.aaa.com
National Automobile Club	☎ 650/294–7000	⊕ www.thenac.com; CA residents only
Major Agencies		
Alamo	☎ 800/462–5266	⊕ www.alamo.com
Avis	☎ 800/331–1212	⊕ www.avis.com
Budget	☎ 800/527–0700	⊕ www.budget.com
Hertz	☎ 800/654–3131	⊕ www.hertz.com
National Car Rental	☎ 800/227–7368	⊕ www.nationalcar.com
Thrifty Car Rental	☎ 888/400–8877	⊕ www.thrifty.com

Child Restraint Law requires that all children three years and younger be in an approved child safety seat in the backseat of a vehicle. Children ages four to seven must be seated in a rear booster seat or child restraint such as a lap and shoulder belt. Car seats and boosters range from $5 to $8 per day.

In Hawaii, your unexpired mainland driver's license is valid for rental for up to 90 days.

Since the road circling the island is usually two lanes, be sure to allow plenty of time to return your vehicle so that you can make your flight. Traffic can be bad during morning and afternoon rush hour. Give yourself about two hours before departure time to return your vehicle.

LOCAL DO'S AND TABOOS

GREETINGS

Hawaii is a very friendly place, and this is reflected in the day-to-day encounters with friends, family, and even business associates. Women often hug and kiss one another on the cheek, and men shake hands and sometimes combine that with a friendly hug. When a man and a woman are greeting each other and are good friends, it is not unusual for them to hug and kiss on the cheek. Children are taught to call any elders "auntie" or "uncle," even if they aren't related. It's a way to show respect and can result in a local Hawaiian child having dozens of aunties or uncles. It's also reflective of the strong sense of *ohana* (family) that exists in the Islands.

When you walk off a long flight, perhaps a bit groggy and stiff, nothing quite compares with a Hawaiian lei greeting. The casual ceremony ranks as one of the fastest ways to make the transition from the worries of home to the joys of your vacation. Though the tradition has created an expectation that everyone receives this floral garland when he or she steps off the plane, the State of Hawaii cannot greet each of its nearly 7 million annual visitors.

If you've booked a vacation with a wholesaler or tour company, a lei greeting might be included in your package, so check before you leave. If not, it's easy to arrange a lei greeting for yourself or your companions before you arrive into Lihue Airport. Kamaaina Leis, Flowers & Greeters has been providing lei greetings for visitors to the Islands since 1983. To be really wowed by the experience, request a lei of plumeria, some of the most divine-smelling blossoms on the planet. A plumeria or dendrobium orchid lei is considered standard and costs $19 to $22 per person.

Information Kamaaina Leis, Flowers & Greeters ☎ *808/836–3246, 800/367–5183* ⊕ *www.alohaleigreetings.com.*

LANGUAGE

Hawaii was admitted to the Union in 1959, so residents can be sensitive when visitors refer to their own hometowns as "back in the States." Remember, when in Hawaii, refer to the contiguous 48 states as "the mainland" and not as the United States. When you do, you won't appear to be such a *malahini* (newcomer).

English is the primary language on the Islands. Making the effort to learn some Hawaiian words can be rewarding, however. Despite the length of many Hawaiian words, the Hawaiian alphabet is actually one of the world's shortest, with only 12 letters: the five vowels, *a, e, i, o, u,* and seven consonants, *h, k, l, m, n, p, w.* Hawaiian words you're most likely to encounter during your visit to the Islands are *aloha, mahalo* (thank you), *keiki* (child), *haole* (Caucasian or foreigner, a derogatory term), *mauka* (toward the mountains), *makai* (toward the ocean), and *pau* (finished, all done). Hawaiian history includes waves of immigrants, each bringing its own language. To communicate with each other, they developed a sort of slang known as "pidgin." If you listen closely, you'll know what is being said by the inflections and by the extensive use of body language. For example, when you know what you want to say but don't know how to say it, just say, "You know, da kine." For an informative and somewhat hilarious view of things Hawaiian, check out Jerry Hopkins's series of books titled *Pidgin to the Max* and *Fax to the Max,* available at most local bookstores in the Hawaiiana sections.

ESSENTIALS

▌ COMMUNICATIONS

INTERNET

If you've brought your laptop with you to Kauai, you should have no problem checking email or connecting to the Internet. Most of the major hotels and resorts offer high-speed access in rooms and/or lobbies. You should check with your hotel in advance to confirm that access is wireless; if not, ask whether in-room cables are provided. In some cases an hourly charge will be posted to your room that averages about $15 per hour. If you're staying at a small inn or B&B without Internet access, ask the proprietor for the nearest café or coffee shop with wireless access.

▌ HEALTH

In addition to being the Aloha State, Hawaii is known as the Health State. The life expectancy here is 79 years, the longest in the nation. Balmy weather makes it easy to remain active year-round, and the low-stress aloha attitude certainly contributes to general well-being. When you are visiting the Islands, however, there are a few health issues to keep in mind.

The Hawaii State Department of Health recommends that you drink 16 ounces of water per hour to avoid dehydration when hiking or spending time in the sun. Use sunblock, wear UV-reflective sunglasses, and protect your head with a visor or hat for shade. If you're not acclimated to warm, humid weather you should allow plenty of time for rest stops and refreshments. When visiting freshwater streams, be aware of the tropical disease leptospirosis, which is spread by animal urine and carried into streams and mud. Symptoms include fever, headache, nausea, and red eyes. If left untreated, it can cause liver and kidney damage, respiratory failure, internal bleeding, and even death. To avoid this, don't swim or wade in freshwater streams or ponds if you have open sores, and don't drink from any freshwater streams or ponds, especially after heavy rains.

On the Islands, fog is a rare occurrence, but there can often be "vog," an airborne haze of gases released from volcanic vents on the Big Island. During certain weather conditions such as "Kona Winds," the vog can settle over the Islands and wreak havoc with respiratory and other health conditions, especially asthma or emphysema. If susceptible, stay indoors and get emergency assistance if needed.

The Islands have their share of bugs and insects that enjoy the tropical climate as much as visitors do. Most are harmless but annoying. When planning to spend time outdoors in hiking areas, wear long-sleeved clothing and pants and use mosquito repellent containing DEET. In very damp places you may encounter the dreaded local centipede. On the Islands they usually come in two colors, brown and blue, and they range from the size of a worm to an 8-inch cigar. Their sting is very painful, and the reaction is similar to bee- and wasp-sting reactions. When camping, shake out your sleeping bag before climbing in, and check your shoes in the morning, as the centipedes like cozy places. If planning on hiking or traveling in remote areas, always carry a first-aid kit and appropriate medications for sting reactions.

▌ HOURS OF OPERATION

Even people in paradise have to work. Generally, local business hours are weekdays 8–5. Banks are usually open Monday–Thursday 8:30–3 and until 6 on Friday. Some banks have Saturday-morning hours.

Many self-serve gas stations stay open around the clock, with full-service stations usually open from around 7 am until 9 pm. U.S. post offices are open weekdays 8:30 am–4:30 pm and Saturday 8:30–noon.

Most museums generally open their doors between 9 am and 10 am and stay open until 5 pm Tuesday–Saturday. Many museums operate with afternoon hours only on Sunday and close on Monday. Visitor-attraction hours vary throughout the state, but most sights are open daily, with the exception of major holidays such as Christmas. Check local newspapers upon arrival for attraction hours and schedules if visiting over holiday periods. The local dailies carry a listing of "What's Open/What's Not" for those time periods.

Stores in resort areas sometimes open as early as 8, with shopping-center opening hours varying from 9:30 to 10 on weekdays and Saturday, a bit later on Sunday. Bigger malls stay open until 9 weekdays and Saturday and close at 5 on Sunday. Boutiques in resort areas may stay open as late as 11.

▌ MONEY

Prices throughout this guide are given for adults. Substantially reduced fees are almost always available for children, students, and senior citizens.

CREDIT CARDS

It's a good idea to inform your credit-card company before you travel. Otherwise, the credit-card company might put a hold on your card owing to unusual activity—not a good thing halfway through your trip. Record all your credit-card numbers—as well as the phone numbers to call if your cards are lost or stolen—in a safe place, so you're prepared should something go wrong. Both MasterCard and Visa have general numbers you can call (collect if you're abroad) if your card is lost, but you're better off calling the number of your issuing bank, since MasterCard and Visa usually just transfer you to your bank; your bank's number is usually printed on your card.

Reporting Lost Cards American Express ☎ 800/528–4800 ⊕ www.americanexpress.

com. **Diners Club** ☎ 800/234–6377 ⊕ www.dinersclub.com. **Discover** ☎ 800/347–2683 ⊕ www.discovercard.com. **MasterCard** ☎ 800/622-7747 in the U.S. ⊕ www.mastercard.com. **Visa** ☎ 800/847–2911 ⊕ www.visa.com.

▌ PACKING

Hawaii is casual: sandals, bathing suits, and comfortable, informal clothing are the norm. In summer, synthetic slacks and shirts, although easy to care for, can be uncomfortably warm.

One of the most important things to tuck into your suitcase is sunscreen.

As for clothing in the Hawaiian Islands, there's a saying that when a man wears a suit during the day, he's either going for a loan or he's a lawyer trying a case. Only a few upscale restaurants require a jacket for dinner. The aloha shirt is accepted dress in Hawaii for business and most social occasions. Shorts are acceptable daytime attire, along with a T-shirt or polo shirt. There's no need to buy expensive sandals on the mainland—here you can get flip-flops for a couple of dollars and off-brand sandals for $20. Golfers should remember that many courses have dress codes requiring a collared shirt; call courses you're interested in for details. If you're not prepared, you can pick up appropriate clothing at resort pro shops. If you're visiting in winter, bring a sweater or light- to medium-weight jacket. A polar fleece pullover is ideal and makes a great impromptu travel pillow.

▌ SAFETY

Hawaii is generally a safe tourist destination, but it's still wise to follow the same commonsense safety precautions you would normally follow in your own hometown.

Be wary of those hawking "too good to be true" prices on everything from car rentals to attractions. Many of these offers are just a lure to get you in the door for time-share presentations. When handed a flier, read the fine print before you make your decision to participate.

Safety Transportation Security Administration ⊕ *www.tsa.gov.*

TAXES

There's a 4.16% state sales tax on all purchases, including food. As of July 2010, a hotel room tax plus the state sales tax add a 13.42% rate to your hotel bill. A $3-per-day road tax is also assessed on each rental vehicle.

TIME

Hawaii is on Hawaiian Standard Time, five hours behind New York and two hours behind Los Angeles for the winter months.

While the U.S. mainland uses daylight saving time from March until November, Hawaii does not, so add an extra hour of time difference between the Islands and U.S. mainland destinations during that part of the year. You may also find that things generally move more slowly here. That has nothing to do with your watch—it's just the laid-back way called Hawaiian time.

TIPPING

Tip cabdrivers 15% of the fare. Standard tips for restaurants and bar tabs run from 15% to 20% of the bill, depending on the standard of service. Bellhops at hotels usually receive $1 per bag, more if you have bulky items such as bicycles and surfboards. Tip the hotel room maid $1 per night, paid daily. Tip doormen $1 for assistance with taxis; tips for concierges vary depending on the service. For example, tip more for "hard-to-get" event tickets or dining reservations.

For single-day guided activities like a boat trip to the Napali, a ziplining tour, or surf lessons, you should tip each guide at least $10–$20 if you feel he or she enhanced

your experience. Oftentimes, the tour company takes the bulk of your booking price, and the locals who are sharing their aloha with you are depending on your tips.

TOURS

Globus has two Hawaii itineraries that include Kauai, one of which is an escorted cruise on Norwegian Cruise Lines' *Pride of Aloha* that includes two days on the Garden Island. Tauck Travel offers an 11-night *Best of Hawaii* tour that includes two nights on Kauai with leisure time for either relaxation or exploration.

EscortedHawaiiTours.com, owned and operated by Atlas Cruises & Tours, sells more than a dozen Hawaii trips ranging from 7 to 12 nights operated by various guided-tour companies including Globus and Tauck. Several of these trips include two to three nights on Kauai.

Recommended Companies Atlas Cruises & Tours ☎ *800/942–3301* ⊕ *www. EscortedHawaiiTours.com.* **Globus** ☎ *866/755–8581* ⊕ *www.globusjourneys.com.* **Tauck Travel** ☎ *800/788–7885* ⊕ *www.tauck.com.*

SPECIAL-INTEREST TOURS
BIRD-WATCHING

Hawaii has more than 150 species of birds that live in the Hawaiian Islands. Field Guides has a three-island (Oahu, Kauai, and the Big Island), 11-day guided bird-watching trip for 14 birding enthusiasts that focuses on endemic land birds and specialty seabirds. While on Kauai, birders will visit Kokee State Park, Alakai Wilderness Preserve, and Kilauea Point. The trip costs about $4,400 per person and includes accommodations, meals, ground transportation, interisland air, an eight-hour pelagic boat trip, and guided bird-watching excursions. Travelers must purchase their own airfare to and from their gateway city. Field Guides has been offering worldwide birding tours since 1984.

Victor Emanuel Nature Tours, the largest company in the world specializing in birding tours, has two nine-day trips that include Kauai. The guide for both tours is Bob Sundstrom, a skilled birder with a special interest in birdsong who has been leading birding tours in Hawaii and other destinations since 1989. *Spring Hawaii* is the theme of the late February/ early March birding trip, when seabird diversity on the island is at its peak. Birders will see the koloa (Hawaiian duck), one of Hawaii's most endangered wetland birds; as well as Laysan albatrosses, red- and white-tailed tropic birds, red-footed boobies, wedge-tailed shearwaters, great frigate birds, brown boobies, and possibly even red-billed tropic birds. Participants in the *Fall Hawaii* birding trip will visit Oahu, Kauai, and the Big Island in October. Birders will see Kauai honeycreepers and Hawaiian short-eared owls at Kokee State Park and Alakai Swamp and seabirds at the National Wildlife Refuges at Kilauea and Hanalei. *Kauai and Hawaii* costs about $3,600/person and *Fall Hawaii* is priced at about $3,900/person. Both trips include accommodations, meals, interisland air, ground transportation, and guided excursions. Travelers must purchase their own airline ticket to and from their gateway city.

Contacts Field Guides ☎ *800/728-4953* ⊕ *www.fieldguides.com.* **Victor Emanuel Nature Tours** ☎ *800/328-8368* ⊕ *www. ventbird.com.*

CULTURE

RoadScholar, (formerly Elderhostel), a nonprofit educational travel organization, offers several guided tours for older adults that focus on Hawaiian culture. With all the tours listed, travelers must purchase their own airline tickets to Hawaii. We've chosen a few of our favorite tours here, but more information on tour subjects can be found on the organization's website.

Best of Kauai's Natural and Cultural Wonders is a six-night tour presented in association with the Kauai Historical Consortium. You'll visit Hanalei, Kilauea Point National Wildlife Refuge, Grove Farm Homestead Museum, Kauai Museum, and Kokee Natural History Museum. You'll learn *lauhala* weaving and other traditional arts and crafts and discover why the island truly is like no other. The cost of this tour starts at $1,475 per person and includes accommodations, meals, ground transportation, and admission fees.

The Best of Hawaii and Kauai is a 10-night tour, split up by five nights on the Big Island of Hawaii and five nights on Kauai. Exploring the natural beauty of these two islands, you'll visit Volcanoes National Park and the Hamakua Coast on Hawaii, then explore the Kilauea Point National Wildlife Refuge and the National Tropical Botanical Gardens on Kauai, learning about these two islands diverse life of birds, marine life, forests, volcanoes and more. Prices start at $2,471 per person and include accommodations, meals, ground transportation, admission fees, and interisland air travel between Kauai and the Big Island.

Contact Road Scholar ☎ *800/454-5768* ⊕ *www.elderhostel.org.*

ECOTOURS

Want to spend a week in Kauai hiking, snorkeling, surfing, and paddling? Kayak Kauai has a seven-day *Discovery Tour* where you will explore Kauai's peaks and canyons, rivers and coastlines, and discover lagoons with crystal clear water and breathtaking waterfalls, sacred trails, and miles of ivory-white sand beaches. Tours are offered every month and include accommodations, airport shuttles, van support during the week, communal gear, linens, all meals, guides, day tours, and activities. *Discovery Tour* is rated moderate but can be challenging at times, and participants should be in good physical condition. With a group of four or more, it is priced at $1,750 per person. Travelers must purchase their own airline tickets between their gateway cities and Kauai.

Contact **Kayak Kauai** ☎ 800/437-3507, 808/826-9844 ⊕ www.kayakkauai.com.

HIKING

Hiking the Garden Island is the theme of a weeklong trip to Kauai sponsored by Sierra Club Outings. In addition to day-long hikes of 5 to 9 miles through many of the rain forests in Kokee State Park, participants will have opportunities for snorkeling and swimming at secluded beaches, as well as bird-watching. Hikers also will help in the maintenance of some of the trails. Accommodations are in shared cabins, and as with all Sierra Club Outings, participants are expected to help prepare some of the meals using only local, fresh ingredients. The trip costs about $1,695 per person and includes accommodations, meals, and ground transportation.

Hawaii Three Island Hiker is a seven-night hiking tour to Kauai, Maui, and the Big Island. Included in the per-person price of about $3,900 are accommodations, meals, interisland air between the Islands, shuttle transportation, support vehicle, professional guides, a T-shirt, and a water bottle. Hikers will spend three nights on Kauai exploring Napali Coast, including hikes to Hanakapiai Falls and the Nulolo Cliffs/Awaawapuhi Loop. Another highlight of the adventure is a cruise and snorkel trip along the North Shore. The trip is rated moderately easy to moderate. The World Outdoors has been organizing and leading adventure trips around the world for 20 years.

Timberline Adventures has a seven-night "Islands Classic" tour that includes Kauai and the Big Island. Participants will hike more than 25 miles total as they explore the rugged southern coastline on the Shipwreck Beach trail, the lush rain forests of Kokee State Park, majestic Waimea Canyon, the incredible waterfalls and cliffs along Napali Coast and even the quiet Sleeping Giant. Then it's island hopping across the chain to the Big Island of Hawaii where participants explore Volcanoes National Park. Included in the per-person price of about $3,095 are accommodations on the West Side and North Shore, Big Island, meals and ground transportation.

Travelers must purchase their own tickets to and from their gateway city.

Contacts **Sierra Club Outings** ☎ 415/977-5500 ⊕ www.sierraclub.org/outings. **Timberline Adventures** ☎ 800/417-2453 ⊕ www.timbertours.com. **The World Outdoors** ☎ 800/488-8483 ⊕ www.theworldoutdoors.com.

LUXURY

For the ultimate luxurious adventure experience, you'll want to book one of the Pure Kauai vacations. Included in all these high-end adventure and spa vacations are private accommodations at elegant estates and villas, all meals prepared by a personal chef, activities, and on-island transportation. There are *Family Adventure*, *Adventure Boot Camp*, *Learn to Surf/Yoga*, and *Romantic Getaway* programs. The company also can create customized vacations with itineraries of any length and theme. Vacationers must purchase their own air between Kauai and their gateway city.

Contact **Pure Kauai** ☎ 866/457-7873, 808/828-6570 ⊕ www.purekauai.com.

▌ TRIP INSURANCE

Comprehensive trip insurance is valuable if you're booking a very expensive or complicated trip (particularly to an isolated region) or if you're booking far in advance. Comprehensive policies typically cover trip cancellation and interruption, letting you cancel or cut your trip short because of illness, or, in some cases, acts of terrorism in your destination.

Such policies might also cover evacuation and medical care. Some also cover you for trip delays because of bad weather or mechanical problems as well as for lost or delayed luggage.

Another type of coverage to consider is financial default—that is, when your trip is disrupted because a tour operator, airline, or cruise line goes out of business. Generally you must buy this when you book your trip or shortly thereafter, and it's available to you only if your operator isn't on a list of excluded companies.

Always read the fine print of your policy to make sure that you're covered for the risks that most concern you. Compare several policies to be sure you're getting the best price and range of coverage available.

Insurance Comparison Information Insure My Trip ☎ 800/487-4722 ⊕ www.insuremytrip. com. **Square Mouth** ☎ 800/240-0369 ⊕ www. squaremouth.com.

Comprehensive Insurers Access America ☎ 800/284-8300 ⊕ www.accessamerica.com. **AIG Travel Guard** ☎ 800/826-4919 ⊕ www. travelguard.com. **CSA Travel Protection** ☎ 800/873-9855, 800/711-1197 ⊕ www. csatravelprotection.com. **Travelex Insurance** ☎ 888/228-9792, 888/457-4602 ⊕ www. travelex-insurance.com. **Travel Insured International** ☎ 800/243-3174 ⊕ www. travelinsured.com.

▌ VISITOR INFORMATION

Before you go, contact the Kauai Visitors Bureau for a free travel planner that has information on accommodations, transportation, sports and activities, dining, arts and entertainment, and culture. You can also take a virtual tour of the island that includes great photos and helpful planning information.

The Hawaii Tourism Authority's Travel Smart Hawaii site offers tips on everything from packing to flying. Also visit the Hawaii State Vacation Planner for all information on the destination, including camping.

INSPIRATION

To get a flavor for the cultural history of Hawaii, many visitors read James Michener's novel, set in the Islands and named, as you might guess, *Hawaii*. Published in 1959, the year Hawaii became the 50th state, this epic work of fiction also serves to educate about life in paradise through tales featuring the first Polynesian settlers from Bora Bora, early Christian missionaries who came from the U.S. mainland, and recent Chinese and Japanese immigrants who have turned Hawaii into a true melting pot.

ONLINE TRAVEL TOOLS
The Hawaii Department of Land and Natural Resources has information on hiking, fishing, and camping permits and licenses; online brochures on hiking safety and mountain and ocean preservation; and details on volunteer programs. The Kauai Visitors Bureau has Kauai-specific information on everything from activities to lodging options and organizes it by geographic regions on the island.

ALL ABOUT KAUAI
Resources Hawaii Beach Safety ⊕ www. oceansaftey.soest.hawaii.edu. **Hawaii Department of Land and Natural Resources** ⊕ www.state.hi.us/dlnr. **Kauai Vacation Explorer** ⊕ www.kauaiexplorer.com. **Kauai Visitors Bureau** ⊕ www.gohawaii.com/kauai.

INDEX

A

Aerial tours, *135–136*
Air travel, *12, 238–239*
Alekoko (Menehune) Fishpond, *61–62*
Aliomanu Beach, *87*
Allerton Gardens, *66*
Aloha Cottages ⌐, *223*
Anahola Beach Park, *87, 89*
ANARA Spa, *171*
Anini Beach Park, *83, 90, 116*
Arboretums, *59*
Aston Aloha Beach Hotel ⌐, *223*
Aston Islander on the Beach ⌐, *223*
ATV tours, *23, 136–137*

B

Baby Beach, *89*
Back Door Surf Co., *127–128*
Bambulei (shop), *163*
Bar Acuda ✕, *191*
Bars, *179, 185–186*
Beach House ✕, *203–204*
Beach House Beach, *95–96, 126*
Beaches, *29, 90*
for children, *22, 82, 83, 89, 91, 94, 96, 97–98*
East Side, *87, 89–92*
North Shore, *43, 77–79, 82–83, 85–87*
safety concerns, *86*
South Shore, *93–97*
swimming spots, *92*
West Side, *97–992*
Bed and breakfasts. ⌐ See Condos, vacation rentals, B&Bs and inns
Biking, *137–138, 143*
Bird-watching tours, *245–246*
Blue Dolphin Charters, *103–104, 132*
Blue Hawaiian Helicopters, *135*
Blue Seas Surf School, *129*
Boat tours, *28, 102–108*
catamaran tours, *50–51, 103–106*
raft tours, *106–108*
riverboat tours, *108*
Boat travel. ⌐ See Cruises
Body boarding and bodysurfing, *109*
Bon Festival, *177*

Books about Hawaii, *248*
Brennecke Beach, *94*
Brennecke's Beach Broiler ✕, *66, 204*
Bubbles Below, *118*
Bull Shed ✕, *195*
Bus travel, *239*
Business hours, *189, 243–244*

C

Café Portofino ✕, *200*
Caffé Coco ✕, *186, 195–196*
Canoe racing, *115*
Capt. Andy's Rafting Expeditions, *106–107*
Capt. Andy's Sailing Adventures, *104*
Captain Don's Sport Fishing & Ocean Adventure, *109*
Captain Sundown, *104*
Car rentals, *12, 240–241*
Car travel, *239–241*
driving times, *12*
Carnival Cruises, *34*
Casa di Amici ✕, *204*
Casablanca at Kiahuna ✕, *204*
Catamaran Kahanu, *104–105, 132*
Catamaran tours, *50–51, 103–106*
Caves, *45*
Children and travel, *22–23*
dining, *189, 191, 196, 211–212*
lodging, *22, 221, 223, 226, 228*
Children's attractions
beaches, *22, 82, 83, 89, 91, 94, 96, 97–98*
East Side, *60, 63*
festival, *177*
kayaking, *115*
mountain tubing, *154*
North Shore, *55–56*
sailing, *104*
snorkeling, *23, 120, 126–127*
surfing, *22–23, 129*
Christ Memorial Episcopal Church, *54*
Churches, *45, 54*
Climate, *18*
Clubs, *179, 185–186*
Coffeehouses, *186*
Communications, *243*
Condos, vacation rentals, B&Bs and inns, *22, 216–217*
East Side, *221, 223–224, 226*
North Shore, *217, 219, 221*

South Shore, *226, 228, 230*
West Side, *232*
Costs, *13*
Credit cards, *5, 244*
Cruises, *34, 108, 239*
Cuisine, *24–25*
Culture tours, *246*

D

Dani's Restaurant ✕, *200*
Deep-sea fishing, *109, 111*
Dining, *5, 13*
American, *191, 194, 196, 197–198, 202–203, 204, 209, 211–212, 213–214*
budget-friendly, *190, 194, 200*
cafés, *195–196*
with children, *189, 190, 196, 211*
East Side, *195–203*
eclectic restaurants, *191, 197, 201, 203, 209*
Hawaiian restaurants, *200, 201–202*
Indian restaurants, *198*
Italian restaurants, *196, 200, 204, 211, 212*
Japanese restaurants, *197, 202*
Luaus, *205–207*
mealtimes, *189*
Mediterranean restaurants, *191, 192, 194, 204*
menu guide, *208*
Mexican restaurants, *198*
modern Hawaiian restaurants, *192, 212*
North Shore, *189, 191–192, 194*
plate lunches, *190, 209*
price categories, *5, 13, 189*
reservations and dress, *189*
romantic dining, *190, 214*
seafood restaurants, *191–192, 198, 200, 201, 211, 212–213*
South Shore, *203–204, 209, 211–213*
steakhouses, *195, 204, 214*
symbols related to, *5*
Thai restaurants, *197, 214*
tipping, *189, 245*
vegetarian restaurants, *197*
West Side, *213–214*
Dinner cruises, *108*
Dondero's ✕, *204, 209*
Donkey Beach, *89*

Duke's Canoe Club ✕, 200–201

E

East Side
bars and clubs, 185
beaches, 87, 89–92
dining, 195–200
exploring, 56, 58–63
lodging, 219, 221, 223–226
shopping, 162–165
Ecotours, 30, 246–247
Eggbert's ✕, 196
Emergencies, 240
Entertainment, 176–179
Etiquette and behavior, 242
Explore Kauai Sportfishing, 109, 111

F

Farmers' markets, 15, 63
Farms, 60, 62, 63
Fauna of Kauai, 40
Fern Grotto, 58, 108
Festival, 177
Fishing, deep-sea, 109, 111
Flora of Kauai, 40, 139–141
Fort Elisabeth, 72

G

Galerie 103, 166
Garden Island Inn 🖻, 224
Garden Isle Cottages 🖻, ,226
Gardens
East Side, 60, 62
North Shore, 43, 45, 55–56
South Shore, 66
Gaylord's ✕, 201
Geology of Kauai, 36, 40
Golf, 134, 143–145
Grand Hyatt Kauai Resort and Spa 🖻, 226
Green tours, 30, 246–247
Greetings, 242
Grove Café at Waimea Brewing Company, The ✕, 213–214
Grove Farm Homestead, 62
Guided tours, 62, 245–247

H

Haena, 41, 43, 45
Haena Beach Park (Tunnels Beach), 79, 90, 120
Halelea Spa, 171, 173
Hamura Saimin ✕, 201–202, 203
Hana Paa, 111

Hanakapiai Beach, 78–79
Hanakapiai Falls, 49
Hanalei, 41, 43, 45
Hanalei Bay, 14, 110
Hanalei Bay Beach Park, 82, 90
Hanalei Bay Resort 🖻, 219
Hanalei Colony Resort 🖻, 219
Hanalei Gourmet ✕, 191
Hanalei Inn 🖻, 221
Hanalei Pier, 43
Hanalei River, 112
Hanalei Valley Overlook, 43
Hanalei-Okolehao Trail, 146
Hanamaulu Restaurant, Tea House, Sushi Bar, and Roba-tayaki ✕, 202
Hanapepe, 67, 69, 72
Hanapepe Swinging Bridge, 69
Hanapepe Valley and Canyon Lookout, 69
Hanapepe Walking Tour, 69
Hawaii, 10–11, 19–21
Hawaii Nautical, 34
Hawaiian vocabulary, 234–236
Hawaiian Surfing Adventures, 128
Healing practitioners, 173
Health concerns, 243
Helicopter tours, 28, 48–49, 135–136
Hideaway Cove 🖻, 228
Hideaway Spa, A, 173–174
Highway 560, 15
Hiking, 146, 150, 152
Napali Coast, 52–53
tours, 152, 247
History of Kauai, 19, 40
Ho opii Falls, 146
Holland America, 34
HoloHolo Charters, 105, 132
Honeymoons, 32–33
Hoopulapula Haraguchi Rice Mill, 43
Horseback riding, 23, 153
Hotel Coral Reef 🖻, 223
Hotels and resorts, 5, 13, 216–232
East Side, 221, 223–224, 226
North Shore, 217, 219, 221
South Shore, 226, 228, 230
West Side, 232
Hours of operation, 189, 243–244
Hukilau Lanai ✕, 196
Hula dance, 27, 180–183
Huleia River, 112

I

Insurance, 247–249
Inter-Island Helicopters, 135
Internet access, 243
Itineraries, 14–17

J

Jack Harter Helicopters, 135–136
JJ's Broiler ✕, 202
Joe's on the Green ✕, 209
Josselin's Tapas Bar and Grill ✕, 209
Just Live (tours), 155, 157

K

Kahili Beach (Rock Quarry), 85
Kai Bear, 111
Kalaheo Café & Coffee Co. ✕, 209, 211
Kalaheo Inn 🖻, 232
Kalalau, 77–78
Kalalau Lookout, 72–73
Kalalau Trail, 28, 49, 146, 150
Kalapaki Beach, 91–92
Kalapaki Joe's ✕, 202–203
Kalihiwai Beach, 83, 85
Kamokila Hawaiian Village, 58–59
Kapaa, 56, 58–61
dining, 195–198, 200
lodging, 223–224
shopping, 162–164
Kapaa Beach Park, 116
Kapaa Sands 🖻, 223
Kapaia Stitchery (shop), 165
Kauai ATV Tours, 137
Kauai Backcountry Adventures, 154
Kauai Beach Boys, 128
Kauai Beach Resort 🖻, 224, 226
Kauai Coast Resort 🖻, 224
Kauai Coffee Visitor Center and Museum, 69
Kauai Cove Cottages 🖻, 228
Kauai Cycle, 142
Kauai Down Under Scuba, 118–119
Kauai Grill ✕, 181
Kauai Marriott Resort on Kala-paki Beach 🖻, 226
Kauai Museum, 62–63
gift shop, 165
Kauai Nature Tours, 152
Kauai Palms Hotel 🖻, 226
Kauai Pasta ✕, 196
Kauai Sea Tours, 105–106, 107

Kauapea Beach (Secret Beach), 85
Kayak Kauai, 113
Kayak Wailua, 113
Kayaking, 15, 28, 112–113, 115, 132
Ke Ala Hele Makalae, 60, 137–138
Keahua Forestry Arboretum, 59
Kealia Beach, 89, 110
Kealia Scenic Viewpoint, 59
Kee Beach, 31, 79, 120
Kee Beach State Park, 43
Kekaha Beach Park, 98–99
Keoki's Paradise ×, 211
Keoniloa Beach (Shipwreck Beach), 93–94
Kilauea, 54–56
Kilauea Bakery and Pau Hana Pizza ×, 191
Kilauea Fish Market ×, 191–192
Kilauea Lighthouse, 31, 54
Kilauea Point National Wildlife Refuge, 54
Kilohana Plantation, 63
Kipu Ranch Adventures, 137
Kiteboarding, 116
Koa Kea Hotel and Resort ☂, 228
Kokee Lodge ☂, 232
Kokee Natural History Museum, 74
Kokee State Park, 74, 150
Koloa, 65
Koloa Heritage Trail, 65
Koloa Landing, 116
Kountry Kitchen ×, 196
Kukuiolono Park, 72
Kukui's Restaurant and Bar ×, 203
Kukuiula Small Boat Harbor, 98

L

Language, 242
Hawaiian vocabulary, 234–236
menu guide, 208
Lappert's Ice Cream ×, 69
Larsen's Beach, 85–86
Lawai Kai, 96–97
Lei greetings, 242
Leis, 167–169
Lemongrass Grill ×, 197
Leptospirosis, 152
Lighthouses, 54
Lihue
dining, 200–203

exploring, 61–63
lodging, 224, 226
shopping, 164–165
Lihue Barbecue Inn ×, 203
Liko Kauai Cruises, 106
Limahuli Garden, 43, 45
Lodging. ⇨ *See also* Condos, vacation rentals, B&Bs and inns; Hotels and resorts
with children, 22–23, 221, 223, 226, 228
East Side, 219, 221, 223–226
meal plans, 5
North Shore, 217, 219, 221
price categories, 13, 217
property comparison charts, 219
reservations, 217
South Shore, 219, 226, 228, 230
symbols related to, 5
tipping, 245
West Side, 219, 232
Lomilomi Hawaiian-style massage, 174
Luau Kalamaku, 177–178
Luaus, 177–178, 205–207
children and, 23
Lucy Wright Beach Park, 98
Lumahai Beach, 82
Luxury tours, 247
Lydgate State Park, 90, 91, 120–121

M

Mahaulepu Beach, 93, 116
Makahuena at Poipu ☂, 228
Makana Terrace ×, 192
Makua (Tunnels) Beach, 116, 120
Mana Yoga Vacation Rentals ☂, 221
Maniniholo Dry Cave, 45
Margo Oberg Surfing School, 129
Massage, 174
McBryde Gardens, 66
Meal plans, 5
Mediterranean Gourmet ×, 192, 194
Mema Thai Chinese Cuisine ×, 197
Mermaid's Café ×, 197
Mission houses, 45, 54
Moloaa Sunrise Fruit Stand, 55
Money matters, 244
tips for saving, 13
Monk seals, 95
Mountain tubing, 154

Movies filmed on Kauai, 184
Museums
coffee, 69
in East Side, 62–63
history, 74
hours of operation, 244
natural history, 74
in West Side, 69, 74

N

Na Aina Kai, 55–56
Napali, 14, 47–53
boat tours, 49, 50–51
helicopter tours, 48–49
hiking tours, 49, 52–53
Napali Catamaran, 106
Napali Explorer, 107, 132
Napali Kayak, 115
Napali Riders, 108
National Tropical Botanical Gardens, 66
Nightlife, 23, 179, 184–186
Niihau (Forbidden Isle), 111, 126
North Country Farms ×, 221
North Shore
bars and clubs, 179, 185
beaches, 43, 77–79, 82–83, 85–87
dining, 189, 191–194
exploring, 40–41, 43, 45
lodging, 217, 219–221
shopping, 161–162
Norwegian Cruise Lines, 34
Nualolo Kai, 49, 126
Nukumoi Surf Co., 130

O

Ocean Quest Watersports/Fathom Five, 119
Online travel tools, 248
Opaekaa Falls, 31, 56, 58
Outfitters Kauai, 115, 132, 143, 157
Outrigger at Lae Nani ☂, 224
Outrigger Kiahuna Plantation ☂, 228

P

Packing, 244
Pali Ke Kua Beach (Hideaways Beach), 83
Papaya's ×, 197
Parking, 240
Parks, 85
East Side, 87, 89, 91
North Shore, 43, 82, 83
South Shore, 66, 94–95
West Side, 72, 74, 97–99

Pedal'n'Paddle, *143*
Pizzetta ✕ , *211*
Plantation Gardens ✕ , *211*
Plantation Hale Suites ▥ , *224*
Plantations. ⇨ *See* Farms
Plate tectonics, *147, 149*
Pohaku hanau, *58*
Pohaku piko, *58*
Poipu, *66–67*
Poipu Beach Park, *90, 94–95, 110, 126*
Poipu Crater Resort ▥ , *228*
Poipu Kapili ▥ , *228, 230*
Poipu Plantation Resort ▥ , *230*
Poipu Shores ▥ , *230*
Poipu Tropical Burgers ✕ , *211–212*
Poliahu Heiau, *58*
Polihale State Park, *99*
Pomodoro Ristorante Italiano ✕ , *212*
Postcards Café ✕ , *194, 195*
Price categories
dining, 5, 13, 189
lodging, 5, 13, 217
Prince Kuhio Park, *66*
Princess Cruises, *34*
Princeville, *54–56*
Princeville Ranch Stables, *153*
Princeville Resort, *145*
Puu hinahina Lookout, *74*
Puu ka Pele, *74*
Puu O Kila Lookout, *72, 74*
Puu Poa Beach, *82–83*

Q

Queen's Bath, *92*

R

Raft tours, *106–108*
Resorts. ⇨ *See* Hotels and resorts
Restaurant Kintaro ✕ , *197*
Restaurants. ⇨ *See* Dining
Rice mills, *43*
River kayaking, *15, 28, 112*
Riverboat tours, *108*
Roadside emergencies, *240*
Rosewood Bed and Breakfast ▥ , *224*
Roy's Poipu Bar & Grill ✕ , *212*

S

Safari Helicopters, *136*
Safety, *86, 97, 125, 244–245*
St. Regis Bar, *179, 185*

St. Regis Princeville Resort ▥ , *221*
Salt Pond Beach Park, *97–98*
Scotty's Beachside BBQ ✕ , *197–198*
Scuba diving, *116, 118–119*
Sea kayaking, *113, 115*
Sea turtles, *123*
Seafun Kauai, *126–127*
Seal-spotting, *95*
Seasport Divers, *119*
Shave ice, *201*
Sheraton Kauai Resort ▥ , *230*
Shivalik Indian Cuisine ✕ , *198*
Shopping, *160–170*
East Side, 162–165
farmers' markets, 15, 63
hours of operation, 244
North Shore, 161–162
South Shore and West Side, 166, 170
Sightseeing tours, *62*
Skydiving, *155*
Sleeping Giant, *59–60*
Smith's Motor Boat Services, *108*
Smith's Tropical Paradise, *60*
Smith's Tropical Paradise Luau, *178, 179*
Snorkeling, *23, 119–127*
tours, 126–127
South Shore
bars and clubs, 185–186
beaches, 93–97
dining, 66, 203–204, 209–213
exploring, 63–67
lodging, 226, 228–230
shopping, 166
Spalding Monument, *60*
Spas, *14, 170–174*
Spouting Horn, *67*
Stand-up paddling, *90, 127–128*
Steelgrass Chocolate Farm, *60–61*
Suite Paradise Poipu Kai ▥ , *230*
Sunshine Helicopter Tours, *136*
Sunshine Markets, *63*
Surfing, *22–23, 90, 109, 110, 128–131*
Swimming, *92*
Symbols, *5*

T

Tavern at Princeville, The ✕ , *194*
Taxes, *245*
Tennis, *155*

Tidepools ✕ , *212–213*
Time, *245*
Tipping, *189, 245*
Titus Kinimaka Hawaiian School of Surfing, *130*
Toi's Thai Kitchen ✕ , *214*
Tours, *245–247*
Transportation, *238–241*
Trip insurance, *247–248*
Tropical Bi-planes, *136*
Tunnels (Makua), *116, 120*

U

Uluwehi Falls, *92*

V

Vacation rentals. ⇨ *See* Condos, vacation rentals, B&Bs and inns
Verde ✕ , *198*
Visitor information, *12, 248*
Volcanoes, *147, 149*

W

Waikapalae and Waikanaloa Wet Caves, *45*
Wailua, *56, 58–61*
dining, 195–198, 200
lodging, 223–224
shopping, 162–164
Wailua Beach, *89, 90, 91, 110*
Wailua Falls, *58*
Wailua Kayak & Canoe, *115*
Wailua Marina Restaurant ✕ , *198–200*
Wailua River, *112*
Waimea, *72, 74*
Waimea Canyon, *31, 72, 74*
Waimea Canyon Drive, *14*
Waimea Plantation Cottages ▥ , *232*
Waiohai Beach, *94–95*
Waioli Huiia Church, *45*
Waioli Mission House, *45, 54*
Walking tours, *62, 69*
Waterfalls
East Side, 30, 56, 58
swimming spots, 112, 146
Weather information, *18*
Web sites, *248*
Weddings, *32–33*
West Kauai Visitor and Technology Center, *74*
West Side
bars and clubs, 186
beaches, 97–99
dining, 74, 213–214
exploring, 67, 69, 72, 74

lodging, 232
shopping, 166
Whale-watching, *131–132*
Whalers Cove ⊤ , *230*
When to go, *18*
Wildlife preserves, *54*
Wrangler's Steakhouse ✕ , *214*

Z

Zipline tours, *28, 155–157*
Z-Tourz, *108*

PHOTO CREDITS